THE PSYCHOLOGY OF BIRTH

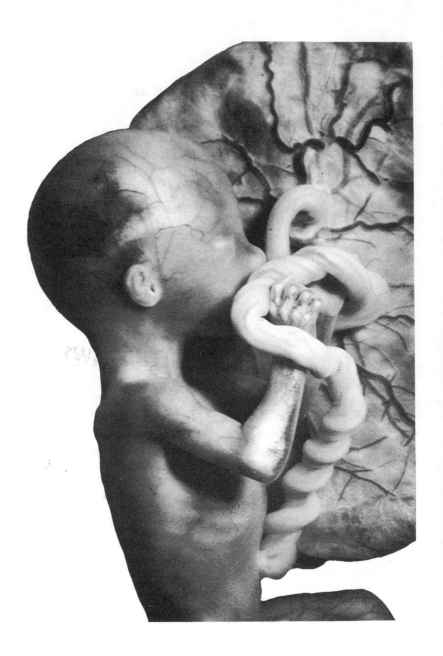

THE PSYCHOLOGY OF BIRTH

ROOTS OF HUMAN PERSONALITY

LESLIE FEHER

With a chapter by
LEWIS E. MEHL, M.D.

CONTINUUM · New York

1981
The Continuum Publishing Corporation
18 East 41st Street, New York, N.Y. 10017

Printed in the United States of America

Library of Congress Cataloging in Publication Data

Feher, Leslie.
  The psychology of birth.

  Includes bibliographical references and index.
  1. Personality. 2. Psychotherapy. 3. Childbirth—Psychological aspects. I. Title.
BF698.F357   150.19′5   80-39993
ISBN 0-8264-0039-6

Frontispiece: Foetus, cord and placenta. Photographed by
Lennart Nilsson, from *A Child Is Born,* Faber and Faber

Contents

DEDICATION

This book is dedicated first to the memory of my three parents:
my mother Elizabeth Fehr whose energy and mental charisma
exposed me to many worlds, my father Alexander Feher, M.D.,
whose dedication to medicine supplied me with real magic and
amazement and Mary, my nani till age five, who truly knew how
to love a child. But most of all I want to dedicate the book to my
beautiful daughter Vanessa who fills me daily with pride and joy.

'The most obvious is the hardest to fathom'
Edgar Allen Poe

AUTHOR'S PREFACE

This book was written for the purpose of formulating a theory about human nature that incorporates the concept of birth. Most personality constructs initiate theory at the neonate or later stages of development, and neglect or slide over the start of life. A few rare psychologists prior to World War II did make some examination of the psychotherapeutic ramifications of birth, but always as an extension of existing theory rather than a new logical order of development. From my own practice of natal therapy – based on the work of my mother Elizabeth Fehr – I realized that some of the old ideas simply did not work, and in fact contradicted the more observable emotional and symptom expressions of those who sought therapy. It was only in turning away from old theory and overlooking its authority, that I was able to review behaviour and reach an alternative organization, and thereby find answers that had previously evaded me. It was only then that feelings took on a clarity that had hitherto seemed elusive, and transitional thoughts that had lain dormant became obvious.

I should warn readers that there is much conjecture in this book. I ask them to bear with this, and to allow themselves to suspend attachment to established patterns of thought and assumption, so as to allow confrontation with the concepts expressed. The book is in part an anatomy of feeling, in part a re-evaluation of past theory about personality. All chapters interrelate in one mental continuum, so that only near the end does some of the material at the start take on the full implications intended. If possible I would have written a circular book, but as with the mind only sequence is possible! It was my intent that the material should be presented with sufficient style and clarity to make the reading of it both a mental adventure and informative for the reader. If I have succeeded it is due in large part to the editorial efforts of my publishers, to whom I owe much thanks.

I also owe thanks to Lewis Mehl, who wrote a special and invaluable chapter to provide the reader with essential facts about the medical implications of birth. It shows clearly that we can no longer leave the experience of birth in the hands of the medical profession alone.

I would also like to acknowledge the help of the following professionals without whom the Elizabeth Fehr Natal Therapy Institute would not have been founded:
Betty Sobel, R.N., M.A., Esther Enterline, Ph.D., David Shiffman, Ph.D., Howard Garell, M.A., Leonard Rack, M.D., Robert Robison, Ph.D., and Attila Toth, M.D. Credit should be given, too, to the two typists who worked diligently on the manuscript these last few years: Linda Lane and Walter Szykitka.

On a more personal level I want to extend my gratitude to all the patients and friends who contributed their thoughts, and to offer special thanks to Ralph Ferney for his continuous support.

Finally I wish to thank those publishers who permitted me to quote from the following books:
To W. W. Norton and Co. Inc. for permission to quote from *A General Selection from the Works of Sigmund Freud*, edited by John Rickman, M.D.; to the Hogarth Press Ltd., and the Institute of Psycho-Analysis, London, and Basic Books, New York for quotation from *The Collected Papers of Sigmund Freud* edited by Ernest Jones, M.D., and James Strachey; to Tavistock Publications Ltd. for material from *Sanity, Madness and the Family* by R. D. Laing and A. Esterson; and to Albert Bonniers Forlag AB for permission to reproduce the frontispiece photograph by Dr Lennart Nilsson, from *A Child is Born*, published by Faber & Faber, London and Delacorte Press/Seymour Lawrence, New York.

LESLIE FEHER
March 1980

1 OVERVIEW

The need for rebirth has apparently existed in man from the beginning of time. The rituals of every tribe, of every religious sect, involve symbols of rebirth in one form or another. In baptism, puberty, wedding and funeral ceremonies, as well as in healing rituals, are to be found variations of birth re-enactment. The sensation of being reborn has been described in every literature, it inspires the poet, the writer, the lover, the saint. Any impulse so all-pervasive through societies and philosophies all over the world must somehow be assumed to fulfil a basic human need.

Freud[1] recognized what we will here call the 'birthing need'. He claimed that birth was our first trauma, and the origin of all the anxieties at the root of later psychic problems. He found that the physiological characteristics of anxiety and hysteria – changes in respiration and heart rates were identical with those of the birth process; and concluded that they were both physiologically and emotionally associated with it. Later traumas were all in some sense repetitions of the first, and throughout life anxiety would be experienced as reactivating the overwhelming anxiety of birth. Freud believed that this primary anxiety was blocked off from consciousness. Yet the anxiety that created the repression – the block – would continue to express itself indirectly even in adulthood, in ways that could be emotionally harmful. The result would be neurosis, that is, cutting off or disconnecting oneself from the feelings that occurred when the trauma happened. It is not the emotion itself, but the lack of expression or the displacement of emotion, that creates the later problems. The displaced emotions connected with the first trauma, the birth trauma, thus set the pattern for all later reactions that may be similarly displaced or blocked off.

Freud claimed that this first trauma was too deeply buried in the unconscious to be reached analytically. Rank[2] broke from Freud on this point. He believed that the birth trauma and its associated emotional reactions could be reached and resolved, and that if this were done all problems that re-echoed the birth would also be resolved. Rank hypothesized that all neuroses originated at birth and were re-enacted in fantasy and dreams. He treated the whole analytic procedure as a rebirth, thereby initiating the concept of a time limit on the therapy process. The termination of treatment for any patient – when he was ready for separation from the therapist – was the point at which he was ready to be reborn. The rest of his profession criticized Rank for concentrating all attention on birth dreams and fantasies, and argued that there should be more to the process than this. Furthermore, Rankians proposed that all children be born by Caesarian section to eliminate birth trauma. Recent evidence, as will be discussed later, suggests that this would in fact be disastrous.

Ferenczi[3] extended and deepened Rankian birth theory. Then Nandor Fodor[4] in the 1940s used the same idea as the basis for a birth psychotherapy which aimed at the patient's emotional rebirth through dream interpretation and verbal dissection of fantasy. Around the same time, Bettelheim and others also noted spontaneous physical birth reenactments in psychotic patients; but they always dismissed these as symptoms, rather than working with them therapeutically or attempting any form of induction to resolve problems connected with them.[5]

Mott,[6] an English dream analyst, incorporated foetal theory in developing his birth material. In a quite overlooked, underdeveloped, physical birth re-enactment with children, he introduced dimension to the idea of the re-enactment of birth as a cathartic tool. His major therapy work, however, like Fodor's, was verbally and psychoanalytically based.

Many new ideas are presently being developed around the birth trauma. Lloyd deMause[7] is investigating a unique approach to what he calls 'psychohistory', attempting to correlate medical practices and social attitudes surrounding birth to historical events and attitudes. In particular, he has analysed the efforts of political leaders to change and mould the world, as re-enactments of their own birth trauma.

Frederic Leboyer, Frank Lake, Lewis Mehl[8] and other obstetricians in Europe and America have been so deeply convinced of the significance of the birth process to the future psychic health of the individual that they are revising the medical procedure for bringing the child into the world. With Leboyer's method,[9] the mother is given little anaesthetic, and may use a Lamaze-type technique for natural childbirth. Soft lights, quiet voices and gentle fondling in warm water greet the child instead of the harsh lights and clinical atmosphere of the high-technology delivery room. He claims that the infant smiles instead of cries in the minutes after birth. The follow-ups done to date have indicated these children to be emotionally healthier as a group than a control sample.* Chapter three contains a more extensive discussion of these medical approaches.

Stanislav Grof[10] is a psychiatrist and author of *Realms of the Human Unconscious* and *The Human Encounter with Death*. From work with some individuals given LSD under close direction, and encouraged to describe the fantasies they experienced, he has concluded that the central metaphor to which all such fantasies return is that of birth. He has formulated what he calls four 'perinatal matrices' of consciousness: symbiotic unity, antagonism, synergism and separation.

The first matrix, 'symbiotic unity', refers to intra-uterine experience prior to delivery. It is described in terms of feelings of security, protection, satisfaction and even cosmic unity, though occasionally 'bad womb' associations occur. 'Antagonism', the second matrix, includes reactions to the onset of contractions: feelings of claustrophobia, physical torment, existential crisis and hopelessness may be mixed with feelings of guilt. 'Synergism', however, once propulsion through the birth canal has started, involves both purpose and energy: a struggle for survival counters the threats of suffocation or being crushed. This is followed by relief and relaxation, as the final 'separation' terminates union with the mother, and initiates independence. Accompanying feelings include terrors of annihilation, followed by spiritual ecstasy.

On the basis of this *coex system*, Grof correlates birth with later life experience. He concludes that reactions from each of the stages he describes can retain influence on later personality structure. Patients, by reliving each matrix, can come to comprehend, resolve and transcend the problems emanating from them. He, like deMause, correlates these processes with social and political trends in the world.

Janov developed his 'primal therapy' rebirth procedure about 1972. Although he, like others before him, had previously observed spontaneous birth re-enactments in patients,[11] it was some time before he set out actually to 'induce' birth, and initially the procedure was rather a crude one, the patient pushing himself through a rubber vagina screaming.[12] From there it evolved to include fantasy regression and a more directed mental encounter. The theory posited

* Personal communication with Leboyer.

that recontacting the buried pain in early events, such as abandonment or rejection, will help alleviate the symptoms and inhibitions
that continue in later life to accompany that pain. Session by session,
the patient is brought back to earlier and earlier points, eventually
reaching the birth itself. Rebirth was however not a goal for Janov
and his colleagues, but a byproduct, resulting from the extension of
screaming and other regressive therapy techniques.

In recent years R. D. Laing, Frank Lake and others mentioned in
Chapter three have also experimented with more extensive fantasy
regressions to encourage birth, and even intra-uterine re-enactments,
as forms of therapy.

And now we come to natal therapy.[13] This was originated in early
1969 by Elizabeth Fehr.*

Elizabeth Fehr approached patients with the concept that everything they felt, experienced or reacted to, had a reality that was
valid to them. No matter how illogical, the effect was real; and so,
too, the cause – even if others could only see them as fantasy.

She had also found from experience that if consistent fantasies
were carried to a point of completion, they were no longer of interest
to the patient. A completed fantasy became a discarded fantasy,
and the unresolved problem it communicated would reach resolution.
Being stuck with the fantasy was being stuck with the problem.

One day a patient who had been in treatment with her for about
a year began having the fantasy experience of being stuck in what
seemed like a manhole. He needed to be pushed through to complete
the fantasy. Instead of intellectualizing the experience and working
it out verbally, she acted it out, joining the patient's fantasy and
involving herself personally, as was her way. She pushed and pushed
and pushed until he felt free of the manhole. Only afterwards did
they talk about birth. However, not only did the contortions and
affect, the release and relief that the patient experienced, identify
the fantasy as a birth fantasy; but the activity made it a birth process
that was carried to a conclusion. In the therapy sessions that followed, emotions related to that birth experience were released, and
repressed anxieties that had long remained blocked off surfaced.
Memories unfolded, sensations and feelings were experienced that
had previously been unknown. With each subsequent session new
associations were formed and repressions lifted. Thereafter, others

* The Elizabeth Fehr Natal Therapy Institute, 444 East 82nd Street,
New York 10028, tel: (212) 988–6617, was founded by the author four
months after her mother's death in 1974.

in group therapy with this patient heard about his experience, and if they too found themselves experiencing sweaty palms, dizziness and stomach flutters – the symptoms of anxiety – when about to face the lifting of a repression or the emergence of a new insight, began themselves to demand the experience of rebirth.

In time Elizabeth Fehr began to induce the experience to *make* the insight emerge, instead of waiting for the lifting of the repression to initiate the therapy.

The natal theory that gradually evolved was developed by the author. This theory recognizes that traumatic anxiety originated at birth. Furthermore, it acknowledges that, because anxiety blocks off memory and the event itself predates language, this trauma is beyond the reach of analytic methods. Only re-experience of the trauma can stimulate memory, and, by breaking through the block of emotion from the traumatic incident, relieve the anxieties surrounding it. Natal therapy, incorporated as an adjunct to traditional psychotherapy, makes this possible.

In this sense, natal theory is an extension of Freudian theory. Unlike primal, which negates the Freudian approach and feels we should bypass consciousness – the ego – and simply overwhelm the patient to break down his defences,[14] natal utilizes the strength and cognitive abilities of the ego to aid the process of the therapy.

Some of the recent research on brain physiology can perhaps further clarify the relationship between trauma and conscious experience. Freud[15] stated that the patient, at the point of trauma, whether at birth or later, splits the emotions connected with a traumatic experience – represses them and pushes them out of consciousness into the subconscious. These emotions are then replaced by anxiety. In 1959 Sperry[16] published his findings on the connection between the two constituent hemispheres of the human brain. These hemispheres, it seems, are not connected at birth; but when the child reaches about eighteen months of age, a membrane called the corpus callosum begins to link them together. The completion of the connection takes place at age seven. Verbal ability now becomes more and more concentrated on the left side of the brain while non-verbal events are separated and integrated on the other side. The connection of the two hemispheres by the corpus callosum, it is hypothesized, enables information to be transferred back and forth, and makes a more integrated functioning human being.[17]

Now these findings correlate closely with Freud's beliefs about the stages of psychic development. The period prior to eighteen months, before the membrane begins to connect the hemispheres, would correspond with what Freud called the oral stage of development. Trauma in this stage, according to him, causes psychosis; and this cannot be corrected through traditional therapies, because introjected stimulus prior to eighteen months is non-verbal. It cannot be transferred to the verbal side, in the light of split-brain theory, because the corpus callosum has not developed. Thereafter there is a connection, what the child experiences can hopefully be integrated on both sides, and it therefore can be reached verbally.

The split-off between emotion and event that Freud describes during the trauma, can thus be expressed quite literally in physical terms: since the material of the episode goes to the appropriate hemisphere only, the emotional portion of the trauma goes to the non-verbal side, and stays locked up there, unable to be transferred to the alternate, verbal hemisphere as would be necessary for healthy integration. In other words, the author suggests, the left verbal hemisphere can actually be seen as the seat of the 'ego', and the right or non-verbal hemisphere as the seat of the 'unconscious'.

Natal therapy, in that it is non-verbal, may be able to reach the material that has been locked into the non-verbal hemisphere prior to eighteen months; and then to transfer it to the verbal side with the later sessions, to create unity and consistency among the hemispheres.* The further emotional ramifications of split-brain theory will be discussed in Chapter seven.

Freud's concepts of undoing, and the repetition compulsion, are also confirmed by the experience of natal therapy. All behaviour, we have found, tends to re-enact birth: emotional, sexual and cognitive patterns all seem to be in some sense duplications of a magnified moment in birth. So Freud's idea of the need to repeat trauma – to work it out and eliminate it – can be seen not only in the re-enactment by individuals of their birth's trauma, over and over in their sexual and emotional lives, but in the universality of the birthing need in society itself.

* The idea that natal therapy could lead to a better balance between the two brain hemispheres was tested experimentally by the author and Elizabeth Fehr. To summarize the experiment, depth perception, which is held to originate in the non-verbal hemisphere, was tested in a group of subjects. The group was equally divided so that each of the two groups had the same total score on depth perception. One group then experienced natal therapy and all were retested. The group that had undergone natal therapy had increased depth perception. Since depth perception is located on the right, this supported the hypothesis that natal therapy increased the dominance of the non-verbal hemisphere.

In women, in our experience, repetition may have a particular meaning, for frequently the mother's unconscious presumes the birth of her child to be a repetition of her own. One woman entered therapy because she was overwhelmed with postnatal anxiety. She had gone through a state of total disorientation when her child was born following a partially induced labour. At her own birth, it emerged, she had on the other hand been held back, so subconsciously she had prepared her mind and perhaps even her body for a similar experience. The doctor had imposed another, a speeded-up labour, and the resulting conflict had not been resolved.

Psychological investigation of birth could discover these subtle variables, and eventually aid in preparing the mother for her own experience. One of the contributions of natal therapy could thus be to facilitate the resolution of depression or panic in the mother before the birth; and to encourage obstetricians and other professionals to give greater consideration to the mental dynamics of the mother as well as to the impact of particular birth practices on the child.

In behaviourism and reinforcement[18] theory we find further theoretical confirmation of the experience of natal therapy.

Birth, the first contact with the world, initiates a whole new series of responses. It involves the child's first physical separation from his mother, the womb, and the umbilicus. Ironically, therefore, although it represents the individual's first individuation and physical autonomy, it is also his first experience of vulnerability and his first contact with external others. The moment after birth, the infant's repertoire of possible responses comprises those stemming from the womb environment – those that are physiologically or hereditarily predetermined, and those introduced to him in the womb or during birth. So, when a stimulus requires a response, he – like every other individual – must choose from his existing repertoire of responses, duplicating or modifying one that is familiar and appears best to fit a new situation. If he chooses a response learned during birth, the response is thereby reinforced and so has a greater possibility of being chosen again. The next time he may again choose and modify it, and again, so that by the time he enters adulthood all his responses may be duplicated or modified birth responses.

Looking at learned behaviour in this way, we can see each second of birth as a separate and unique unit of experience. And we can also see that those birth moments that were distorted or disturbing at the time will become magnified as whole distorted patterns in adulthood. By revising experience of the original birth moment in therapy, we can hope to revise the developed magnification of it and the behaviour arising from it.

Labour and birth cannot but be key psychic experiences. Except in unusual conditions, for instance when the cord is tangled, the foetus before labour begins may be said to feel only sensations of floating and limitlessness. The tightening of the uterus with the onset of labour is the first experience of restriction. Since this is a sudden rather than a gradual change, this sense of confinement is sharply distinguished from that of a tight womb. Then the pressure is equally suddenly released. Pressure brings awareness to each body part, while release brings knowledge that freedom exists. So just as the foetus encounters for the first time the sensation of a physical limit, simultaneously, when contraction is released, it experiences freedom. It takes the existence of a boundary to create the awareness of limitlessness; and the experience of freedom to acknowledge limits. Both concepts are profoundly important to the definition of self.

Quite contrary to Rank,[19] then, we see individuals who have had Caesarean births as having missed something essential to their psychic development: the contractions themselves. So we re-enact contractions in therapy, and find that these patients gain a stronger identity and a new contact with the world around them. If the Caesarean baby does not feel uterine boundaries, it has no awareness of being freed from them.

The enclosure and relaxation of labour can have many effects on specific subsequent body awareness. Both elements of pressure and release make up a total experience. Particular body parts, such as the head, the hip, or the shoulder, may have received more or less contraction contact than others: so after natal therapy patients may experience increases of sensation capacity in arms, chest, genitals or other parts of their body. A limb, for example, that suffered reduced blood circulation during birth – perhaps through constant pressure without alternating release – may retain a numbness throughout life which is so subtle that the individual realizes it only when sensation increases. Later cognitive development parallels this physical correlate: the grasping of abstractions such as time, space or logic is in part dependent upon this birth experience.

As will be seen in later chapters, emotional maturity and the development of skills in forming relationships also have much to do with contraction training. Since the contraction is the first direct physical communication of mother to child, this experience deter-

mines the development of later verbal, sexual and emotional patterns
with external others. Closeness to the mother creates awareness of
separation. The impact of labour is, thereby, one of the most important determinants to healthy functioning and the strengthening
of identity.

Patients undergoing natal therapy, just like the very first in the
manhole, often experience the sensation of being stuck at various
points of the body. Being stuck in the rebirth is like being stuck in
the fantasy: the person must get unstuck to evolve emotionally,
and the place where he feels stuck – whether head, shoulder, hips
or feet – is a clue to the problem itself. For example, many patients
who were delivered by forceps, or who tried to push out before the
mother was ready, feel stuck in the head. These are often 'head
people', characterized as over-intellectual, who use verbal therapies
not to resolve problems but as mechanisms of defence. Natal therapy
can get such a patient past his defence of over-cognition and into
his feelings, which can then be brought back to a verbal session and
reintegrated there.

One man who has stuttered all his life suddenly began after natal
therapy to speak normally. We discovered that the umbilical cord
had been tied around his neck during labour. A woman who had
long lacked feeling in one leg began to walk normally. We found
that during birth this leg had been entwined around the foetus of
her dead twin. Another woman, who had spent her whole life in a
hysterical frenzy, was slowed down during her natal therapy experience and gained a new calm in her daily life.

Separation anxieties, family and sexual malfunctions, problems of
responsibility for the self, and a variety of other disturbances can
be dealt with and resolved in this way. When a woman went into
a severe depression after her natal therapy experience, it turned out
that she had contacted feelings about a father who had died when
she was two and whom she had never previously mourned. In later
discussion she described an undefinable sense of loss, and recalled
previously buried memories of her father's death. Because she had
been so young at the time the death had been associated with feelings of guilt and 'grandiosity' – the child's feeling of omnipotence
that makes him feel that whatever happens he has *made* happen –
and these still negatively affected her life until they too were reached
and finally understood.

Another patient was unable to function sexually with his wife in
any satisfying way. Although he could ejaculate, he had little physical

sensation and none of the accompanying orgastic emotional outlet in elation or a sense of fulfilment. In checking out his birth history, it was discovered that just prior to delivery his mother had been given excessive amounts of anaesthetic, so he arrived in the world asleep. By re-experiencing the moment of birth with attentiveness, and feeling the satisfaction of the climax, his orgastic capacity increased. The concept of a correlation between birth and sexuality will be discussed further in Chapter twelve.

Still another patient complained of a state of immobilization and tendencies towards procrastination. He recognized in therapy that these feelings arose from his sense of fury at being yanked from the womb before he was ready. His passivity during his first natal experience showed his general sense of helplessness in life. When he became more active and creative in his movements in the birthing, his daily functioning too became more autonomous, self-reliant and effective.

We are however just beginning to find and understand the correlations between birth and ensuing emotional states. Natal therapy is now in its own birth: we are witnessing the inception of a new therapy. But natal therapy cannot, as many have expected, impose insight; it can only facilitate. It can function as a tool to gain insight and expand awareness. But, as with all other tools, its effectiveness is dependent upon the user, and upon his active participation.

This book is intended to act as some sort of guide towards the recognition of the importance of being born.

Birth is a significant and specialized area of study that has been too long ignored.

It is my hope that this presentation will encourage others to find ways of extending the thoughts I have expressed, to challenge them and develop new insights of their own. The following chapters, setting out the theory that developed from working with birth, are therefore not definitive; but they may act as catalysts to inspire whole new ways of thinking about ourselves.

We begin with the start of life, and a mental journey to 'the world of the womb',

2 WORLD OF THE WOMB

The world of the foetus consists of a continuous endless experience of the self. He is joined to the limits of his world – the wall of the uterus – by the umbilical unit of the placenta and the cord. One thing is connected to another which is connected to something else, so that there are no separations between the foetus and his environment. The world without is one with the world within. There are no value systems, no judgements, no comparisons. It is an existence that is warm and growing, devoid of fear, pain, or competition; a totality and a utopia, resembling the visions, dreams and goals of poets or prophets.

This is the environment that we are now to investigate. To do so, we must force our imagination to travel almost as far as if to a distant planet: we must draw on science, on speculation, on conjecture to see this world, for we know so little of it. So some of the formulations set out below are based on concrete fact, and some on mental fabrications made up of bits and pieces of logical deduction, intuition and dream. They cannot be presented as truth, only speculation. For this I beg the reader's indulgence.

We will begin with the physical world of the foetus, for there is the particle of knowledge we have at hand. From there we will shift slowly across theories and fantasies, and build a picture of the possible, even if we cannot prove that it is real.

Physical World of the Foetus

We know that the sounds of the internal mechanisms of the mother – her heart beating, her blood pulsing, and the liquids slushing through her digestive system – are a definite reality to the foetus, to which it attends and responds. One author at least has claimed that the foetus can hear noises outside the womb, and even suggested that it has some form of sight, which gives it a sense of light and imagery, although limited and distorted.[1]

We know also that life in the womb is dark and warm. But we cannot postulate any awareness of concepts of darkness or warmth, since the foetus has no real experience of light, or cold. These perceptions are part of the child's awareness only after birth. On the other hand, it is almost certainly the post-womb experience of cold, in contrast to the warmth of the womb, that gives us the powerful emotional meaning we attach to concepts of warmth and cold. It is surely not coincidental that we can be considered warm or cold emotionally, or warm or cold in terms of sensitivity or sexuality.

Life in the womb is also thought of as quiet. We find throughout the literature references to this intra-uterine quiet – which is in striking, even surprising, contrast to all the activity of which the foetus is capable once it is born into the world.

Stimulation and Response

This quiet, we are told, obtains because stimulation in the womb is so limited. But if we re-examine this idea, we may come to a different conclusion: that in fact the foetus is not so much quiet, as just not making responses that we define as responses. The overt expressions by the foetus that are observable may appear relatively lethargic. Yet even apparently minimal external reactions could represent considerable internal activity: the foetus may be going through periods of adjustment to the novelty of his ongoing development – the extraordinarily rapid and intense development of the unborn. Only as the newness becomes mastered does the foetus become more visibly energized. So although outwardly passive, the foetus may be seen as working internally at conquering and mastering his situation. When each growth alteration is assimilated, he becomes more outwardly vigorized. Put another way, we could postulate that the degree of activity increases as the novelty within the womb decreases. It is well known that an energetic foetus will stop movement when there is change, as for example a climatic shift should the mother travel while pregnant.[2] We know that even as adults, novelty frequently breeds inertia, till familiarity frees reaction. Should this be so in the womb also, we would conclude that there is a constant form of stimulation there, and a constant form of arousal.

Understood this way, the increased activity when the foetus enters the world represents a continuation of techniques for adaptation that have been already learnt, and that will be used throughout growth. Change has been conquered in terms of internal adaptation, and therefore external adaptation becomes manifest. This view is in contradiction of the literature, which perceives the foetus as a passive dependent creature; and it initiates the alternative view, that he is in fact dynamic and independent.

This view is substantiated in part by physiological research on cognition, myelinization and physiological development.

Consciousness

Greenacre,[3] in a fascinating discussion of foetal biological development, says that some research workers believe that there is a forerunner of consciousness in the womb. They base their conclusions on observation of periodic activity in the foetus, as though he had waking and sleeping cycles. Other studies identifying apparent fatigue in the womb seem to agree with this idea.

Myelin is a coating on the nerve that conducts neutral and other impulses.[4] Although reactions are sometimes possible without it, the response is slow and the stimulus must be more persistent and extreme. Messages to the nervous system from the organs of vision, hearing and touch – especially messages of pain – can be reduced and even eliminated without it. Demyelination diseases[5] frequently result in paralysis and loss of muscle control.*

The fact that myelinization mainly takes place after birth has been used to argue that the foetus lacks consciousness. However, recent[8] evidence shows that myelin deposits in the spinal nerves appear as early as the fourth month in the womb. The process is not complete till after birth, so that it is unlikely that a pain response could exist for the foetus; but some cognitive activity or memory retention might be possible. Langworthy[9] in 1933 wrote the first major work on this process, which is still used for reference today. His research indicated that nerves become myelinated as they become functional. Stimulation seems to facilitate that process, so if vision is inhibited till days beyond birth, so is the myelinization of optic nerves.[10] The process of birth, as he points out, because it involves extreme stimulation, particularly of the head, promotes increased myelinization and thereby possibly cognition, as well as sensitivity to pain. According to another source,[11] the process increases further at the end of the first year, and thus coincides with the establishment of bowel movement control and the beginning of effective toilet training.

* Although no research seems to have been done into the question, the author suggests that there may be connections between demyelinization and some mental illnesses, since loss of bowel control, for instance, is part of psychotic symptomology. Injections of vitamins B–6 and B–12 have been valuable in reducing symptoms not only of such diseases but also in coping with schizophrenia.[6, 7]

Body Movements

Body movements in the womb are also significant in that they may affect later emotional states, and mental development. According to one author,[12] movements create sensations which have patterns. These patterns are actually imposed on the musculature, and then on the cortex itself, as imprints or memories, which remain like a permanent 'motion picture' to influence our consciousness and future reactions. Motion is not initiated by the foetus in the first place, but movement can result early on from stimulation. And when it does occur, it is a massive organismic response: that is, the whole body responds. Only later do individual muscle responses begin, and finally reflex movements. Muscular reaction first takes place throughout the body and becomes more localized with development.[13]*

By the same principle, in psychosis, almost every textbook on abnormal development reports findings that with regression a reversal of this process takes place: decreased body functioning starts with single responses, and only later do the massive responses stop functioning.[15] For example, severe anxiety shows symptomatically in a loss of swallowing, speech or bowel control; then eventually, if it reaches the disintegrative stage of catatonia, all body functioning becomes immobilized.

Explanations by psychotics of their reality may therefore be another way through which we can discover something about the way the foetus must feel and experience. For example, hypersensitivity to vibration is one of the symptoms of the psychotic episode, and is used as a rationale to verify delusions. Sensing vibrations in this

---

* If we look at very early foetal development[14] we find that prior to the growth of the umbilicus the yolk sac is the primary organ. Its functions include:
1) providing nutrition to the embryo;
2) acting as a digestion tube;
3) originating the germ cells which later find their way to the foetal reproductive centre and become sperm and egg cells for the next generation; and
4) forming the first source of blood supply and the beginning of blood vessels.

This yolk sac is one continuous system that later divides into oral, anal and urogenital components at about four weeks of life, that is, just before the beginning of myelinization in the spinal nerves. Within the following days, its usefulness begins to end as the umbilical cord develops and takes over its functions. This phenomenon exemplifies the reality base of physical as well as emotional inter-reaction later.

way may well be a womb phenomenon, emanating from the umbilical flow or chemical transmission that is felt by the foetus as a primary area of communication with the mother. The healthy development from this early sensitivity to vibrations is to be found in feeling for music, rhythm and the dance.

It is also no surprise that experiments with sensory deprivation, where the confined environment closely resembles that of the womb, often elicit psychotic responses.[16] Freud indicated that psychosis has its origins in the oral stage of development after birth. It may therefore be useful to see what connections can be made between psychosis and the oral stage in foetal development.

It is known that an oral reflex[17] – the foetus moves its leg when the lips are stroked – appears at the beginning of the second lunar month of intra-uterine life. This phenomenon indicates a connection of response throughout the body. Opening and closing of the mouth appears as a discrete and localized reflex at about the eighteenth foetal week; while sucking and swallowing are developed as early as the third or fourth month. Even the hand-to-mouth reaction begins in the uterus.

We also know that in adults, sucking results in a pulling in of the stomach. This observation led the author to speculate that there is an association, starting in the womb, between sucking and the drawing in of food through the umbilicus. The experience of sucking the thumb might thus be used by the foetus to facilitate the flow of food through the umbilical cord, or more probably to control the degree of sensation around the navel area. This self-stimulating response, if indeed it exists, would be a basic conditioned reflex: the food flows into the foetus' body through the umbilical cord, and then after a time he begins to learn to manipulate the flow so that he is in control.

Since no experimental investigation has been made, this is a purely hypothetical concept. But it is at least possible to conceive of the stomach muscles as being contracted by the sucking responses, and of these muscles as modifying the stimulation and flow of food or sensation from the cord. The foetus learns first passively, then actively, just as he learned to be active in movement.

Genital development occurs approximately at the same time that the heart develops, at about twelve weeks.[18] It also so happens that about this time, one of the two veins (and two arteries) present in the umbilical cord when it first developed, is liquidated.[19] This fact supports the idea of a developmental connection between genital sensation and umbilical development, which the sucking response may reinforce. The nerve relationship to the genitals is something even the adult can feel by applying pressure to the navel.

Again, reference to psychotic experience seems to support the hypothesis. Sensations of flowing, connected perhaps with the amniotic fluid and also with the umbilical cord itself, can be a component in psychotic fantasies,[20] in most of which body fluids tend to feature. The ability to self-stimulate with the navel may also be a precursor to masturbation, and interestingly psychotics have a period prior to breakdown where there is an increase in the need to masturbate.[21]

Mastery and Competence

Expressed in terms of conditioning theory, then, there is a reward concept in the womb, the reward being food or increased sensation, and a degree of mastery, or control, of sensation. And if in fact this first experience of competence occurs at this point, this is very significant to control concepts for the individual after birth. Whether the foetus has unrestricted control over the flow of nutrition, or only limited control, as when the cord is wrapped around his body or his feet, may determine many later emotional reactions. *Therefore, the forerunner of the concept of competence is part of womb experience*; but so is the first experience of vulnerability, as well as the distress connected with it.

Post-womb reality, however, will determine and shape the meaning of this pre-birth experience in the life of the individual, for as long as any aspect of foetal life remains isolated and unconnected to the outer world, it cannot really be described in terms of concepts as we understand them. For example, it is impossible for vulnerability, which to us has components of dependency, fear, deprivation, anxiety, guilt, etc., to exist fully until after birth. The superimposing of reality, society and the external physical world on to intra-uterine life changes its meaning. As in the case of the contraction training described in the last chapter, the future experience changes the meaning of the past.

Relationship

In the womb the infant also has his first experiences of relationship. He can relate to his thumb by sucking it, he can relate to the placenta and the umbilical cord and to the walls around him. He can suck or release his thumb – which skill may even be a forerunner by association of contraction training during labour, although sucking is controlled by him, and contractions during birth by the external uterine wall. The degree of the foetus' involvement with his own thumb is clear in some of the photographs taken of infants while still in the womb: some children are even born with callouses on their fingers from thumb-sucking. And there are actually pictures of a nine-month foetus having what might be called a temper-tantrum, after losing control of his thumb.[22] Rage would thus appear to be the first emotional response of which the foetus is capable, or at least the first emotional response that we can identify.

Rage

The idea that infantile rage may be a womb-originating phenomenon is reinforced if one observes the body postures of rage reactions after birth. Post-birth rage always has elements of irrationality, of a physical reaction which seems to control the whole human being, bypassing the ego. That rage is predominantly physiological as opposed to emotional in expression, would support the idea that it is a more primitive reaction, stemming back to a pre-logical stage of development, than for instance anger and aggression, both of which encompass a mental reference to the existence of others. Rage just *is*, and renders the subject oblivious to others. To this extent it is lacking in conscious awareness and surprisingly conflict free.

At this point the author will risk the assertion that rage can be classified as womb experience, in that it does not need learning or any environmental phenomenon in the real world to create it, and that all instances of rage in childhood and adulthood are potential reflections of this type of rage within the womb. Anger, assertion, rebellion, on the other hand speak of world experiences, and represent a 'higher' stage of development. This is an important conclusion to reach, for one of the purposes of birth psychology is to differentiate between emotions that relate to intra-uterine experiences, and emotions that are more highly developed. The more non-womb reality to which the individual is capable of adapting – i.e. the more he can assimilate the complexity of life – the healthier and more mature he will be.

The First Contradiction

When the child is inside the womb, he relates only to a few things. He can experience his own body. He actively attends to his fingers, specifically the thumb, and at six months, he practises the sucking response with it. He relates to the umbilical unit and the walls of the womb. However, there is some contradiction in the idea of relationship, when the whole is a single life-support system of which the foetus is a part. The umbilicus, placenta and womb might be considered as extensions of his self, or actually as parts of him. On the other hand, they are in some sense distinct, alien to the self. So the beginnings of post-birth conflicts concerning individuation and differentiation can be detected in this intra-uterine contradiction. But the conflict is without emotional content; and, as with many womb events, it is later reality, the feedback of the external world, that will determine its meaning and outcome.

Embryo Parents

The embryo is physically dependent upon the umbilicus. And at first it is huge: originally larger than he. It looks down upon him, a massive 'phallic' symbol. It fills his sky, and surrounds him, protects him, feeds him and is always there for him. It is the first real parent: it gives him security and he clings to it.

This grasping response originates at approximately four weeks, and it is obvious that the most graspable thing within his environment is not himself, nor the massive placenta but the cord. So his first relationship evolves with this. The cord starts as massive compared with himself, but as he grows, he comes up to meet its size. Similarly, during his teen years, he will catch up with the size of his parents, and the emotional relationship with his parents at that time may even re-enact in some way the 'umbilical unit'-to-foetus interaction prior to birth.

The father is the first cord substitute after birth, so the forerunner of the relationship with the father is the infant's relationship to the cord within the womb. The mother, on the other hand, represents the placenta. This parental symbolism in the pre-birth development of relationship will be elaborated in greater detail in the chapter discussing the crisis umbilicus. However, the metaphorical significance is important to note at this point, especially when one examines the process of birth itself.

Before birth, placenta and cord are the foetus' total environment, his security and source of life. Then as he goes through birth, he slowly feels the placenta being pulled downward, away from him. Sometimes he feels entangled by the cord, or it gets tied around his neck and chokes him and cuts him off from the rest of the world.

His food supply becomes erratic. Much can go wrong during birth with the placenta and the cord, which can keep him from being born or cut off his oxygen.

Up till then, the umbilical unit was his friend and protection, and suddenly it becomes his enemy, at the very time when the womb has become too restricted a space for him.

The Concept of Difference
The onset of birth also lays the foundation for another concept – that of difference. When the infant is in the womb there are no differences and no comparisons – there is no 'other' with which to compare. With the first contractions of labour, the pressure followed by the release of pressure is the first real 'difference' in sensation of which the infant is aware. From this other differences can be generalized after birth – concepts such as greater and lesser or better and worse, good and bad or big and small, which are all phenomena of the real world and not of the womb world.

The Organization Principle
Freud identified a need in the child to find a logical organization in experience, and this drive towards organization he called the Ego.[23] Our imaginative reconstruction of womb life suggests that there is also a logic that is within the womb, and that this is as strong as the ego that develops later – it is *modified* by the ego to adjust the infant to reality. This theory is contrary to that of Freud, according to whom ego is non-existent at birth and begins to evolve only after the age of five to create a logic in reality.

But it is the author's conviction that the organization principle is present in the baby upon entry into the world, and that it originated in the womb. We shall call it 'Logos', or the logic of the womb. This is differentiated from the concept of ego by the fact that it does not include reality. The ego – reality organization – combines with logos after birth for full adjustment.

This logos, as we will see in Chapter five, can be lost to the infant when he encounters his vulnerability in the new environment; or it can become strengthened, if adequate emotional sustenance is offered him.

The development of the organization principle is thus continuous from the beginning. And the pattern of the foetus' physical growth in the womb is the basis for the order of mind. That is, the pattern of one thing built on another, one thing growing out of another, reflects a development to more definition and identity, which is logos. Anything that reverses this tendency by making for less definition, or that breaks the continuity of movement by imposing abrupt change without transitional phases, is anti-logos and leads to confusion.

In this sense, the work of Leboyer[24]* and others who have tried to encourage gentler and more 'natural' birth practices, has added transitional steps on a physiological level in the passing of the infant from the womb into the world, and so contributed to the preservation of logos. Possibly these steps should be extended even further. For example, the experience of darkness could be extended after birth into a period of days rather than minutes. Warmth could be simultaneously prolonged over a period of time, so that the infant could more slowly adjust to the alien experience of coolness. Fulfilment of the infant's demands for feeding also seems more desirable than scheduling, since post-womb practical orientations can jar the preceding order. A slow withdrawal of attention, and ready response to needs, particularly those for food and sleep, would give the baby time to adjust. Sudden discipline may result in incipient feelings of deprivation, dysfunctional adjustment or later resentment and rebellion against authority.

Reality and Truth
Womb psychology gives a special meaning to the concept of reality testing, or finding what *is*, as distinct from non-reality, which is a distortion of what is, and is used to cover up reality. Truth, in the sense that the word is used here, means the logical transition – according to logos – of a concept from the womb into the world. Truth implies a direction, a goal and a sense of organization that inspires a drive for mastery of the environment. The transition from the womb to life, of the concept of relationship with the umbilicus to relationship with people, is an obvious example of such truth, and a transition which we have to work very hard to get wrong.

Distorting or 'getting wrong' what is logically consistent, is what breeds confusion, disorientation, self-negation, emotional prostitution, seduction and the whole range of problems arising from birth trauma that will be discussed in the following chapters. The world, according to birth psychology, is *exactly* like the womb, and when we are born no tremendous modification of our response to environment in terms of logic is necessary. We go in this sense from one

* See Chapter three.

type of womb into another, the womb on the outside, or the world, containing only variations or modifications of the variables that we have already experienced in the womb 'inside'. If the child's experience of an essentially consistent environment is in fact consistent, adaptation to the world will be appropriate. But if it is illogical – because of distortions in the people who deal with him – the child learns inconsistent modes of dealing with the environment. He picks up from those around him ways of responding, dealing and adapting. Inconsistent forms of feedback will be incorporated in his attempts to adapt. The result will be a distortion of that healthy form of response, that is, womb response modified appropriately and logically through the ego. Distortion means a break in logos and this in turn results in deviations from feelings of identity, and consequent defence reactions that further confuse and stunt psychological development.

Learning

The most basic learning pattern that the infant seems to incorporate even before birth is *imitation* – he learns to do what has already been done to him: first it's done and then he imitates it. First he is moved and then he moves; first he receives the flow of nutriment through the umbilical cord and then he attempts to control that flow. After birth, first he experiences the mother's love and then he gives it back. We only give back what we have already received.

Logical development moves from simple and general, to complex and specific: touch is experienced in the foetus throughout the body and then becomes localized; adult complex behaviour arises from the child's simple behaviour, and this in turn comes from the foetus' even simpler behaviour.

In the sense that in utero it is externally initiated and the foetus copies it, imitation is a learned response. The foetus is pushed, and this is his first experience of movement. Movement is imposed on him. Then he goes on to moving by himself by copying and repeating. 'The original passive movement of the foetus depends on the change of the position of the mother from standing, lying, walking or even breathing as well as impacts on the maternal abdomen with external objects. Every time an external object causes a change in position, a dislocation of the embryo within the uterus, there is an imposed movement upon the foetus.'[25]

That 'imitation' is an early conditioned response, dating back to

the womb experience, appears to be confirmed by the fact that
regression to imitative behaviour is common in psychosis.

Imitation is however only one elementary form of education that
may be seen as originating within the womb, then developing contin-
uously in adjustment to reality after birth. The basic concept the
author wishes to convey is that embryonic learning is a real possibility, and that the idea has repercussions throughout life; and a
hypothetical survey of possible base learning patterns started by the
foetus would include the following elements.

Reproduction of past behaviour takes place when a past circumstance
recurs, and the infant duplicates the behaviour he has already used.
This concept includes both historical reference, and reward; and
it is here that a mode of cognitive initiation is to be detected. But in
life, exact reproduction of past learning to a specific incoming
stimulus *can* be inappropriate, if the surrounding feedback is ignored.
Distortions of perception that result from attending only to fragments
of reality, and responding solely to them, will be discussed in Chapter
six.

Degree variation is a technique of changing response by exaggeration
or diminution, to facilitate adjustment. Over-reaction and detachment may be misapplications of this learning, and when either is a
consistent pattern into adulthood, an early disruption of the basic
cognitive organization can be assumed to have taken place. This
conclusion is even more obvious if not only the degree of response is
inappropriate, but reproduction is inappropriate – or displaced –
as well. For example, a man who becomes not only irritated but
furious because his wife shows affection to their son, may be re-
experiencing childhood jealousy that he felt when his mother hugged
his brother. He is not only over-reacting, he is displacing his reaction
altogether, for the childhood situation has nothing to do with the
current one.

Reversal is the process of switching a concept into reverse, or creating opposites. If this has a womb origin, it may be in the physical
event of the reversal of blood circulation after birth. This may sound
obscure, but much current thinking about 'mind' suggests that all
responses at the level of cognition or emotion may be traced back
to a simple physical counterpart that precedes the more complex
response.

Substitution or 'symbolization' takes place when the child cannot find exact correlates to a behaviour he understands. So he revises or generalizes from an earlier behaviour, incorporating new intro-jected elements. Since the earlier behaviour itself derives from ex-periences in the womb, the roots of symbolization too may be said to lie there, and future research may throw further light on its beginnings. The use of words is the most developed form of symbol-ization, and humour is an example of an even more complex tech-nique – a defensive one – developed from language.

The sixth learning pattern is *modification,* which is very close to symbolization except that it involves a slight deviation to adjust to external change. Finally, in *combining,* two forms of simple behaviour – which according to the theory of logos derive originally from the womb – are blended into another response. It is in these last four forms (reversal, substitution, modification and combining) that the new elements of the world and reality are essentially in-volved.

The first three forms of learning are the most simplistic, and are primarily assimilated in the womb. Only with birth, cognitive develop-ment, and the introduction of reality do the other four evolve to their full potential, and all are used in the process of adapting the womb world to the real world. If the learned processes of intra-uterine life are *not* found to be applicable in post-birth existence, confusion and distortion set in. Neonatal exposure inevitably adds elements that complicate and expand adjustment: anxiety, limitation, anal sensation, pain and communication all add to the learning repertoire and introduce new needs to organize responses in growing, coping and surviving. When these new non-womb elements are added in unpleasurable ways, convolution of the original learning into defen-sive coping mechanisms results.

Womb to reality
Within the confines of the womb the foetus is often thoughts of as being dependent, because of his total connection to his mother, who is his sole source of food and oxygen. However, if we view his situation from the foetus' own point of view, we may revise this interpretation: we may see him as seeing himself as a completely independent creature capable of total self-sufficiency, with his own life-support system. Provided his trip into the world is consistent

and his needs are fulfilled, he maintains this feeling of independence and autonomy that originated in the womb. He is not aware of his own dependence. This has to be shown to him later on, after he is born. It can be shown in a negative way, which undermines or totally eliminates his original sense of independence; or in a supportive way, so that he can learn to re-experience his original independence in the real world, and to integrate it with reality.

Reality as we all know is one of Freud's major concerns, so it may be useful at this point to consider how his theory fits in with the world of the womb.

Embryonic life, as has already been suggested, is in a way a mirror reflection of the Freudian stages of development in early childhood: in the womb, genital development comes first at twelve weeks of intra-uterine life, and the sucking response comes last at six months.[26] After birth on the other hand, according to Freud,[27] development of the sucking response comes first, at birth, and genital development comes last, at puberty.

And thumb-sucking, as we now know, occurs in the womb, prior to breast feeding. But Freud concluded that the thumb was a *substitute* for the breast. Does womb psychology suggest that the reverse may be true, and the breast is a substitute for the thumb? Since thumb-sucking in the womb promotes muscle flexion and somehow controls sensation from the umbilical cord, it would make sense to see it as in some sense a preparation for breast feeding. Thumb fixation is also therefore probably more primitive, and more concerned with control of self-indulgence, than breast fixation, which has more secondary characteristics and speaks of dependency that is other-oriented. This differentiation of points of fixation correlates with what will be later discussed as the Narcissistic-guilt dichotomy – narcissism being in these terms a regression to thumb fixation, whereas guilt originates with breast fixation.*

Womb life and birth also present the perfect metaphor for the need to merge and the need to remain separate, the drives called Eros and Thanatos in Freudian theory. The need to unite in the ego is a healthy form of merging, and the need to separate, in its healthy form, is individuation.[28]

Separation is for identity, self-sufficiency, self-awareness and independence, just as the cells separated in creating the child. Merging takes place when the cells combine to create a new being

---

* Narcissism is not itself thumb fixation, but a regression to it, which occurs *after* first contact with the breast. See Chapter ten.

and represents uniting, meeting and communicating. The need for separating can become aggressive, detached, narcissistic, rejecting and controlling. Merging, on the other hand, can become dependent, demanding, guilt-ridden and grasping. The antagonism between the two, merging and separation, can also create problems, as we will see in later chapters. The process is a pulling together and a pulling apart, represented in birth by the need to stay in the womb and the need to be born. Each can be used for healthy or maladaptive behaviour.

In our reality we continue to carry the womb world with us throughout life. The ultimate truth is that each of us is totally and completely alone in our lives, just as we were in the womb. When we hurt others, we hurt ourselves; when we are hurt by others, we are still hurting ourselves. Every dream character in a dream is really the self.[29] The perception of others in the world, our philosophy of the world, every aspect of our being, is ourselves, and affects and modifies our awareness of others. The self is the womb-self continued. The others, who and what they are, are totally dictated by our own perception. Each person is a separate universe. Not accepting one's aloneness in the ultimate sense, either by being dependent or by negating the positive aspects of being alone, means a rejection of the world and represents a form of womb return.

If the world of the foetus consists of a continuous endless experience of the self, however, we want to learn to modify that perception to include the requirements of post-womb existence. The first contact with the world starts with the onset of labour. And so we now leave the boundaryless realms and fantasies of the womb and travel further beyond to inspect the bridge to reality . . . birth.

3 PSYCHOPHYSIOLOGICAL ASPECTS OF CHILDBIRTH

by Lewis E. Mehl, M.D., Director of Research, Center for Research on Birth and Human Development, Berkeley, California; and Medical Director, Berkeley Family Health Center.

Childbirth is of central importance in every culture. Every society has fertility rites, birth myths and art, and persons whose duties to the community involve attending births. Because birth is so necessary for the preservation of the society, childbirth practices tend to reflect the deepest values of the culture. This is true also for the other rites of passage, including the transition to adulthood, marriage and death, but birth has been more difficult to study anthropologically because it has usually been a private family-friend affair, whereas these other events tend to involve the entire community.

Childbirth can involve unparalleled intimacy and emotional power or can be stripped of both by technical procedures and impersonal attitudes. Such depersonalization has been progressive in most of the developed countries of the West, where the process of making birth and death technical rather than significant life events has succeeded to an unprecedented extent during this century. This reflects a deeper process whereby technology has taken control of many facets of our lives.

Emotions come to be controlled by chemicals rather than expressed in a healing environment. R. D. Laing has written extensively about this.[1] Death takes place within a sterile hospital atmosphere. Preserving life as long as possible has become a goal rather than making death a meaningful, dignified life experience for the individual and the family. Jessica Mitford[2] and Elizabeth Kübler-Ross[3] have written eloquently about this. In the same way, birth has become technical rather than emotional. Such cultural changes have profound changes upon the life of the family and the individual.

This book deals with the impact of birth upon adult psychology, and with the therapeutic implications of this. In this chapter we shall explore some of the psychohistory of current childbirth practices, and the changes that are currently taking place. We shall elaborate on current birth practices as they may have affected the psyches of most of us.

Changes in Birth Practices in Recent Years

Birth practices have changed dramatically in recent years among developed Western nations, and are yet in flux. Through the century there has been a move from the traditional practice of birth at home, attended by a midwife (or in recent times perhaps a family doctor), to birth in hospital, where mother and baby are separated from their family (and from each other as well), and surrounded by medical professionals and machines. Yet today a new movement to humanize childbirth is growing, as women demand control over their own labour, the emotional support of their families rather than anaesthesia to deal with pain, and immediate contact with their babies. This new consciousness seems to reflect a growing level of self-awareness, or conscientization in Frieri's term,[4] and a cognizance of the psychological importance of the process of birth. At its most self-aware, the new consciousness accepts the painful aspect of parturition and assents that pleasure can exist parallel to pain,[5] insisting on complete sentience and even finding childbearing a transcendental experience, ecstatic to the mother and, perhaps, also for the child. There is a growing concern with how to make the birth experience a source of profound personal growth for the mother and a psychologically/spiritually positive experience for the infant. This book is itself an outgrowth of this new awareness.

The birth practices developed from the 1920s to the 1950s, against which new generations of mothers are rebelling, remain pervasive in the West, mainly through the uniformity of teaching of obstetrics in the medical schools throughout allopathic medicine. This allopathic tradition involves reliance upon drugs and surgery to relieve symptoms, rather than more holistic techniques aimed at preserving health, via good exercise and a healthy lifestyle. Allopathic medicine tends to ignore the psychological factors affecting health, as well as the traditional organic herbal pharmacopias. It represents the medical model as we know it today.

Giving birth under this regime became a very sterile undertaking, literally and figuratively. In America, typically, the woman came to the hospital early in labour. Once she had been admitted, her pubic hair was shaved, an enema was given, and an intravenous solution was usually begun. No husband or support person was allowed to be with her, even in the labour room, so the course of birth was very lonely. Twilight sleep[6] was still common in many maternity wards, and the norm was general anaesthesia at the time of the pushing stage with forceps delivery[7] of the baby over a wide episiotomy.[8] Pain medications such as meperidine (Pethidine), morphine, and Nysentil were routinely administered during labour. During delivery the woman was flat on her back on a delivery table with sterile drapes over everything except her vagina and perineum. Everyone present would be garbed in caps, masks, sterile suits and sterile operating garb. There was little place for humanity. Doctors and nurses would chatter, as they do during surgery, about sports and politics, well spiced with sexual innuendos and sexual game playing between doctor and nurse. Once the patient was under general anaesthesia, she would not infrequently be the object of humour or ridicule. After birth the baby would go to the nursery. The mother might not see her child for the first twenty-four hours, and thereafter only every four hours for feeding during the day.

This situation has changed remarkably in some American hospitals in recent years, as it has in the U.K. and in parts of Europe. There has been a progressive humanization of the process, although it has by no means reached every institution, and the United States norm probably still more closely resembles the practice of the 1950s than that of the most progressive centres of the 1970s.

Routine Technological Delivery in the U.S.
In routine technological delivery, it remains common for the woman to enter the hospital in very early labour – 2 cm cervical dilation – largely because she has never been adequately instructed about the feelings to expect. So she is put to bed, and conditioned to a passive role, both physically and mentally. She spends hours lying around, as little happens to move labour along, whereas in fact walking and activity, and an active energized mind, are most useful for good labour to progress.[9] In our experience 'passivity' is a common cause of failure of the uterus to contract effectively, and hence the necessity to encourage the contractions with the hormone oxytocin, which carries its own risks for mother and baby.

A passive mental attitude also tends to an augmenting mode of sensory perception – that is, more pain: if there is little sensory input, what there is becomes more intense. This then further enhances passivity, and when hard labour begins it seems much more intense than it might otherwise be.

The supine position (flat on the back) which the woman finds herself in, too, is the worst position for labour. The pressure of the uterus on the large arteries of the body – the aorta and vena cava – may actually interrupt the blood supply to the womb and cause the baby to become distressed.[10]

A prep (shaving off the pubic hair) is usually done at this stage. Since this procedure has actually been found to increase infection rates,[11] it must have more cultural and ceremonial significance than medical. Many women describe the experience as humiliating. Ostensibly it is done so the doctor will have an easier time later repairing the episiotomy (a cut made in the perineum from the vagina towards the rectum at the time of delivery). This also is of no scientifically proven value, unless the infant is in distress and needs to be born quickly.[12]

Next, an enema is commonly given. The justification for this seems to be that it prevents the woman from passing faeces while the doctor is working. It too thus has psychological roots (an obsessive desire for cleanliness as a defence against sexual/libidinal impulses) rather than medical ones.

Electronic foetal monitoring may follow. It requires artificially rupturing the bag of waters (amniotic sac), placing a catheter through the vagina and cervix past the foetus' head into the uterus, then applying a metal electrode to the baby's scalp. These two devices respectively record the strength of uterine contractions and the baby's heart rate.

Pain relieving drugs are ordinarily given after 4 cm cervical dilation. Epidural anaesthesia may be given at 5 to 6 cm of cervical dilation. This is done by threading a catheter through a needle into the space around the dura (the covering of the spinal cord) in the low back area of the spine. The anaesthetic is infused through this catheter to bathe the nerves and cause numbness in the areas reached by them, including the abdomen and the lower legs. The ability to move is greatly diminished, and occasionally there is significant hypotension (low blood pressure) at the time of placement of the epidural. This can cause distress in the baby by decreasing the amount of blood (and therefore oxygen) received from the placenta. Spinal anaesthetics are similar to epidurals, but they involve more risk.

In some hospitals it is routine practice for all women having their first child to be given epidural anaesthesia and to have a forceps delivery. This can be simply because the resident physicians (registrars) want more training and experience in the use of forceps. The residents (registrars) and nurses encourage the woman to accept drugs and epidural anaesthesia by telling them how good it will feel to be free of pain, and that it will not harm the baby in any way. This constitutes a powerful indirect hypnotic suggestion (see Bandler and Grindler[13] and Erickson et al[14] for a discussion of indirect hypnosis). After delivery the mother then feels she could not have given birth without the aid of forceps and medical intervention, not realizing that the anaesthesia made her unable to push and therefore necessitated the use of forceps (for a more scientific discussion of this see Haire,[15] Mehl,[16] Arms,[17] or Ettner[18]).

In this way, women become socialized into being dependent upon physicians and the medical establishment to cope with their normal, natural physiological functions (childbirth, menstruation, family planning, menopause). Sandia Danziger[19] has written about the importance of the medicalization of childbirth as a social tool to teach women a dependent, patient role. Ivan Illich[20] has described similar techniques of socialization to the dependency role in relation to general health care in *Medical Nemesis*. Both authors describe a process which might be recognized as indirect hypnosis, as a powerful means of convincing women who are in a naturally vulnerable state while in labour that unnecessary procedures are essential, so that they in turn become grateful to the physician-rescuer. According to Illich, the essence of such socialization is the creation of a class of women willing to allow their births to be controlled by technology.

Medical Procedures in Complicated Deliveries
Later in this chapter, we shall look at the alternatives to technological birth in normal deliveries. Before we do so, however, let us consider the problems of complicated deliveries. I shall describe the procedures that would be used in the context of my practice, with our consultants, and also attempt to give an impression of the range of variation in the management of these complications.*

Breech
The breech presentation is abnormal in that the baby presents with

* A wider discussion of these can be found in the book *Human Labor and Birth*[21] and in any general obstetrical or midwifery textbook such as Friedman's obstetrics[22] or Myles' textbook of midwifery.[23]

the feet or buttocks first. There is widespread disagreement about how this should be managed since it is difficult to assess the risks of the breech presentation *per se*. An inordinate percentage of premature infants are breech and, as prematurity itself carries inherent risks to the baby both in terms of immediate and long-term outcomes, it is difficult to separate these from those attached to breech birth alone. There is a greater incidence of congenital anomalies and malformations among infants who present breech compared with vertex (head down) infants. The reasons for this have not been adequately explained, though complications or deaths arising from such abnormalities are obviously not due to the type of delivery.

The major risk to the infant from vaginal breech delivery is that the body will descend through the cervix and the aftercoming head, which is the largest part, be caught by the cervix. The foetus can then suffer damage from lack of oxygen while the head is being manipulated out, or from the obstetrical manipulation itself. There is also danger of prolapse of the cord, if it is trapped while coming through the vagina so that it stops functioning, thus abruptly stopping the baby's oxygen supply.

In conjunction with our perinatal consultants, we manage breech deliveries in a hospital in a regular delivery suite, generally with electronic foetal monitoring of the baby. We attempt natural delivery as long as the course and pattern of labour appear normal and there are no obvious signs that the baby is too large in relation to the mother. If such signs do arise, then Caesarean section is seen as the best option. The procedure for a Caesarean section will be discussed later.

We are conducting a research project on psychophysiological integration techniques to convert the baby from breech presentation to head down before delivery. We use deep relaxation coupled with guided imagery and visualization, in an effort to utilize the mind-body connection to help turn the baby. This has been effective much more often than would be predicted on the basis of chance, and we are very excited about this approach to turning breech infants to vertex.

In some hospitals the routine is Caesarean section for all breech infants. There are in our opinion insufficient data to warrant this. The psychological implications for both mother and infant of a Caesarean section are tremendous and, for the most part, not sufficiently considered by physicians. Caesarean birth poses a nine times greater risk of the mother dying than vaginal delivery,[24] and maternal mortality rates have been on the increase in recent years along with the multiplying Caesarean birth rate. Infants born by Caesarean also have a ten times higher incidence of child abuse than infants birthed vaginally.[25]

There are ways to make Caesarean birth a more human experience than it is in many hospitals, and in particular to facilitate the bonding between mother and infant that would follow vaginal delivery.

Twins

For the management of twins, our practice is to use the labour and delivery suite of a hospital, ausculating both foetal heart rates, and often using the ultrasound foetal stethoscope (a small, hand-held unit which enables one to obtain the baby's heart rate quickly with ultrasound). The birth takes place in the delivery room because of the somewhat increased risks to the second twin, but it is done as humanly as possible without intervention unless necessary. If a twin is breech, then the usual considerations for breech infants apply.

The most important aspect of managing the twin pregnancy is preventing prematurity. We work with the woman on this, using intensive nutritional counselling, discussing appropriate activity levels for late pregnancy, and offering relaxation training and visualization sessions (psychophysiological integration techniques).[26]

Forceps

The chief indication for the use of forceps for delivery is foetal distress in the pushing part of labour (second stage), at a point where the baby can be delivered. Foetal distress usually takes the form of the foetal heart rate dropping well below normal levels (bradycardia), or beating very rapidly (tachycardia). When to use forceps is not always an easy decision. Observing the colour of the baby's scalp can be very helpful: a pink scalp is reassuring; a blue scalp is potentially ominous. In general, forceps are applied when the heart rate during a contraction is dropping very low and not recovering well or quickly between contractions; when the beat-to-beat variability (instantaneous change in heart rate from beat to beat) is flat or minimal (a sign of decreased oxygen reaching the baby); and when foetal scalp colour (or pH taken from a sample of blood in the scalp with a special speculum-like instrument) is not reassuring. When properly used, forceps can be very helpful.

Forceps have been abused in many ways. Often they are used

electively for the doctor's convenience to decrease the time he/she must stay at the delivery. Friedman[27] has found that the use of forceps in itself increases the infant mortality rate significantly, so it is obvious that forceps should not be used unless the benefits clearly outweigh the risks.

The procedure for forceps delivery involves creating a sterile field using sterile drapes, since an instrument is actually being inserted into the vagina and manipulated. The person(s) who will be doing the delivery usually scrub their hands and wear surgical garb, but only the person actually handling the forceps really needs to wear full sterile garb, including cap and mask – we feel the other individuals in the room do not affect the infection rate, if they are not involved in the actual birth. Usually pudendal anaesthesia is adequate for a relatively easy forceps delivery. This anaesthetizes the vaginal opening and walls, but does not totally eliminate the sensation of giving birth. It is given by injecting anaesthetic through the vagina into the pudendal canal where the pudendal nerve runs. An episiotomy is necessary when forceps are used.

When a fairly difficult forceps delivery is contemplated, which may not succeed (rendering a Caesarean necessary), epidural anaesthesia is used. The purpose of this is to obtain complete relaxation, so as to facilitate birth if possible. If vaginal birth proves impossible, then the proper anaesthetic is in place for a Caesarean. There is no reason, if the baby is normal after forceps delivery, why it cannot be with the mother to receive, comfort and love, just as with a normal vaginal birth.

Caesarean section

Caesarean section is a very useful operation for certain kinds of complications and can be life-saving. But when applied uniformly, as in some U.S. hospitals, it creates its own complications quite out of proportion to its benefit. The main indications for Caesarean section are foetal distress when delivery is not imminent, and cephalopelvic disproportion – when the baby is for one reason or another too large to pass through the birth canal. Cephalopelvic disproportion is diagnosed by inserting a uterine catheter (as described earlier) to measure pressure inside the uterus; and confirmed if the contractions are found to be strong, even though dilation is not occurring and there is no progress. One consultant, O'Driscoll,[28] however, has found that the administration of dilute oxytocin (a hormone to stimulate labour) at this stage has decreased the number of Caesarean sections that he performs for cephalopelvic disproportion to 0.9 per cent among women having their first child. Our team has found psychophysiological integration techniques used prenatally helpful in preventing the need for Caesarean section.

When a Caesarean is necessary, it can be made more human than it usually is. In many institutions a Caesarean section can be a nightmare. The woman may receive general anaesthesia and not see her baby for 24–48 hours afterwards, and then only infrequently. The psychological implications of this experience can be profound. In our unit, however, the mother is prepared by shaving her abdomen and pubic area, and cleaned with a betadine antiseptic solution to remove skin micro-organisms which might cause infection. Then an epidural rather than a general anaesthetic is used to allow her to be conscious during the procedure. We try to have a support person present with the mother, sitting at the head of the table next to the anaesthesiologist to give her support and encouragement. Using epidural anaesthesia there is commonly some discomfort from pulling and tugging on organs, and the presence of a support person helps make this more bearable. The mother and the support person can interact with the child after it is born while the mother's incision is being closed. Bonding can proceed normally during and after a Caesarean section, assuming the baby is normal. If the mother has trouble caring for her infant after a Caesarean because it is difficult for her to get out of bed, the support person, father or friend can stay with her to help. We have had several clients who have described such a positive experience after a Caesarean that listeners were sure that they had had a vaginal delivery. But there is still far to go to make operating rooms and the surgical process itself more human. Vaginal deliveries for subsequent pregnancies are also common in our hospital, assuming that the reason for the Caesarean section is non-recurring.

Induction or Augmentation of Labour
Induction of labour means causing labour to start artificially. This may be done with a controlled infusion of a natural hormone, oxytocin (which may be synthesized), or of another biological agent, prostaglandin. Oxytocin causes rhythmical uterine contractions which mimic normal labour. Prostalglandin softens the cervix and stimulates uterine contractions in a different manner. Augmentation of labour is used when uterine contractions are weak and ineffective.

The U.S. Food and Drug Administration has recently revoked its authorization for the use of oxytocin to induce labour electively (that is, for the doctor's or patient's convenience); but oxytocin can be used to induce labour when toxaemia of pregnancy is becoming severe, for diabetic pregnant women who do best to deliver somewhat early, and when the waters have been broken for too long.

In our unit we use the electronic foetal monitor with a uterine pressure catheter for the induction or augmentation of labour. This provides better control of the dose, and makes sure that if the augmentation is not working, it is not because we are using too little drug. This helps eliminate unnecessary Caesarean sections. The woman is in the regular labour room with an intravenous solution delivering the oxytocin, and a machine (an IVAC) to control the rate of administration. We feel that uterine inertia is very much a psychophysiological event, and can often use psychological interventions.*

Foetal Monitoring

Electronic foetal monitoring is a recent development. The first electronic monitor was developed at Yale University by Dr Hon in 1963. There are two types of monitoring – internal and external. Internal monitoring has already been described. External monitoring uses a belt strapped around the mother's abdomen, with an ultrasound unit to detect the foetal heart rate and a unit to measure uterine contractions by changes in hardness of the uterus against the body wall. The woman is relatively immobile with the external monitor, since there are only a few positions in which it will work. Once she is where it will function, everyone tries to keep her there.

Some physicians and hospitals mandate routine electronic monitoring. They claim this reduces the number of still births and brain-damaged infants, by detecting subtle changes in the baby's status early. The counter-argument is that these changes will be detected soon enough if someone listens relatively frequently with a foetal stethiscope. Haverkamp et al[30] have presented data showing that ausculation by a nurse is as effective as electronic monitoring for intermediate risk patients, and there is no doubt that the emotional impact of a human being with a stethoscope in an alternative birth centre is very different from that of attachment to a machine in a traditional hospital labour room. But the foetal monitor has an important place for certain women with high risk problems, such as high blood pressure, toxaemia or premature labour. Significant drop-

* This has been described elsewhere.[29]

ping of the foetal heart rate during labour is also an indication for
foetal monitoring.

A major disadvantage of the monitor is that once it is placed staff
will pay attention to the monitor and not to the labouring woman.
In some hospitals there are telemeter units so that the monitor signal
is displayed on a console at the nurses' station. There are positive
aspects of this, but a negative one is that nurses can watch the screen
without seeing the woman.

Pain Relieving Drugs and Anaesthesia

Drugs for pain are commonly used in technological delivery settings.
Yet we very rarely encounter a request for drugs during labour.
Drugs and anaesthetics are not discussed in our childbirth classes,
even for women planning hospital births. When clients ask about
them, we assure them that they will not be required and that even
though labour will be painful, they *will* be able to handle the pain
with the help of their family, friends and us. This is a good reason
for bringing a team of two to each birth – to provide that extra support if it is not forthcoming from friends and family. In general, each
effective support person is worth a minimum of 50 mg meperidine
(Pethidine) per hour.

During the second childbirth class we emphasize the painful
aspects of labour. We want to prevent women from denying pain to
themselves, and we stress that pain and pleasure can exist together.
Playing audio tapes of women in labour is especially useful, and
vocalization is encouraged as an effective coping style. While it is
easy to romanticize visual slides of birth, it is difficult to do so for
birth sounds.

'Pain-relieving' drugs (analgesics) may indeed make a normal
abour high risk. They seem to change the mother's time sense, so
hat labour is perceived as longer than before the drug was admini-
:tered. And they tend to decrease the infant's ability to cope with
:tress, and to lower the threshold at which stress becomes distress.

The effects of the regional anaesthetics (epidurals, caudals, spinals)
actually eliminate sensation, and this has the effect of eliminating
the emotional experience as well, as though the woman were watching herself on a video screen.

Infant Resuscitation

Resuscitation is needed for depressed infants who do not breathe after birth and remain very blue ('blue babies'). We try to avoid this through good obstetric practice. There are many signs which can aid in deciding whether levels of foetal stress and/or distress warrant intervention. An infant in trouble will drop its blood oxygen level and blood pH. These are usually reliable indicators, but when they are not, and the baby is born depressed, it must be resuscitated. When such depression is severe, this is termed birth asphyxia. There has been some speculation about the feelings of the foetus when this happens – suffocation, perhaps, and panic – and their impact on future consciousness. Accurate phenomenological data on this may well be obtained with the birth regression techniques described in this book.

When a depressed baby is born, it is cyanotic (blue), and limp. It is not breathing, has a slow heart rate, and does not respond well to outside stimuli. The umbilical cord is clamped and cut immediately. Sometimes stimulation by rubbing the back or the feet vigorously will suffice, but if not, a mask is placed next to the child's mouth and nose and oxygen is passed into the lungs by squeezing an oxygen-filled bag (an Ambu-bag). This is continued until the baby responds. If he does not, an instrument (laryngoscope) can be put into the baby's throat to visualize the vocal cords. A tube (endotracheal tube) is then placed through the vocal cords into the windpipe (trachea), and taped into place in the baby's mouth. A ventilator machine can be used for forcing oxygen-enriched air through the tube into the lungs using positive pressure. Various drugs can be given to combat the effects of acidosis (accumulation of acids and low pH), or the depressant effects of narcotic drugs, including bicarbonate of Narcan.

High Risk Infant Care

High risk care for the sick newborn has recently become more and more technologically sophisticated. Smaller and smaller (more and more premature) babies now survive who would otherwise have died.

The sight of a baby in a nursery or neonatal intensive care unit (NICU) can be frightening to a new parent. Usually there will be a tube travelling into the child's umbilicus (navel), inserted through an artery in the cord. This is used to monitor the concentration of oxygen and other gases in the blood. Often there is also a tube into the baby's windpipe (larynx), through which a machine assists the baby's breathing. Electrodes are attached to the baby's skin, continually recording its heart and breathing rate. Such electronic foetal monitors make a perpetual beeping sound with each heart beat, so that a constant beep-beep-beep at different sound levels (made by different brands of machine) provides the background noise of the nursery. Other machines may measure the blood pressure, the oxygen concentration present in the blood vessels in the skin, and other parameters.

The sight of a one-kilogram baby surrounded by these machines is indeed formidable. The effects of these procedures over many days upon the baby must be tremendous, and we hope that more of the kind of work presented in the remainder of this book will shed important light on this.*

Emotional Aspects of Physicians

Every physician is a human being with basic intrapsychic and intrapersonal needs, desires, and conflicts which he or she brings into the relationship between doctor and patient. He or she has learned certain communication skills, which are also brought into the doctor-client relationship; and particular value systems. The physician's beliefs about women and childbirth and the roles of women in society are particularly relevant.

One important capacity of the individual physician is the ability to tolerate, encourage, receive and express emotion. Family centred, non-medicated childbirth is an intense emotional experience – the more so, the more family oriented it becomes.

At least a partial obsessive-compulsive character structure seems common to many physicians. Such individuals do poorly with emotion. They have often experienced a symbiotic mother-child relationship in which emotion was seen as threatening because it represented engulfment by the mother. Intimacy and intimate experiences are to be defended against, since they may herald attack on the ego by the overly involved object. The hospital environment with its asepsis, masks, gowns, and inhibiting effects on feeling can be seen as a defence against intimacy, and the expression of emotion. Technical childbirth strips birth of its emotional power.

Another important intrapsychic factor which affects the individual physician and patient is the physician's ego strength and relative narcissism. The greater his ego strength independent of neurotic needs, the more he can tolerate and respect the patient's differing needs and value systems, and so work together with the patient in an equal relationship. If the physician's relative narcissism demands

* More information on procedures used in NICUs is available elsewhere.[31]

continual feeding, and he receives ego gratification from the dependence of his patients, he will be poorly tolerant of disagreement and differing value systems among patients. To defend himself against narcissistic injury the physician must subjugate the patient's desires, needs, and values to his or her own.

There is indeed a neurotic need underlying some physicians' choice of medicine as a career. For these, feelings of low self-worth are bolstered by the idea that others' lives are dependent upon their skills. The gratitude and subjugation of their patients become extremely important to them. With our model of the passive, dependent, weak, needy patient and the active, aggressive, strong, knowledgeable physician, the projective nature of these doctor-patient relationships is not amenable to reality testing. The flooding of anxiety aroused in such doctors by any attempt to make a transition from the paternalistic medical model to a client-centred approach, continues to block change.

Anxiety is a fact of life on most obstetric wards, and all feel it. One of the most consistent reactions from nursing staff who have been trained in a traditional hospital setting, then exposed to home delivery, is surprise at the lack of anxiety present in the home setting. They had imagined it to be *more* anxiety-provoking than hospital delivery. For a variety of reasons, partly related to the narcissistic needs of physicians already described, childbirth tends to be regarded in hospital as fraught with danger, as if each birth were a life and death crisis. Rigidity serves as an important social defence against this anxiety.

Primary defences applied by physicians include:

1. 'Splitting off' the relationship with the patient. The core of the anxiety for the physician lies in the relationship with the patient. Childbirth can involve an extremely intimate relationship between patient, husband, family, friends, and physician. The closer and more concentrated this relationship is, the more likely is the physician to experience anxiety. When the birth takes place in a hospital environment, a nurse and/or resident (registrar) is responsible for the management of the labour under telephone supervision of the attending doctor. The physician thus withdraws physically from the scene of childbirth, and places it on the resident and the nurse – who have developed their own defence mechanisms. These may include the substitution of a foetal monitor for direct patient contact, restricted contact between any one nurse and one patient, and use of obstetric analgesia and anaesthesia as a substitute for personal

intimacy, emotional support and encouragement for the individual.

2. Depersonalization, categorization and denial of the significance of the individual. At one hospital we studied in Wisconsin, all women receive pudendal anaesthesia regardless of their desire. All individuals in most delivery rooms wear caps and masks, except the mother. She is covered with sterile drapes, pubic hair shaved, and placed flat on her back with legs tied up and apart. Depersonalized, denied personal individuality, she is categorized as an obstetric patient – a class with only one recognized set of needs.

3. Detachment and denial of feelings. Physicians typically do not share feelings with patients or staff. Emotional expressions from any element of the system are discouraged. The disturbing feelings that arise within relationships are denied, and, in fact, in the guise of professional detachment, attachments are not permitted to take place.

4. Eliminating individual decision by ritual task performance. All obstetric patients are treated the same. Each physician has a somewhat unique idiosyncratic routine, but within a narrow range of variability. Nurses keep cards describing the routine orders of each physician.

5. Reducing the weight of responsibility in decision-making by a 'standard-of-care approach', so that broad categories of events dictate one and only one approach. One decision logically follows another as the only possible option, regardless of particular appropriateness.

6. Avoidance of change. Change is inevitably an excursion into the unknown. It implies a commitment to future events that are not entirely predictable, and to their consequences, and inevitably provokes doubt and anxiety. Any significant change within a social system implies changes in existing social relationships, and thus change in the operation of the system as a defence system.

Why the high rate of Caesarean sections?

The Caesarean section rate has risen steadily since 1964 in the U.S., so that in many urban hospitals 25–50 per cent of *all* women having babies are having Caesareans, even while in the Netherlands, for instance, the rate has held constant at 2.8 per cent.[32]

The reasons for this extraordinary situation must be sought in the social context.

Malpractice

One important factor which affects relations between physician and client, certainly in the United States, is the client's consequent view of the physician as made rich with money derived from his patients. Physicians tend to enjoy both high incomes and high class status. Yet the average obstetrician has been calculated to spend *five* minutes per patient on each prenatal visit. If one assumes an initial hour for a history and physical examination and an average of twelve pre-natal visits, this is a total of two hours. He or she usually manages the patient's labour by telephone with the help of nurses, and if all proceeds smoothly, arrives only in time to 'catch' the baby. This may require up to another one and a half hours. He or she may see the mother for ten minutes on each of the first three postnatal appointments, and again for ten minutes at six weeks. For a normal delivery, then, the doctor may spend in all little more than four hours with the patient, who (in California) would be charged an average fee of $1000 (approx £480).

Pregnancy is so significant and emotional an experience for the mother, notably for the first baby,[33] that it is easy to see how she may feel resentful at making such an expenditure without receiving what she can consider a fair return. It is easy to see too that the woman may have an incentive to develop problems during pregnancy in order to receive more attention and caring; or to have a difficult labour in order to involve the doctor earlier and for longer.

In the U.K. and other countries with socialized medicine, where doctors are paid on salary, it may be that they too have an interest in spending as little time as possible with each patient, in order to maximize the income received in relation to hours worked. European countries have also developed a tendency to look to the United States for models of medical technology, which bring along attendant pro-cedures and attitudes. The depersonalization of obstetrics is thus well under way in most countries of the West, and not in the United States alone.

A process has been recognized in intergroup relations whereby one group (in this case women, or couples) may project positive attributes on to another group (physicians), and deplete their own self-worth in relation to the idealized group. Psychohistorically, it has also been demonstrated,[34] that physicians have encouraged this idealizing projection and fostered it in their own economic interest. This process dates as far back as those French physicians who from the twelfth to the eighteenth centuries aspired to be 'priests of the body and of morals',[35] just as their counterparts in the clergy took charge of the soul.*

This tension between the devalued and the idealized means that the psychically impoverished group will seek every opportunity to obtain their just revenge from the group to whom they have surrendered their own positive attributes: 'By God, my oppressors should have to pay for my suffering. They're the strong ones, and I'm so weak. They have all the resources, and I have none.'

Hence, in the U.S., there is a plethora of malpractice suits brought against physicians. Further, in malpractice litigation, it is not uncommon for the court to rule for the damaged plaintiff even though the physician has demonstrated his or her lack of culpability for the damage – because the jury identifies with the plaintiff as a fellow sufferer and a member of his or her group. Malpractice suits thus represent a symptom of a continuing class struggle in a capitalist society, a symptom with its own particular psychohistorical origins.

Malpractice and Caesareans

This threat of suit against the physician for malpractice, then, has an effect on his decision-making. He (or she) modifies his behaviour to protect himself from liability. So the argument in relation to Caesareans, as Schneider[37] states, runs as follows: 'If one is aggressive and intervenes with a C-section – you're a hero if it's good. If the C-section doesn't go well, at least you tried. If the physician lets nature take its course, however, and things turn out badly, you haven't got a defence.' Yet according to recent findings, Caesarean section increases maternal mortality nine times over vaginal delivery, with over half of these deaths directly attributable to the procedure. In spite of this, C-section currently renders the doctor protected against liability in a way that vaginal delivery does not.†

Almost half of all Caesarean patients in the U.S. (4,000 a year in the period 1958 to 1976) have one or more operative complications, including a respectable number of severe complications (such as to compromise future childbearing, or potentially lethal).[39] These

_____

* In another paper, we have argued that this process was essentially a struggle between the Archetypal Masculine and the Archetypal Feminine, with a phytoid-like beginning in the early Hebrew tradition of individuation (Masculine Consciousness) and alienation from Yahweh.[36]

† Charles[38] has expressed concern that 'the pendulum might swing too far in one direction, so that physicians will feel that every woman should have a C-section because (they will think) that is the safest way to deliver'.

potential complications, in order of frequency of occurrence, are intra-uterine infection (35–65 per cent if internally monitored in labour, 20–40 per cent if not); bladder infection (cystitis); infection of the lining of the abdomen (peritonitis); abscesses; overwhelming infection throughout the body (sepsis); haemorrhage; adhesions between internal organs; open channels (fistules) between vagina and bladder, ureter and uterus, uterus and bladder, etc.; opening of the incision (dehiscence); rupture of the uterus in subsequent pregnancies; injuries to internal organs, including ureter, bladder, bowel, or nerves; complications of blood transfusion; blood clots causing stroke or other damage; pneumonia from breathing intestinal contents into the lungs; death or brain damage from anaesthesia; and cessation of the heart (cardiac arrest).[40] For the baby the risks include jaundice requiring treatment; increased irritability; respiratory distress caused by water in the lungs not being squeezed out during passage through the birth canal (lung-water syndrome); other causes of respiratory distress (breathing difficulty); drug effects upon the infant's brain and/or behaviour; abnormal neurological findings; prematurity (from repeat Caesareans having been done too early); acidosis (low blood pH); anaemia; and blood clots causing bodily and/or intellectual damage and/or death.[41]

Sexuality and its Relation to Caesarean Section
De Tocqueville,[42] in the beginning of *America*, described the typical American man as part of a 'nation of conquerors who submit themselves to the savage life without ever allowing themselves to be seduced by it'. The typical American man left the social 'bosom' that has nurtured his early years, his 'natal earth'. Avoiding 'staking' his life 'on the throw of the dice or the destinies of a woman', he converted his desire 'into the labours of the wilderness' with an obsession that stirred de Tocqueville to awe. The anxieties of this frontier world, however, had consequences for American women. As Barker-Benfield[43] has described, they shaped a common male view of women. Women were usually ignored or fled from. The arena for the development of American gynaecology was characterized by a growing polarity.

Both de Tocqueville and Cooper[44] noticed that young democratic women in America were uniquely free before marriage. This freedom, however, contrasted starkly with their status after marriage. The American wife was 'burdened' and 'sobered' with 'matrimonial duties'. Then came the Industrial Revolution, which superimposed a new view of women as frail, weak, sentimental and destined to remain in the home having children. Barker-Benfield uses the expression 'strong men over orderly women' to describe this. Similar changes were also occurring in England and Europe.

One feature of the move to consolidate male power over women made possible by the Industrial Revolution was the elimination of midwives. Birth has archetypically been one of the most important expressions of female power.* In myth, legend, sculpture and art, the mysteries of the Archetypal Feminine are consolidated in the birth process. For men to gain complete control of this from a technological 'scientific' view was to break open a mystery.

It also provided a means to socialize the free young democratic women described by de Tocqueville and Cooper. Birth – especially the first birth – serves as a ritual passage into the role of woman/ mother. To gain control of this could serve to 'properly' socialize the young woman to the mores desired of her, those elaborated by J. Marion Sims,[45] Augustus Kingsley Gardner[46] and other influential nineteenth-century gynaecologists and social changers – including the Reverend John Todd.[47] Such control could also serve to acculturate immigrant families: professional obstetricians symbolically opened up the immigrant family to 'penetration' by 'outside' male expertise, thus breaking tight European family bonds.[48]

The importance of the sexual metaphor here cannot be underestimated. The whole country was in a state of penetration and insemination of the virginal, fertile wilderness. Freud has described the element of sexual fear in the man who fled the creative union and left home – for the sea like Captain Ahab in *Moby Dick*, or for the frontier as did Kit Carson, John C. Fremont and others.

In order to convince women, as the 1800s began, to come to male physicians for gynaecological care, it was necessary to convince them that birth was dangerous and required the presence of a 'trained' physician. This led to strategies of unnecessary intervention and manipulation. An obstetric textbook from the 1840s,[49] for instance, advises the physician to break the waters and stretch the cervix, then to go away, telling the woman that this will hasten her delivery. If she delivers before the doctor returns, this attests to his work, for which he takes credit; and if she does not, he performs an operative delivery, again taking credit. Over a century later, a similar logic may lie behind the widespread American practice of amniotomy

* Neumann's work, *The Great Mother* attests to this.

to hasten labour: even in the face of Roberto Caldeyro-Barcia's[50] finding that amniotomy can prolong labour and contribute to foetal distress.

Doctor-attended deliveries in the mid-1800s serendipitously (for the doctors) fulfilled their interest in making childbirth dangerous. Doctors did not wash their hands between infectious processes, autopsies and obstetrical cases. The incidence of lethal uterine infections after birth rose dramatically. This phenomenon was attributed to the physical and moral decline of American women. Birth indeed was becoming a dangerous process, rising to as much as 20 per cent maternal mortality under some doctors. This figure can be compared with the records in the diary and logbook of a Maine midwife in the 1700s, who experienced one maternal death in 800 cases.[51] Intervention was not without its risks.

The next step was to convince women that anaesthesia was an integral part of childbirth, to fit the cultural notion of passive female dependency. J. Marion Sims and others had actually been travelling to wealthy homes to anaesthetize women for sexual intercourse.[52] The belief was that the more passive a woman was, the more attractive she was to her husband and the closer she was to the state nature intended for her. It was not a great step to attempt to transform women from active birth-giver to passive, being-delivered object.

Unanaesthetized birth, giving birth actively, is always very emotionally powerful. Women who give birth successfully have a sense of personal power and strength through the pregnancy, labour and birth. They are actively central to the process and not peripherally involved. On the other hand our current research has indicated that the nineteenth-century beliefs about women, forced upon them by men, actually interfere with their capacity to give birth. Passivity, dependency, low self-esteem, subservience and sexual conflicts tend to interfere with the physical process.

We have been particularly struck by observing that when a woman sees herself and her body as a mere sexual symbol, and presents herself in such a way as to fulfil the sex-role expectations of the male culture, she may find giving birth very difficult. Conforming to role expectations includes giving up strenuous physical exercise and developing a passive relationship to her body. For a woman who has never used her body, the stress and energy of labour may be overwhelming. If, on the contrary, she has an open, expressive, active sexuality grounded in a sense of her body as *hers* entirely, then the incidence of birth problems is diminished.

Avoidance of Intimacy

Another consequence of the Masculine-Feminine polarity which
contributes to the high Caesarean section rate is the tendency to
avoid intimacy. Existentially, this represents a choice for non-
relatedness, against love, community and communication.*

Birth is always intimate and sexual, although the intimacy and the
sexuality can be masked. My own personal experience of the birth
of my children confirms this. My feelings throughout my wife's
labours I can describe only as those of a very close, physical-
emotional, sexual union with her and what I felt to be the transcen-
dent force flowing through her. The sensation was warm and soft,
like making love, but was also strong, forceful and awesome. Each
time the experience changed my life and allowed me a glimpse of
the transcendental.

That this could be a potentially frightening experience – to see the
world divested of its usual constituted meanings, especially if one
is unprepared for it – is clear. For many, it may require the resurrection of strong internal defences against anxiety. Working with
women in labour, supporting them and their men and friends through
a powerful rite, can often reactivate disturbing memories and feelings, including libidinal impulses. So for the physician deeply
threatened with anxiety in the face of such intimacy, the safe choice
is anaesthesia and/or operative delivery. The clinical atmosphere of
the hospital, sterile drapes, isolating labouring women from the
support of their friends, the use of analgesia and anaesthesia, and
the choice of birth by Caesarean section are all means by which
intimacy and sexuality can be denied.

The historical trend toward operative delivery is clear. As far
back as the 1920s Dr Phillip DeLee recommended routine forceps
delivery and generous episiotomy to protect the infant's fragile
skull from the mother's vagina. He compared the situation of the
infant's head in the birth canal to being slammed in a door. The
sexual overtones – castration fear, and fear of engulfment by the
Feminine Principle – are obvious here. At this time, women had

* Neumann, in *The Origins of Consciousness*, argues that this split of
the Archetypal Masculine manipulative, operative skills from the deeply
feeling, intuitive Archetypal Feminine intimacy was necessary for the development of consciousness. It seems to us however that this path was one of
many Western society could have chosen, and that now an integration of
these polar dialectics may be required for our very survival in a violent,
competitive nuclear-armed society.

already been taught to demand anaesthesia – and under anaesthesia often could not give birth without forceps.

This trend continued unchanged until 1960, around the time when the natural childbirth movement was born. The International Childbirth Education Association was founded in 1961. The first electronic foetal monitor was designed at Yale University in 1963, and the natural childbirth movement was a clearly visible force in the U.S. by 1964. It was the same year that the Caesarean rate began to climb: if one plots memberships of childbirth organizations, or number of childbirth books published each year, with the figure on Caesarean section, the curves are almost identical. This does not prove a relationship between the two phenomena, but it is strong circumstantial evidence that the use of Caesareans was in fact a response to the attempt by women and their families to regain active control over the birth process. Once anaesthesia no longer functioned as a social enforcer of medicalized birth, new methods had to be devised. With advances in antibiotics, surgical techniques and blood transfusion, Caesarean section became less dangerous, and in some U.S. hospitals 20–50 per cent of women had Caesareans. The old message is confirmed: women's bodies really are inferior, women really can't give birth, and technology is required to aid weak, ineffective, inferior Nature. The result of this process creates a positive feedback loop, in which women become more hostile and angry with their physicians, but their anger only reinforces their dependence.

Feelings of fear, frustration, disappointment and failure are common after Caesarean birth.[53] Relief and shock are also common reactions, along with a sense of loss of control, and loneliness at having been separated from a spouse when parents most want to be together.

Denial is a common grief reaction, as are anger, self-blame, and depression – for a woman's self-esteem often suffers tremendously after a Caesarean, as does her body image. This has later consequences for both mother and infant. We[54] have shown that the best predictor of infant cognitive development at six months is the mother's self-esteem in relation to mothering. Caesarean families have been shown to be at a higher risk for difficulties with infant bonding, just as correlations have been shown between difficult pregnancies and birth (including Caesareans) and later child abuse.[55]

Dr John Hobbins of Yale[56] on the other hand has credited the widespread use of Caesarean section with helping to reduce rates of infant death at delivery. Yet there have been many advances in caring for high-risk infants in recent years, and the fact that Dr Hobbins chooses to put so much weight on Caesarean section only confirms a climate of belief in medicalized birth. That the attitudes of doctors in the nineteenth century are still with us can also be seen in the advertisements in medical journals: Lynn Shearer and colleagues[57] made a study of advertisements in obstetric journals, and concluded that they were as sexually exploitative of women as those in *Playboy* or *Penthouse*! Obstetric advertising depicts woman as the same passive, weak hysteric as nineteenth-century medicine portrayed her, totally dependent on the advice of her physician. Women are portrayed as not intelligent enough to give informed consent. The American College of Obstetricians and Gynaecologists is actually suing the U.S. Food and Drugs Administration to prevent patient information from being included with obstetric and gynaecological prescriptions. ACOG maintains that such inserts interefere with the doctor-patient relationship, arguing that the ACOG (a predominantly male organization) is the appropriate guardian of women's emotional and physical health care – a claim vigorously refuted by women-controlled groups such as the National Women's Health Network.

Psychophysiological Aspects of Birth
In the Center for Research, our approach to birth is phenomenological, in that we attempt to understand childbirth from a presuppositionless position, with the emphasis on data obtained from first person experience. In this way we are discovering interesting and important relationships between philosophical and psychological states and the physical outcomes of pregnancy and birth. The relationships are complex. We have learned that as a woman lives, so does she give birth – and, we presume, so will she die. We are deeply interested in why an experienced doctor or midwife can have an intuitive feeling that a woman will have a difficult birth, and so often prove to be right,[58] and have compiled a psychophysiological needs assessment form on the basis of our own experience. This list of important factors affecting the body process of birth is then used to provide immediate feedback to women about any psychological conflicts they may be involved in, the resolution of which might encourage a more emotionally satisfying and problem-free birth. Consistent with our phenomenological approach, however, we make no assumptions about how given factors will operate for a specific individual. These must be worked on experientially by the individual

person. The nature of the interactions between psychological attitudes, beliefs, expectations and lifestyle-in-the-world, and the physical processes of the body become apparent as the process of pregnancy and birth unfolds.

We see pregnancy and birth as a continuous process, amenable to detailed phenomenological description, and full of 'fringe facts'[59] (events which cannot be precisely measured), both emotional and psychological. We thus oppose the more conventional view of birth as discrete, with entirely separable phases. In keeping with Selye's general theory of the physical effects of stress, we have found that the *gestalt* of how a person fits on a number of parameters is more important than any one individual factor. There may be a low rating on one, or even five, of the key factors, but if the overall sense is positive in relation to giving birth, our experience of the process will usually be such. We are currently looking for clusters of psychological attitudes which may prove relevant to particular physical conditions, but are not assuming that we will find them. It may well prove that, though the factors we have identified may predispose to problems, any specific problem is a function of other processes. In fact, any specific problem manifested may have its genetic basis, its basis in the organ system of the body weakest in relation to stress, its environmental basis, and perhaps even an astrological basis, as Kautz and Kimball have noted and are currently researching at Standford Research Institute. The phenomenological position is that it is best to make no assumptions · but since no one can be perfect at that, we make the fewest assumptions we can.

Other researchers have examined influences of psychological factors on labour. Niles Newton[60] found that when mice labours were environmentally disrupted, the pup mortality rose significantly, along with abnormal labours. Murray Enkin at McMaster University found shorter, easier labours with women who attended childbirth preparation classes, compared with women who desired to attend childbirth preparation classes, but for whom no places were available.[61] Researchers at Northwestern University found decreased medical complication rates among women using prepared childbirth techniques.[62] Some of this may be simply a function of the avoidance of analgesia and anaesthesia, which have been shown to increase risk iatrogenically.

Childbirth Education

The two major childbirth education approaches may be represented by the LaMaze technique[63] and the Bradley technique. The LaMaze technique was begun by Dr Ferdinand LaMaze in France, and is also termed the psychoprophylactic technique for pain relief during labour. The Bradley technique was founded by Dr Robert Bradley in the U.S. Similar in principle to Bradley is the Read technique, started by Dr Grantley Dick-Read in Britain. And yet another approach is currently being developed at the Berkeley Family Health Center.*

The LaMaze technique distracts the woman's attention from pain to enable her to cope with the pain of labour: she and her husband are taught breathing exercises to do in time with the contractions. The assumption is that labour can be painless with sufficient distraction, but not all LaMaze teachers now accept the assumption that painless labour and delivery is possible. Further, LaMaze characteristically teaches a very stereotyped way of pushing: the woman takes a deep breath, holds it, and bears down. Noise is discouraged, as are vocalizations.

LaMaze is essentially a 'dissociative' coping style. Studies on long-distance runners have found two distinct coping styles,[64] in one of which the runner dissociates from the pain and stress of running by trying to imagine other things, creating the illusion of a cool mountain stream for instance, or simply removing him or herself from the body sensations. In the other, associative style, the runner accepts the pain and welcomes it. He/she builds on the pain and allows it to be a part of him or her, embracing it and pushing through the 'wall' until he or she enters an altered state of consciousness 'beyond the wall'. Here perceptions become sharper and pain is transcended, but still experienced.

The Bradley and Read techniques are similar to the associative running style. And the method in use at the Berkeley Family Health Center actually uses these findings about runners. Runners using the dissociative style, while relatively successful, are never champions. Champion runners use the associative style. And this is also true for childbirth. An associative style of coping is much more predictive of success in labour than a dissociative style. Many women trained in the LaMaze technique but who by nature live in an associative style do quite well during labour, and women who live in the dissociative mode may need additional training in using the associative mode to accomplish labour.

* More information is available from the Center in the form of a book currently in preparation by Gail Petersen entitled *Psychological Foundations for Childbirth Education: A Model for Personal Growth.*

The weakness of the dissociative mode is shown when it fails, or even succeeds too well, in suppressing pain, as the result is often uterine inertia, leading to ineffective uterine contractions. This reflex loop, caused by a sequence of neurohormonal events, has been described elsewhere.[65] LaMaze then is an externally directed skill for pain reduction.

In the Bradley technique, slow, deep breathing is taught. The teaching encourages the woman to focus on the sensations within her and to allow these feelings to exist. Although many Bradley teachers do not teach the associative mode directly, theirs is a more internally directed style and is more consistent with allowing the woman to be in touch with her own body processes.

The Bradley method is simpler from the coach's point of view, less steeped in technique and more real in allowing feelings and emotions, and it also permits the support person to respond to the woman rather than direct her. Bradley recognizes that some women do not need to push except with their uterus, and then not consciously. More options for coping methods, in short, are open to women using the Bradley method.

The Leboyer Technique

Frederick Leboyer[66] has had an obvious impact upon birth, not only in France but elsewhere in Europe and America. He recommends that the baby be born silently, without lights or under dim lights, and then placed in a warm water bath to recreate the environment of the womb. The baby is then symbolically reborn as it is removed from the water, and only then handed to the mother to hold. The theory is that childbearing is always traumatic, that the infant needs to be put into water gradually and tenderly to allow it to re-enter the womb-like environment, and that this rids the child of birth trauma.

What is good about Leboyer's technique is what is human about it. But there are rigid and limiting aspects of the method as well. Some couples using it maintain such a rigid rule of soundlessness that they prevent themselves from experiencing the wonder and joy of spontaneity in birth.

Our aim is for parents to be as completely spontaneous and open as possible. Since the foetus hears noise through the uterine wall during pregnancy,[67] it does not seem natural for him to hear no sound during labour. In fact, one could even argue that it might be frightening, if he has up to now gone through the normal cycles of noise during activity and silence during sleep, to be exposed to silence during such an active, intensive experience as birth. The infant at birth is already a conscious person who can know and sense love. If affection and support are spontaneously being expressed all through the labour, as they are in a non-interfered-with natural birth, he or she will experience the love received after he or she is born as a continuation of the labour process itself.

At the Berkeley Family Health Center, once the shoulders are birthed, we often ask the mother to reach down and take her baby. Every mother who does this exclaims with joy, and puts the infant on her chest and abdomen so that its head is essentially between her breasts. She then strokes the baby's head, cheek and back. This has happened so often during normal, natural births, that we have come to see it as a possibly specific behaviour of humans. Similar kinds of contact have been described as species-specific behaviour of primates.[68] There is nothing quite like this warm, close, skin-to-skin contact for the infant to know it is desired and wanted. Its shouts of happiness can easily be interpreted by any living being as shouts of gladness, rather than as fear.

We have not seen a neonate react negatively to its mother reaching down after the shoulders are born and lifting it out of her vagina with her own hands, exclaiming in elation and placing him/her on her breast.

These children seem quite contented, and it may indeed be harmful to delay this immediate mother-infant contact. For couples who want to use the Leboyer bath, we recommend that they do so some time after the birth, to give the baby the chance to experience that warm skin-to-skin immediate contact with the mother, and the father too. On a belief level, another failure of the LeBoyer method is that it seems to reflect the attitudes of most American obstetricians – that all birth is very traumatic and difficult for the baby. We do not accept that this is so. Birth is a process which can be easy or hard. The work of Leslie Feher described in this book, like that of David Cheek[69] and Helen Wambach,[70] in helping people to re-experience their own birth, makes it clear that not all childbirth is painful for the child. For many, birth has pleasant aspects for both mother and baby. What is distressing is the separation from the mother afterwards. Routine hospital care, drugging the mother and removing the newborn from her, reinforces distress and negates the positive experience.

Alternative Birth Centres and Home Birth

One of America's most innovative birth centres is at Mount Zion Hospital and Medical Center in San Francisco, California. Mount Zion has alternative birth rooms designed to provide a home-like setting and atmosphere, with proximity at the same time to hospital equipment and facilities in the event of complications. The prototype room is carpeted, with a double bed for the parents. There is a stereo receiver. There are bean bag chairs, hanging plants, a recliner chair, a rocking chair, a table, a private bathroom and shower, and a fold-out sofabed. As many family and friends as are desired can come to the delivery. The woman spends her labour attended by a nurse trained in the parents' chosen coping method and such other individuals – such as childbirth education teacher – as they may wish. There is no required position or procedure for delivery, and the atmosphere is very human.

Some other hospitals are developing alternative birth centres, though many of these, in fact, only present traditional delivery techniques in a nicer setting – alternative birth is as much a philosophy as a setting.

At the Berkeley Family Health Center, with which I am affiliated, we use Mount Zion's alternative birth facilities and thus provide clients with a very positive opportunity of a non-technological birth. We also attend home deliveries for screened, selected low-risk clients.

Our approach to prenatal care has been to attempt to develop a kind of preventive birth psychology. By working with women prenatally using a variety of techniques, we try to eliminate risk factors which could make intervention necessary. Childbirth classes at the Center are based on a theoretical grounding in current neurophysiological research – such as that of Buchsbaum and colleagues at the National Institute of Mental Health,[71] and the research on long distance running already quoted – and on our own observation of the applicability of these concepts at a practical level. Because our childbirth teachers also attend deliveries and see first-hand the success or failure of their teachings, there has been constant modification of our techniques. Indirect hypnosis and hypnotic suggestion are used by the teacher to augment the training.

Research on preoperative preparation of patients undergoing major surgery has shown that explanation of the process greatly decreases anxiety and also decreases postoperative pain.[72] Childbirth education techniques accept this principle that sharing detailed information removes fear of the unknown, and thereby decreases perceived pain. Some childbirth teachers, consciously or unconsciously, also use indirect hypnotic suggestion that the woman will deliver without complication and without anaesthesia or analgesia. (Many people are natural hypnotists and use this art commonly in their daily life.) With other teachers, who have had natural childbirth experiences themselves, modelling may be sufficient inspiration to students. Relaxation procedures include to some degree the principles of hypnotic induction, and help to induce a mild trance state in class participants, making them amenable to suggestions to avoid drugs.

Buchsbaum and his colleagues have studied a brain mechanism called the sensoristat.[73] Its function seems to be to control the amount of stimulus reaching the cerebral cortex at any given time. This sensoristat can function in either a reducing or an augmenting mode. When it operates in a reducing mode, experimentally induced pain is perceived less intensely than when it is acting in an augmenting mode.*

The function of hypnosis, meditation, and various visualization techniques may be to change the brain's sensoristat from an augmenting mode into a reducing one. This is the function of hypnoanalgesia during surgery. In our childbirth classes, we play down labour by telling clients they must know they are not in labour until there is no other choice. They are also given indirect hypnotic suggestions that if they should believe they are in hard labour and we find they are in fact less than 3 cm dilated, they will reset their brain sensoristat to a reducing mode, and so increase their pain

---

* The role of the sensoristat may be studied by computer-averaged evoked potentials taken from electro-encephalographic recordings. Experimental stimuli are repeatedly presented to the subject over the course of four minutes, and electroencephalographic responses from various brain areas are stored in a computer. The computer averages the response and, after four minutes of repeated reactions, can display an evoked potential, or a cumulative response in brain rhythm to the stimulus, on an oscilloscope. Alternatively, another way of measuring the reducing or augmenting modes prior to the development of the evoked potential technique is by using a psychological test termed the Kinesthetic After Effects Test.[74] In this test the subject is blindfolded and asked to match the size of a test wooden bar felt with the right hand, to the diameter of a tapering wooden bar felt by the left hand. The subject's left hand moves back and forth along the tapered bar to the rhythm of a metronome. After two minutes the subject stops at the place on the tapered bar which he or she feels to be the same size as the test rod. Reducers tend to pick a point on the tapered shaft smaller in diameter than the experimental rod, and augmenters are inclined to choose a point of a larger diameter.

tolerance to allow the pain enough space to grow to permit active labour to develop.

Visualization processes permit clients to get in touch with their own body process during birth before being taught the process in classes. Relaxation techniques let them, and include suggestions to help them, develop an associative mode of coping with labour. There is no recipe for handling labour. Singing is fine, vocalizing is excellent, yelling is healthy, dancing is good, breathing exercises are nice, praying is fine: whatever works is acceptable. What is important is that the coping style be such that pain is given permission to exist, and that an associative mode is used to manage the pain.

Using this approach, we have been very successful in helping women to avoid medication, and in fact, in over 300 deliveries, have had not a single woman who has taken our classes and had a normal delivery, need it.

When people spontaneously do what is natural, without culturally enforced inhibitions, they tend to do what is right for them. This belief relates to a basic faith in the natural instincts of human beings. As existentialists, we believe in a model of humanity which celebrates the ability of people to grow, change, learn and do spontaneously what they need. Deficit models of humanity on the other hand preach that people can be taught 'the right way'. In Leboyer's approach, women in labour are assumed to need to be taught how to handle their baby so that it becomes more aware and open to love. The writings of the Golds[75] make the same assumption. We believe that people are intelligent creatures, and that if not interfered with, that is they are not stifled by prior conditions, birth will be joyous and loving for them – and the baby will obviously know it.

This book is concerned with the ways in which the birth experience of the infant affects its later psychological make-up. As important is the way the birth experience affects the mother, her sense of herself and her feelings about her own abilities as a mother. These, in turn, have long-lasting effects on how she parents her infant. These factors can be worked with later in life. We can, as well, work to change current birth practices to humanize them.

Overall, our hope would be that with intensive prenatal physical and emotional support for mother and baby, birth trauma *can* be eliminated, and every birth become a normal one. As the notions of health optimization and holistic health care become more prevalent in our society, perhaps we will eliminate the deeper causes of birth abnormalities altogether.

4 *LABOUR, BIRTH AND THE ROOTS OF PERSONALITY*

The foetus is a being boundless in possibility, yet bounded by the confines of his physical self. Since he has just so many senses, organs, cells and synapses in his brain, he can learn within a predetermined range of ability and no more. Should he choose one set of learning he inhibits other learning.

Once born, he is limited by concrete reality – by what is, and what has been. His mind can wander, and partially transcend its concrete limits, but he cannot even begin to comprehend that which his own physiology precludes. Thus he can have abstract thoughts, but he cannot express them without returning to the world of substance.

It is the contention of this book that all patterns in life are metaphoric re-enactments of birth. As we have already suggested in the chapter 'Overview', these patterns come from the foetus' first experiences of movement, from interaction in the birth canal, and from his first radical change in environment: birth itself. Birth is thus his initiation into the experiences of travel, of pressure from without, and of exposure to non-womb substances. The foetus has experienced only muscle, tissue, organic liquids and chemicals: his was a physiological environment. Once in the world, he has to deal not only with the touch and hands of new people, but with new elements: air and water, plastic, metal, wood, glass, cloth. He is faced with a variety of new sensations. On the degree to which the transition into the world is continuous, or modified bit by bit in small steps rather than large, sudden and jarring ones, will depend the success with which the newborn adapts.

Based upon the components of his birth experience, the neonate will select out from the world that which is continuous with birth. Initially he can attempt adjustment only to a limited number of alternatives, on which he will later expand and build. So those stimuli that he chooses to cognitize will be those things that have some meaning in terms of his own past, whether through familiarity or novelty; and the ways in which he chooses to respond to them will reflect back to some historical connection with a previous pattern of response. In this sense, birth determines all life responses.

As we have already said, in the womb the foetus cannot distinguish between himself and his environment, since everything is continuous. He and his environment are one. During birth, contractions are external, but he cannot yet know this. We see in natal therapy that when the patient re-enacts his birth, he does so by pushing himself. He acts both the mother and the foetus. It seems that at first any activity the foetus experiences is *his* activity. And we see this over-identification with external phenomena again in the psychotic[1] episode which is characterized by regression, sometimes to the point where an introjected environment is actually felt once more to be synonymous with the self.

Autonomy

The mother's autonomy in pushing the foetus out is experienced by him as his autonomy. The foetus identifies with the mother and what she does, he is doing. When her body contracts, he feels as though he is contracting and when he is moved along the canal he feels he is moving himself. Only when the mother is helped externally (with forceps) and the natural flow of birth is disrupted, is his sense of competence threatened. If she pushes the child out too soon, on the other hand, he may continue in life to feel pushed into independence before he is ready. The pattern of birth can be affected in turn by the mother's experience of her own birth, which may predispose her to repeating it symbolically with her own babies.

Differentiation

The capacity for differentiation begins with contraction. The process of differentiation – individuation – is a stage Mahler[2] has identified as taking place between eighteen and twenty-two months after birth. But in Chapter five we shall trace back its origins to the cutting of the cord, and argue that on the baby's reactions to that first crisis will depend the success or failure of what Mahler calls the 're-approachment' phase of preparation for the separation from the mother.

Simultaneously with the initial break from the placenta, the child seems to have a feeling of suffocation until he begins to breathe on his own, so that one finds that suffocation is often associated with crises of differentiation in later life.

The idea of differentiation, or self separated from others, is connected also with the infant's initiation into other anti-womb experiences, such as pain, or cold, since homeostasis was the condition in the womb. In fact any extreme, even extreme happiness, is anti-womb in this sense. Emotional extremes can be seen as counterparts of contraction extremes, and contractions as the first experience of comparison or evaluation.

The rhythmic movement and exact timing of the contraction is experienced by the foetus as his own timing, and he introjects it. But imposed contractions, controlled by the doctor who administers a spinal anaesthetic for instance, will be introjected as artificial control, to which he is compelled to respond.* Speeding up contractions or inducing them may affect the child's response timing in later interactions.

After birth the infant continues to perceive the environment and the behaviour of others as extensions of himself, until differentiation takes place. Acceptance of separation is a world phenomenon; while rejection of separation – as in imitation, and projection – is a return-to-the-womb experience. Failures in separation, or differentiation, may thus echo problems in dealing with the first disruptions of identification and introjection during birth, or after.

The author hypothesizes that 'other' is initially identified in terms of touch – anything that feels unwomblike (e.g. metal) is 'other'. Only later is 'other' experienced through sight; as something seen but eliciting no sensation in the child's own body. Identifying body boundaries is thus essential to dealing with reality. Because 'other' is originally defined by touch or feeling, projection, identification or empathy can break down visual discrimination relatively easily, to make 'other' felt as self. But because sight plays a more and more important part in individuation, the sense of vision remains highly significant in determining later identity and self-image.

Self-image

The birth itself has a great deal to do with the development of the child's self-image. If the birth was in some way externally determined – by induction, or forceps – the child's predisposition will be likely to be towards a dependent or weak self-image. With a freer, less externally controlled birth, he will be more likely to rely on his own self-evaluation. And since externalized criteria for assessing his responses are less important to him, he will not be as much

---

* Compulsion to respond inappropriately may later be translated into the hypnotic aspects of seduction, as discussed in Chapter eight.

damaged by them if they are, in fact, negative. So the degree to which the demands of reality are capable of compounding a mal-adaptive response may be at least in part modified by the degree of self-direction permitted the infant during birth. Maladaptive responses will be discussed in Chapters five to ten.

Ego Development

It is the development of what Freud calls ego in the child that enables him to deal with the world – with 'outside' reality. The ego, as defined here, means both awareness of appropriate demands of the environment, and mastery in adaptation. And it may be that the amount of contraction during labour actually helps enable the child to define the world he is about to face, to adjust to it and gain autonomy. Lack of contraction experience on the other hand may result in ineffectuality and needs to return back to the womb – that is, towards an alternative autonomy. The type of adjustment to reality chosen by the child may in short be determined to a large extent by the physical experience of birth.

Some delineation of the boundaries of reality is necessary in order to exist with others, and to function.[3] Since there are no beginnings or ends in the womb, one must make a transition from the womb into the world to conceive of limitation. If this transition is not fully experienced the individual may not learn effectively to distinguish the boundaries between his own body and the environment, or even, conceivably, to conceptualize.

On an emotional level, too, the individual's needs must be distinguished from the needs of others, and this ability too may be based upon birth. Some individuals cannot define their interaction with others because they cannot define the difference. This inability may be said to reflect earlier difficulties in separation between the child-self and the parents, and even earlier difficulties in separation between the foetus and the placenta or cord. Without some sense of that distinction in labour, the child may continue to feel the umbilical unit as one with his image of himself, so when it is cut off at birth *he* feels cut off: and nothing in his life can repair that.

To experience life one must accept, relate to and conquer the parameters within the environment. These, perhaps like labour contractions, can benefit rather than restrict, can be experienced as a hug rather than pressure. The only real restrictions are not in the boundaries, but in our lack of understanding of how to use them. So to some extent the degree of maladaptation in this world can be measured according to lacks in ability to create mental margins, or to distinguish social compartments.

Federn,[4] in talking about ego feeling, describes how one can cathect one's own body image, that is, take one's own internal energy and invest it in an object. Cathecting may be a feature of psychosis. This process too relates to contraction, for in that the contraction contact helps define body image, it helps identify borders of experience. Megalomania[5] is another condition that allows no limits, boundaries, or definition. It is a womb state, and it too can be seen as having originated for lack of contraction in labour, and thus a lack of internalized thresholds.

Words constitute one of our primary methods for controlling our environment cognitively. A word has outlines, limitations, definition. Our bodies have these qualities as well, and we find that people without cognitive boundaries also cannot perceive the contour of their own bodies. They are totally unaware of themselves. Interestingly, people born by Caesarean, who never experienced contractions, are among the most susceptible to this confusion.

There is no right or wrong way to be born. But our society is organized in a specific manner, and some types of births set up personalities more compatible with it than do others. Thus individuals may have maladaptive behaviour that corresponds to a maladaptation in the environment (e.g. competitiveness), and they will find greater success and achievement in life than a hypothetically super-healthy neurotically free individual.

Stimulation

Rado[6] refers to the narcissistic bind of the ego, which Greenacre[7] connects with the contractions of birth as stimulation for the physiological system. They see birth itself as a kind of massage: massaging the head, toning up the skin, stimulating the muscular system, and preparing the mouth for sucking. From this point of view, the birth experience is primarily positive. And equally positive is the idea of being born as being released from a state of entrapment. It is a way of gaining further independence. It may also be that contractions, rather than painful to the baby, are as pleasurable as a hug; and that sexuality – sexual arousal and awareness – is part of the experience of birth to both mother and baby.

Immediately after birth, a regression takes place in the functioning of the baby's central nervous system. This has been viewed as a result of fatigue due to the trauma of birth.[8] Fatigue after birth lasts three days, or longer with more severe births, when sleep cycles are prolonged and the infant wakes only to feed. We can trace back patterns of regression in the face of later life crisis to this point, where the infant's initial pattern is established. But there is also a longer post-birth sluggishness, which is different from the fatigue, which affects some babies more than others. In Chapter five this is interpreted as a sort of mourning response, which may be the beginning of passivity problems in adulthood.

Consciousness

The moulding of the infant's head by the contractions of labour, and the subsequent moulding by forceps, can also be seen in relation to the emergence of consciousness.[9] It is possible that anaesthesia, and the use of instruments – creating head pressure – modify cognition. On the other hand, pressure may be essential for the infant's mental adaptation during the post-natal period, and then later on for his adjustment to reality. And the degree of pressure may make many physiological, emotional,* and intellectual modifications which represent the beginning of personality structure. Both the degree, and the point during labour, of any loss of consciousness in the foetus, from drugs, forceps, or contraction, may also affect how he re-enacts birth in his daily life; for instance, some people use a degree of lack of awareness to cope with situations symbolically corresponding to birth. One woman complained that she had a severe fatigue reaction just before the climax of critical events. If she were invited to a party she would find she was energetic and excited until just before she was due to leave, and then a feeling of exhaustion would overwhelm her. Any project or task had a similar pattern: just before completion her vitality and enthusiasm would fade. It turned out that she had lost consciousness just before birth, because of the sudden introduction of anaesthetic during labour.

There are all manner of similar correlations to show the impact of birth on later behaviour patterns. For example, one patient always woke up at two in the morning to raid the refrigerator. It turned out that 2 a.m. was her first feeding time after birth. Another had increased concentration abilities about four in the afternoon. It was no surprise to discover that this was the hour she had woken after

---

* Spitz[10] in his work in orphanages, found that children die in the first year of life if they are not touched sufficiently – that is, the need for hugging and physical contact may be another need continuous with the womb and the birth experience.

her first post-birth sleep. Case material, and analysis of similar correlations, will be specifically dealt with in Chapter twelve.

Animal Birth

In the animal kingdom, birth is a natural extension of pregnancy,
and totally integrated logically into the past experience of the animal.
According to many veterinarians, there is for animals no disconnection, no altering of physical or emotional reality, between womb and
world.* Taking this as a model, birth for humans too could perhaps
be only a pleasant experience. It seems ironic that humans should
until recently have neglected such an important concern. Leboyer
has shown that post-birth stimulation creates calm and a healthier
transition to the world, just as in the animal world the instinctive
response by the mother to lick the infant after birth increases body
functioning. Perhaps one reason why the human infant takes so long
to be self-sufficient in comparison to animals is because of the radical
nature of the changes with which he must deal. Easing this transition
is clearly an area for future research.

Bonding

Birth is also a more autonomous experience for some animals than
others. At the Bronx Zoo in New York City, spectators can watch
chicks hatch from eggs. For about twenty-four hours, the chick
works diligently, pecking till exhausted, resting and then pecking
again. He breaks out finally, looks haggard but exhilarated, and
then sleeps. He has no contraction to push him, he strives for freedom by himself. Yet, the plaque on the exhibit reads: 'Sometimes
prior to hatching chicks communicate with other chicks in adjacent
eggs, and with their mother hen. They produce call notes and click-
ing sounds.' What facilitates this bond with others so soon? What
motivates this determined movement into the world with such exact
timing?

The mother animal's bond to her young is almost instantaneous,
unless, as some monkey studies have shown, there has been interference, including maternal deprivation, in her own history. But
bonding in humans is a great deal less certain, and takes time to
develop. Physical communication with the mother may occur prior
to birth – through chemical transmission – but sound expression,

* Personal communication with veterinarians at New York Veterinary
Hospital, Animal Emergency Clinic and the Animal Center in New York
City.

even on the most non-verbal level, begins to develop only afterwards.

It is interesting that Caesarean children have been found to be more open, as a group, to abuse, apparently because of lack of bonding.[11] Pain itself has been predicated, by some professionals, as essential to the bonding process. Similarly, some mothers have also blamed post-natal depression on not having gone through the expected pain of labour because they received drugs. But the author takes argument with these conclusions. The assumptions by such mothers seem to be maladaptive, misleadingly reinforced. The real problems behind depression and feelings of alienation result not from any lack of pain, but lack of contact. In Chapter eight, sadistic seduction will be shown to be a substitute for real affection in some parental-child interactions; the mother's requirement for pain in labour may be a similar substitute for positive physical contact.

Pain

Pain is usually assumed not to be experienced by the foetus during labour; but it may be that endorphins or similar substances known to affect pain are transmitted from the mother to the foetus during labour. If so, the degree of pain she suffers may affect him, and have repercussions on his consciousness.

The birth process is already known in some way to initiate myelinization of the baby's nerves.[12] It is possible that the passage of endorphin through the placenta, combined with contraction pressure, is what begins myelinization, since endorphin and myelinization are closely associated physiologically. If this is true, there will be a correlation between the degree of pain experienced by the mother and the degree of myelinization of nerves in the infant after birth.

As will be indicated in Chapter six, endorphin and myelinization may have something to do with later cognitive development, and with mental illness. If this is so, it is a further argument for natural childbirth, without unnecessary medical intervention or anaesthesia, since the mother's experience of pain will be assumed to be just as important to the well-being of the infant as his own direct experience of birth.

If this speculation is correct it is specifically relevant to humans, since animals do not experience labour pain. One hypothesis is that pain in humans is the evolutionary consequence of walking on two legs, and thus modifying the structure of the backbone and pelvis.[13] The traditional medical view is that pain in labour is functionally healthy, despite its inconvenience, so the negative effects have not often been seriously examined. The consequences of pain for the foetus have never been fully considered by the medical profession.

False Labour

During pregnancy many women experience false contractions. Since the onset of birth may well be a moment of total chaos for the foetus, this false labour may perhaps be a valuable preparation for the actual birth. It possibly helps to prepare the way physiologically, in getting the membranes ready for the contractions; and we are here hypothesizing that it also prepares the way emotionally. Long periods of very mild contraction prior to heavy labour may, contrary to what has previously been believed, be positive, in that they lay the basis for eventual adult capacities to make emotional preparations for change. On the other hand, they may also help to eliminate spontaneity.

Contractions may have something to do too with subsequent handling of anxiety and tension. Anxiety represents half a contraction: a tightening of the muscles without immediate release. The continued need for contraction can however also be associated with a verification of life, and for the baby it is possible that the long relentless contractions help to confirm his drive towards birth, and achievement.

Introjection and Identification

Freud showed in *Mourning and Melancholia*[14] how the loss of a loved object leads to an identification with the person who is lost, so that his or her personality is taken into that of the mourner and becomes part of his identity. So too perhaps with the loss of the umbilical unit when the individual is born: identification with or introjection of the placenta and the umbilicus takes place, which in due course turns to a projection on to the parents when the internalized characteristics are transferred into the external environment. So the mother acquires for the infant some of the characteristics of the placenta – stability, consistency, possibly passivity – and the father those of the cord – movement, inconsistency, assertiveness.

Identification and introjection perhaps need at this point to be distinguished. In identification, the individual feels similar to another in a specific way, and sees parts of himself in them; while in introjection he incorporates that person's whole personality into his own. Freud states that the two processes become less distinguishable the younger the infant, and the nearer to birth. In his paper 'Ego and Id',[15] for instance, he finds that during the nursing, or oral, period, identification and introjection are hard to distinguish. It follows that within the womb they may be so close that they are the same.

If this is the case, the foetus simultaneously introjects *and* identifies with the umbilical unit, and after birth projects all these associations outward on to parents. The possibility of differentiation between introjection and identification begins at birth with the separation of the infant from the umbilicus; but at this stage what is done subjectively is still also done concretely. When the placenta is cut off from the foetus on the concrete level, he symbolically feels cut off as well.

Freudian Theory

It will become clear to the reader through this book that what the author is doing is not contesting Freudian theory, but extending and modifying it to include pre-birth experience, birth and the cutting of the cord. Our disagreements with Freud centre on his concepts of fixed stages of development – oral, anal, oedipal, latency and the later genital stage – because we see all behaviour patterns as continuous: initiated in the womb, imprinted at birth, then remaining dormant until they become manifest at later critical stages of development. The key to how these patterns develop is to be found at birth, in the 'crisis umbilicus'.

Thus, for instance, the Freudian trauma of toilet training can be seen as symptomatic of birth trauma, because the key sensation of separation and extreme reactions to letting go reflect the same reaction to birth. This specific reaction to birth has remained latent until the anal period, when it is enhanced by the new traumatic experience.

Things that happen in the womb before the child is born can also affect eventual development: that is, traumas can be inflicted upon the foetus from outside the womb. These intra-uterine traumas will then interact with the conflicts of birth to create a compound response, which after birth will condition the individual's reaction to social and environmental traumas, be they fire or floods, business losses, death or loss of important others. The choice of reaction that the individual makes is somehow always indicative not only of early development, as Freud insisted, but also of a predisposition from the birth experience or the womb environment itself.

One trauma added to another trauma creates a stronger trauma, and all emotions are compounds, as in the chemical formula where $A + B = C$, as distinct from $A + B = A + B$. A new component is added with every additional step. And the more primitive the point in development – the earlier the chronology – the more densely are the elements compounded. So every fixation can be seen in each stage of development, but at each stage a certain element may become dominant. For example, you can see compulsiveness in the three-month-old, but only later will this become clearly manifest in a full-blown problem. On the other hand it may remain latent and become less and less important to the child's make-up. Similarly you can see in a child at six months traces of the Oedipal complex described by Melanie Klein[16] in the three-year-old, or find traces of an anal fixation well before toilet training.

The personality can thus be traced back to the very first days, where its initial form is laid down. Later expressions of this form can be modified to incorporate the demands of the particular environment, and make variations on that personality structure. In this sense Freudian theory is seen in the light of natal theory as a guideline, a tool and an aid, but not as a dogma.

Birth Trauma

The first trauma is birth. The severity of the discord that results will vary, according to whether experiences are healing or exaggerating of the original conflict. Since reactions to subsequent trauma are compounding, however, a child may not appear traumatized perhaps until trauma 73, even if he has been emotionally battered earlier on. On the other hand if he has not been exposed to previous discord, trauma 73 need not be destructive. The degree of conflict involved in each trauma also affects the outcome.

Thus birth trauma is of the utmost importance; yet it is only important because it is the first.*

If birth as the first trauma affects all responses to trauma thereafter, we see reflected in all maladaptive responses this first intro-

---

* That there is a particular significance in any first experience is confirmed by an experimental psychology technique involving nonsense syllables. Three or four letters are put together to form meaningless words. Subjects are asked to memorize the list of strange words, and then tested for retention. Findings indicate that the first and last, but primarily the first, nonsense syllables are the best retained.[17] So too with emotional experiences, particularly if they are novel. All trauma has novelty attached to it, but birth, which is the first, is certainly the most novel. It is reasonable to suppose, therefore, that it must be uniquely powerfully retained, and must accordingly affect later organization.

duction to reality; and the last chapter of this book will analyse some of the emotional tendencies that have been found to mirror birth variables such as Caesarean, forceps and premature births. But before considering specific birth repercussions on individual types of personality, the following chapters will attempt to investigate and integrate more general birth effects as they interact with reality and society.

The individual comprises all that came before birth and all that follows. Birth is only the bridge to a new dimension, in which a revolution of perception, feeling, thinking, being, engulfs the child. It is a passage that can lead to depression or elation, peace or insight. But is is only one stage in a longer process, through which the adult in each of us must be born. And this can happen only when the potential for the freedom we initially only suspect, survives.

5   CRISIS UMBILICUS

We have shown how the womb was a self-contained world that began the shaping of the foetus' psychic core. The umbilicus shares this environment and, in birth, as the infant travels down the birth canal, shares that journey as well. The parting between these first friends occurs just before the infant takes his first breath of life, and thus corresponds to his introduction to reality.

This umbilical unit of cord and placenta has been literally an extension of the foetal body, a major organ more important than hand, eyes, ears or nose, more important indeed than any other part of the body because it was the source of oxygen and food – a total life support system which permitted the foetus within the womb the extraordinary autonomy we have already described.

Then, when he comes into the world, this major extension is suddenly cut off, and he has to become dependent upon the external environment for the first time.

We already know that when an arm is amputated, the individual experiences a phenomenon called the phantom limb. The arm is still felt to be there. Since the cord is so much more consequential than an arm, would one not imagine that once cut, it too would continue to be felt as a phantom limb, the residual memory of which stays with the infant on some level long after birth, and perhaps throughout life?*

One concept hypothesized here, then, is that there is such a thing as a Crisis Umbilicus, that may occur at birth when the cord is severed, or later, when the infant experiences extreme trauma such as abandonment by its mother. It would seem logical that no privation in later life can ever be greater than the loss of the umbilicus, for no vulnerability that follows can be compared with that imposed on the newborn babe by its first encounter with external reality. The cord, the first object of security, represents the first loss that the infant ever encounters, and every loss experienced in childhood or adulthood becomes a symbolic re-enactment of that one. And we

* Lloyd deMause has also suggested that a group can act as a 'phantom placenta' to the individual.

may conclude that a major trauma occurs if the cord is cut off too soon, and oxygen temporarily decreases and causes a degree of suffocation.

On its relationship with the umbilicus in the womb, too, may depend the newborn's predisposition to later experience. If this relationship has been secure, the baby may be expected to come into the world a 'loving' child, accepting of parents, encouraging them to respond to him; if it has been an insecure one, abruptly ended, he may come into the world without trust, expecting to be cut off in the world as he was at birth. Environmental factors may modify these tendencies, but the predisposition remains as a historical fact to affect future experience.

Let us examine how the relationship between foetus and cord may develop. The restriction of the womb, as the months go on and the foetus grows and becomes equal in size to the umbilicus, can make either a hugging relationship or a smothering one. The fact that this embrace becomes too close, too entangled and too inhibiting to movement may even be one of the reasons why the baby decides to be born. Yet at the same time the cord has been a constant companion from conception on, from the beginning of his formation. So his feelings are mixed. These mixed positive and negative feelings can be extended into world experience as the conflict between love and hate familiar to everyone.

If the infant is lucky, the umbilicus is permitted to remain with him until the air cuts off by itself, and the cord disintegrates natur-ally and drops off from his body.[1] If he is very unlucky, the separation is made too soon and there is an increase in trauma. Most of us had an experience somewhere in between. Whatever happens with the cord, however, will influence the ways in which the baby later responds to deprivation, and the ways in which he relates to objects that are important to him, including his parents.

Emotional reaction to the loss of the umbilicus can of course be offset by subsequent attentiveness toward the infant from the environment, particularly by the love of his parents. There need be no overt crisis. But should an abandonment precipitate one, its severity will largely depend on when in the child's lifetime it takes place. The later the point of the onset of the crisis, the more chance there will be that logic and adaptation to reality have developed sufficiently to offset the mourning and the depression that must ensue. A crisis in adult life is likely to have less severe consequences than one in childhood.

The individual's sense of autonomy, then, can be destroyed in infancy, childhood, adolescence, or adulthood and bring on the umbilical crisis. It can remain latent, or be regressed back to at later points when vulnerability becomes extreme. This emotional revolution has a variety of symptoms which will be described in the following paragraphs. Modes of counteracting and adjusting to the crisis will be discussed in the chapter 'Adjustment to Reality'. It is maintained here that the crisis umbilicus is the first fixation point.

Penis as Substitute Umbilicus

The Freudian stages of development start with the oral stage during nursing. In this book, we are extending the continuum back to the moment of birth itself, and the loss of the umbilical unit, for within all the later stages of development are to be seen many of the features of that crisis. Using this concept of a fixation point even earlier than those recognized in traditional psychoanalysis, we can make various interpretations of human interactions that were not previously possible.

Let us start with the all-important phallus. According to psycho-analytic theory, the penis is the phallus, is *the* phallic symbol. But what if the phallus itself represents something else? On closer examination we can see it as a physical representation of a huge umbilicus, as the embryo must perceive it. The infant, who as a foetus was comfortable grasping this elongated object, begins to search for something similar to replace it. If he is male, he finds his penis. This is not only the object most easily reachable but it bears the closest physical resemblance to what he lost at birth. An auto-matic association and substitution will be made.

This theory casts new light on castration anxiety[2] and penis envy.* What is castration anxiety but the fear of having something cut off? If the penis is in fact a substitute for the umbilicus, that fear would be obviously justified because the cord *was* cut off at birth. The concept of castration anxiety, in this light, becomes much more reasonable, logical and acceptable. Castration anxiety has an origin in experience and that experience refers to birth, as do many of the problems connected with it.

Umbilical theory also may provide some insight into the psycho-

---

* Castration anxiety in women has been identified and distinguished from penis envy by Abraham and others.[3] No Freudian explanation seems ade-quately to account for this symptom.

logical aspects of the almost world-wide phenomenon of male dom-
ination over women.[4] The man is perceived as more total because his
penis is a substitute for the cord. Since the umbilicus is a life support
system, which thus implies self-sufficiency, the larger the extension
of the genital organ the more capable the individual is perceived
as being. Recognition of the male as having more of the umbilicus
left after birth than the female may be a psychological basis for male
chauvinism.

The woman, on the other hand, must depend for her substitute
umbilicus on a man. How many times do women feel suffocated,
stifled, incomplete when a relationship with a man breaks up?[5] Is
it because of the man, or because the substitute umbilicus has been
taken away?

Freud's concept of penis envy[6] is one with which many people
disagree. Some women have experienced it and some have not. Penis
envy may also be said to be reflected in men when they compare
the length of their penises. Why, when the size of the male penis has
been shown to have little correlation with sexual enjoyment,[7] is size
so important? Why even conceive the idea of penis envy? The feeling of having something missing, of being incomplete . . . does this
echo what was taken away at birth?

Many children have security blankets, or a pet toy that is held
as dear as life itself. Is this too a substitute for the umbilicus? Many
little boys clutch tightly to their penis. This is usually seen as purely
a search for sexual sensation; but in the light of umbilical theory
it could well be a search for the security of the womb. One study
by Greenacre[7] of erections in infants found that the primary time for
these erections was feeding time, particularly when breast feeding
was being ineffectual. This conclusion would tend to confirm the
idea that the penis becomes for the infant a substitute for the umbilicus. Feeding and the umbilicus are so deeply connected, and the
physical resemblance between penis and cord so obvious, that the
idea of erection during feeding as a re-enactment of womb experience is not far-fetched.

The frontispiece of this book is a picture of a foetus. What strikes
me about it is how descriptive, visually, the placenta is of the
breast, with the cord seen as an extended nipple; which in turn looks
like a large penis. The foetus is leaning comfortably against the huge
placenta-breast and seems content, serene and comfortable. Here
the mythological, sociological and psychological concepts of large
breast or large penis as sexually desirable acquire a new meaning.

Gender and Sexuality

Many other phenomena previously identified in our culture as phallic symbolization could equally be seen as representing the foetal relationship to the unit. For instance, the cord is movable and can be seen as active, while the placenta is stable and therefore passive. Gender identification can perhaps be attributed to which part of this life support system is introjected during fetal psychological development: those identifying with the cord would have greater independence and 'masculine' assertiveness, while those identifying with the placenta would have more 'feminine' attributes. So it may be that gender identification begins in the womb.

We have already referred to a connection in sensation between the genital area and the navel. Suppose self-stimulation does, as hypothesized in Chapter two, begin in the womb, when the foetus finds that he can control the flow from the umbilicus. Application of conditioning theory tells us that when the foetus feels the pleasurable sensations surrounding the navel, he is being rewarded, so he will try to repeat the experience. By contracting the muscles, perhaps, he learns to draw the food into himself to a minor extent, and thereby create the sensation; or at least, if he cannot actually increase or decrease the flow, he may be able to increase or decrease the sensation connected with the flowing. If this happens, it can be seen as the first form of masturbation, whose centre could, after birth, be transferred to the genital area. During prepuberty, in other words, the genital area probably has a sensuality for the child similar to that of the umbilicus for the foetus, and masturbation reinterpreted becomes a form of regression back to womb life.

When this hypothesis is set against Greenacre's[8] evidence that excessive masturbation occurs prior to psychosis, we have the beginning of a theory that self-stimulation may be one defence, used in collaboration with other defences, to avoid illness. The way one masturbates – the method, the emotional investment, the associated fantasies and so on – in any case gives symbolic clues to the psychotherapist about early trauma associated with the crisis umbilicus, and this fact too reinforces the notion of cord-to-genital substitution.

Sexualized orality too may be connected with nutrition coming from the cord. Just as masturbation with the cord is initiated when the foetus learns that if he moves his body or moves a muscle within the body, he can stimulate the umbilical sensation and bring nutrition, so later on these associations can be replicated not only in the genital area, but also in the lungs and mouth. Some cord associations go upwards towards the mouth and are focussed there because we breathe and get nutrition from the facial area; so habits such as smoking, compulsive eating and certain ways of responding to sexuality can all be analysed in terms of the relationship of the foetus to the umbilicus.*

These transfers of sensation and function occur for the first time after the cord is cut. Depending upon the timing and circumstances of the cutting, the transitions may be complete or partial.

As stated in the first chapter, the genital area is one of the first to develop in the foetus, in fact next after the umbilical cord itself. So it is reasonable to assume that sensation would relate the two, even if the nerve connections did not exist.† Sexuality and sensations connected with the genital area are experienced first in the womb, before vision, before taste, before sound, before smell, so we might therefore expect that they will be reflected in every other experience thereafter. In our dealings with patients we have found that this expectation holds true, for sexuality is reflected in all aspects of life, although all aspects of life are not necessarily reflected in sexuality.

There are many forms of sexuality, which Freud labelled libido.[11] There is sexuality as expressed in the sexual act itself. There is sexuality that is sublimated. There is sexuality in singing spiritual songs, in mass hysteria, in dancing, talking, thinking. There is also sexuality between parent and child, which is of a much quieter, more affectionate, less self-indulgent quality than that between adults. The way any of these aspects of sexuality is expressed is often determined by the individual's original experience of the umbilicus,

* Symbolical of this, we can sometimes see men with facial hair in terms of a displacement upward from the genital area. The concept of the vagina dentata,[9] or the vagina with teeth that can castrate, is particularly obvious in the case of the goatee. And frequently, according to our experience in therapy, the emotional and sexual behaviour of such men reflects this. They often have problems arising from switching roles emotionally with the female, so that they are metaphorically the ones with the vaginas and the women females with the penises. Such men have a tendency to gravitate towards women who would fulfil the concept of the phallic or aggressive woman, and the whole pattern is furthered when the men find themselves almost simultaneously rendered impotent. Certainly if a displacement upward can occur in so obvious a form, it is not too far-fetched to see displacement upwards from the umbilical cord: castration anxiety being a feature of both phenomena.

† In fact a residual membrane left from the umbilicus does, even in the adult, connect umbilicus with the genital area.[10]

for which the genital area has became a substitute, but which still determines the emotional pattern of the experience.

The richness and depth of umbilical symbolism is well illustrated in a repetitive dream that was brought to us by one young man, in which he is going through a dark tunnel at the end of which is light. A skeleton holding a knife greets him as he goes through the tunnel and there is tremendous anxiety connected with the fear of death and cutting. This can be interpreted as a dream of death or a dream of birth, with the tunnel representing the vaginal canal; but if we look closer it can also be seen as a dream of castration. We find three immensely powerful ideas simultaneously; castration anxiety, birth, and fear of death – and they *all* originate with the cutting of the cord. Similar images can be found in many dreams and fantasies that individuals express during therapy.

Anality and the Fear of Death

All fear of death, too, can be traced back to that first moment of vulnerability on giving up the umbilicus and the autonomy with which it is associated. The symptoms are similar to those associated traditionally with anal fixation from toilet training.[12] Feelings of being cut off and disconnected, of stubbornness, and holding back, possessiveness, jealousy, stinginess, hoarding and ritual-making might all apply equally to someone who is made to feel the loss of the umbilical unit too quickly, and is holding on for dear life because more than anything else the umbilicus *represents* life.

Many patients have expressed to us feelings of incompleteness, disconnection and a general dissatisfaction with themselves. In our analysis of their behaviour in therapy, tracing patterns back to trauma in toilet training has been able to bring consistency to these conceptions. One young man remembers playing with his faeces in the crib. His mother reprimanded him and took them away from him. Even into adulthood he could still attribute a variety of angry hostile feelings, and his tremendous need to continue to hold on and never let go, to this trauma. Frequently such people also have a critical attitude towards others and a need to be unique, or special, which we will discuss in other chapters.

But we have also found that experiences of holding back physically or emotionally, of constipation or rigidity, can be attributed to the outcome of the umbilical stage. This suggests that one is a re-enactment and a manifestation of the other: that is, that the tendency to react strongly to the anal stage of development originates at the umbilicus stage. If the crisis is traumatic, but held latent, it can become manifest at this point. The toilet training stage, where an extension of the body is given up (and must be given up, voluntarily, for the first time), is of course a landmark in development and leads to various behaviour patterns that have been identified throughout the psychoanalytic literature.

We can now conclude that there is a connection with the crisis umbilicus, not only in the oral stage and the genital stage, but also in the anal stage: in short, a fixation point can in each case be traced back to an origin at birth.

Arthur Beebell,[13] President of Hypnotic Communications Ltd, has indicated that patients undergoing crisis in giving up smoking or overeating usually request more birth experiences than any other group. This would invite a leap to the conclusion that habit formation, as well as the symptoms discussed above, may in some form be a regression back to the birth period. People often substitute overeating when giving up smoking simply because they are replacing one function of the umbilical cord with another. So breaking habits such as smoking, overeating, or addiction to alcohol must actually involve giving up dependency itself. The individual must be permitted to accept autonomy, thereby dispersing the separation anxiety connected with the habit. There is self-stimulation and a sense of control associated with smoking, drinking and overeating, very similar to the sensation the foetus has with the umbilical cord in the womb. By re-enacting that experience of mastery, the individual may in some sense return to the womb, back to when there was no vulnerability.

Drug addiction could be seen to have a similar origin. It is interesting that consciousness exercises, such as those prescribed by Transcendental Meditation, which re-enact the trance-like state of the womb, help facilitate the break in habit.

Some authors[14] have noted that certain schizophrenic patients try to cut themselves with a knife. This is interpreted as the schizophrenic's need for imposing pain on himself. A closer look might indicate that in fact this is a repetition compulsion, a re-enactment of the original cutting of the cord at birth. The schizophrenic, in his obsessive need to cut, is usually so totally oblivious to the pain that one might question whether the pain has anything to do with the event. And the lack of pain sensation, as in the psychotic episode, could in itself be seen as a return to birth when pain did not exist, prior to the myelinization of the nerves. It is also perhaps no accident that stomach aches are very frequent complaints of psychotic patients. In one recorded case a patient had such an excruciting stomach ache that when the doctor said there was nothing wrong medically, he committed suicide. Is this phenomenon of pain in the navel area not an obvious reference to the crisis umbilicus?

Sexuality towards important others, too, can be seen in terms of the umbilical cord which the other represents symbolically. In 1911 Freud described, in the Schreiber case,[15] how 'The individual . . . unifies the sexual instinct which has hitherto been engaged in auto-erotic activities in order to obtain a love object. He begins by taking himself, his own body and only subsequently proceeds to the choice of some person other than himself as his object.' If a sexual connection is transferred from the self to others, it could be seen as well as transferred from the umbilicus in the womb, to others as substitute cords.

The development pattern would be that other people to the infant are first objects and extensions of the cord and placenta; and then, slowly, become perceived as human beings on the adult autonomy level. The primary individuals in our environment, at least when we are children, are surely all cord substitutes. In learning to adjust to reality, through maturation, we can let these substitute objects become people. Yet some preconception of them originates in the womb, and whether they can meet these expectations will in part determine our acceptance or rejection of them.

Umbilicus as Parent

This womb predetermination most immediately affects the infant's relationship with his parents. We have already identified the two prototypes, of feminine and masculine in the placenta and the cord. The placenta stays stable and concrete within the womb: it is not subject to the whim of the foetus, and, in order to have contact with it, he must move to it. With the cord it is quite the reverse: the foetus can move the cord at his will, and have active control over it. His behaviour is much more active in interaction with the cord. It might follow that not only is he born with the tendency to perceive the male as he did the cord, and the female as the placenta, but his responses in the environment are also predisposed in the womb, so that according to what role the parent plays, active or passive, the infant will have an already conditioned reaction. For example, if the foetus felt smothered by the placenta in the last months of womb life, or he felt chained or tied up by the cord, this might set up a predisposing hostility towards one or other parent, which could of course be modified by interaction with the parent but would remain a factor, initiated before birth, in the relationship.

If parents at the beginning are objects to the infant and substitutes for the cord and placenta and nothing more, they are dispensable, in so far as anyone or anything else can serve the same purpose. No loyalty or love or dependency is due to father or mother just because he or she is a natural parent. The omniscience that the infant attributes to the parent, the respect he offers, is projected from within the child himself, for it is left over from his attitude towards the placenta and cord. Since they were in fact his life-support system and were required for life functioning, at first he perceives the parents as the same, part of him physically. But he discovers that they are not part of him, that there is a distinct difference which he must confront and accept if he is in the end to become autonomous.

If he does not learn to distinguish the parent as an umbilical substitute from the parent as a person, problems of separation anxiety in childhood and later in teenage years will arise, with concomitant feelings of guilt and hostility, or even a refusal to grow up altogether. In order to transcend the infantile state, the child must give up his parents as objects and recognize their irrelevance as objects. The person who can see his parents as people, fully and totally, without having to encompass their image as a life-support system, has reached adult maturity.

One of the purposes of natal therapy is to aid the individual to differentiate between his perception of his parents as objects, and his perception of them as people. Often when an individual feels himself to be in the control of a negative parent, the parent turns out to be all object and no person. The minute he is perceived as the object he is and not in any sense a person, the recognition itself is enough to eliminate any need to submit. The more negative the parent, the more he remains an object to the individual.

Mourning the Object Parent

The transition between giving up the parent as an object and accepting him as a person involves a mourning period. Just as there is a depression, or a mourning, after the loss of the umbilicus, so too there is a mourning after the loss of the substitute umbilicus. We must each mourn the object perception of our parents before we can transcend that perception. Only when we have done so can we recognize ourselves as individuals in our own right, and feel our true autonomy.

The teenage years are the time for much of this differentiation to be made. Those parents that are only objects get discarded and rebelled against, while those parents who are people are accepted and integrated. Most parents are a combination of both, so they face the problem of having a part of their personality, the object part, rejected, which in healthy development is the final cutting of the umbilical cord. This can be an extremely difficult and conflicting time for all concerned.

The parent who treats the child as an object, as many do, automatically implies that he must be treated as an object as well. Yet rejection of a parent is virtually prohibited by society, particularly rejection of the object parent. This is considered a nasty thing to do and no one wants to be nasty. Also, the more the parent rejects the child, the more that parent becomes the object, and the more difficult it becomes for the child to go through the turbulent period of mourning the loss of that object.

This mourning process involves facing the parent's faults, openly criticizing, and acknowledging the fact that the child does not need that person as an object any longer. A person-parent could accept this independence in the child; an object-parent never could, and would reject the individual. The child then suffers guilt, for people feel guilty when they admit that they don't need someone else who expects them to be dependent. Assuming one's autonomy in this way takes an awful lot of guts, energy, confrontation, psychic pain, and the courage to acknowledge lack of love. But it is harder still to try to remain constantly dependent on another being, subject to their whim and rule. We must work hard at dependence, so there must be a reason why we do so, and why we are so afraid to give it up.

It would be consistent with our theory to see dependency itself as connected with the lost umbilicus, and an inability ever to relinquish it. If this is true in some sense, whether symbolically or psychologically, the dependent individual must be given the umbilicus back in therapy, in order to be able to give it up voluntarily.

One component of infatuation, as of other illusions centred on people, is a preference for the fantasy person over the real one. We place the burden on them of giving us a feeling of completion, such as we had within the womb. But this is a misleading experience that inevitably gives rise to disappointment and anger, for eventually the substitute cord must be found lacking. Psychotic or neurotic symptoms often disappear when one falls in love, because at that point one has found a substitute cord; but they return as soon as the illusion ends, and the false autonomy gives way again to un-resolved dependence.

Mourning and Regret

When we mourn the loss of someone, the depth of the mourning increases according to the degree of our dependence on that person as a cord substitute, for the first thing we mourned was the loss of the cord itself. Since transference takes place first from cord to parent, and then to other important others, such as mate, friends or thera-pists, mourning the loss of the cord can take place at any of these stages, or several. This can occur when the person is still alive, or years after they have died. When we have fully mourned someone, it means that they have died as an object and been reborn as a person to us – if there is anything left of them! Regretting someone's death is a whole different matter, for regret is for the person.

Where I have made a distinction between regret and mourning, Freud[16] speaks of the difference between mourning and melan-cholia, believing that the latter is much more deeply rooted in the unconscious. However, the general characteristics are similar. The features of melancholia, according to Freud, are 'a profoundly pain-ful rejection, an abrogation of interest in the outside world, loss of the capacity to love, inhibition of all activity and a lowering of self-regarding feelings to a degree that finds utterance in self reproaches and self reviling and culminates in a delusional expectation of punishment'. He says that the same features are present in grief, except that melancholia involves fallen self-esteem and grief does not. According to umbilical theory, fallen self-esteem would be related to the cutting of the cord, and the sense of vulnerability associated with it.

In mourning, concentration on the lost love object has priority over anything and anyone else, and the individual has no capacity to find a substitute object until the mourning period is over. Once a substitute object can be found, however, the loss experienced be-comes minimal. The minute a new object is found the symptoms associated with that mourning disappear. Some people mourn the loss of their cord their whole lives, and have difficulty relating to the rest of the world because of it. They devote themselves to mourning the cord, as in the melancholia Freud describes. This devotion is so great that it tempers all energy until a substitute is found. Such people in-between relationships become immobilized, indifferent, self-negating and rejecting.

Freud claims that mourning means work. It involves reality testing, and learning that the love object no longer exists. In the process, all energy or libido has to be withdrawn from its attachment to the object, and this involves a struggle sometimes so intense that the person must temporarily give up a certain amount of reality in giving up the object. However, reality is regained and the mourning ended once the individual can acknowledge that the love object is truly lost. To reach this point he or she must go through each of the memories and feelings connected with the object in order to resolve the memory bit by bit.

So too in therapy, in the resolution of the cord trauma or the relinquishing of a hold on an object-parent or mate. If this process can be fully resolved, the individual is able to give up not only the object-person but the dependency on the relationship itself.

During the mourning period the individual becomes inhibited and feels trapped within it. Once the work of the mourning has been completed, however, 'the ego becomes free and uninhibited again'.[17] We can conclude that individuals who spend their whole lives feeling inhibited and in a prison are experiencing symptoms of unresolved umbilical mourning, while individuals who are free and uninhibited are expressing a resolution of that loss. If we can apply this idea therapeutically to individuals who are still fixated at the umbilical stage, by duplicating the resolution of that loss, we can possibly undo some of the neurotic connections. Freud feels that the testing of reality that goes on during the grief period is what allows truth, and the acknowledgement of the loss of the object, to emerge. Slowly, the ego becomes itself again: a total and fulfilled human being. This is a hope and a goal of natal therapy.

6 *ADJUSTMENT TO REALITY*

Life immediately after birth, it is said, is a 'buzzing confusion'[1]
through which stimuli are gradually differentiated, identified and
categorized. Then other, contradictory, stimuli begin to impinge
upon these original percepts, forcing the individual to make choices
in order to maintain consistency. Without this process, chaos would
result.

Shibutoni[2] refers to this process as 'selective attention' – the individual attends to that which will reinforce his present attitudes
or perceptions; while Sullivan[3] sees it in reverse, as 'selective inattention', that is, the individual inhibits stimuli that would threaten
consistency. And Piaget[4] is describing essentially the same thing
when he says that the infant's primary intellectual function is to
determine the principles of organizing reality.

This the child accomplishes through manual and interpersonal experimentation. But the adult too has to make constant efforts to
maintain his acquired organization, and protect it. Role playing,
stereotyping and categorizing are some of the mechanisms used by
the adult for the protection of his ontology. In a similar way, society
maintains cohesiveness by establishing institutions, traditions, moral
judgements, and rejects deviant theory or behaviour that may jar
its sense of order.

Shibutoni[5] defines reality testing as a social process – 'consensual
validation', as he calls it – through which we determine our identity.
Interaction with others is required for this. As this testing in the
course of interaction modifies and reaffirms reality, we assimilate
more and more divergent perspectives and our ontology becomes
more comprehensive. By becoming aware of what we may expect
of our environment, we gain confidence in our ability to control our
fate, which then permits greater freedom of action, greater security
in the presentation of our self, and, finally, an increased assuredness
in our own identity.

Goffman,[6] Sullivan[7] and others have described how we use cues
to help interpret the behaviour of others during interaction: an-

other's posture, dress, tone of voice and whole presentation of the self help define our expectations of them. It is through picking up cues, both verbal and nonverbal, that we clear up uncertainties and make the consensus valid or complete. If we find contradictions, we rationalize, reinterpret and reorganize the percept till it regains its logic and consistency. If contradictions cannot be eradicated, our identity is threatened and we experience anxiety.

Adaptation to Anxiety

According to Sullivan, we all adapt, some better than others. The degree to which our adaptation is adequate is determined by the type of interaction we encounter and the type of information we receive. When uncertainties develop, anxiety makes us rationalize and thus distort our sense of reality. In an anxious state, the individual acts in the opposite direction of needs. For example, the anxious infant rejects the breast although he is hungry; then, having rejected it, is further confused because he has no other means of satisfying the persistent hunger. So anxiety increases and reality is further distorted.

Anxiety undermines the adult in the same way. Energy which is being used for dealing with the anxiety cannot be used to resolve discrepancies in the environment, and the distortion sustains itself. Additional behavioural and communicative attempts simply magnify the perceptual or emotional confusion. Unless this vicious cycle can be broken, ontological insecurity and identity loss ensue.

Coping, or eliminating this anxiety, can be achieved in a variety of ways. *Recategorizing* is one way. Categories, or labels, make reality reliable and the individual secure. Becker[8] points out that Alice in Wonderland experienced anxiety until she began to label unknowns. Categories also aid in the processes of selective inattention or selective attention that we have described.

A second way is to change attitudes and *conform to group expectancies*. Ash, Sherif and others[9] have done experiments supporting the conclusion that individuals will modify behaviour or attitudes to conform to a group, even when the behaviour and attitudes are 'inappropriate' ones. If conforming to the group does not reduce tension, changing groups may do so. Encountering a new terminology identified with new ideas among new people in a new situation can reduce stimuli, change the perspective of the individual, and aid him, if not to reassert his old identity, to gain a new one.

Third, Mead[10] suggests that *changing the vocabulary*, finding new phraseology to define the same behaviour patterns, can in itself reduce anxiety and reassert identity.

In short, it seems to be agreed that some form of change must occur, either in perception, in attitude or in the presentation of the self, for the individual to break the cycle, regain an identity and reduce the tension arising from insecurity.

Conflict as Threat

The problem, however, in this conflict is that behavioural or emotional modification is usually threatening in itself. Sullivan[11] describes a dynamism which he terms the self-system, used primarily to protect coherence in the personality. This dynamism fights change and defends the present identity. In so doing it can force the individual to maintain rigid characteristics: of the superficial role player, the dogmatic tyrant, or the hypocrite, for example. The self-system, Sullivan explains, may resist change in the face of any but the most elaborate or prolonged experience of threat. For the individual, such experience may have to be as drastic as imprisonment in a concentration camp (for society, it may need the overthrow of a government).

When a contradiction is open and alternative responses are possible, the individual *can* change and reduce the conflict. However, when there is no resolution possible, when the conflict is closed and offers no alternatives, the individual has recourse only to internalizing. This is the situation that Bateson describes when he writes of the 'double bind'.[12] He gives two pertinent examples: 1) A schizophrenic patient was told that his mother was waiting to see him on visiting day. He ran to her with open arms. But when he hugged her, her body stiffened. So he withdrew. She responded by saying, 'What's the matter? Don't you love me anymore?' The young man was in a situation where he could not do the 'right' thing. By stiffening her body, she had rejected his attention; by her statement, she had rejected his appropriate response. Whether he expressed love or withheld it, he was rejected. 2) A child stood at the kitchen door with muddy shoes. The mother yelled, 'Come in immediately, but don't get the floor dirty.' He too had no 'right' course of action to follow. If he went in immediately, he would get the floor dirty; if he took the time to take his shoes off, he would be disobeying her.

In a double bind, no matter what action is taken, the results are undesirable. It is in this type of situation that the individual cannot externally modify the event, or change himself to produce favourable adjustment. He must do something, and the only possibility is to internalize the conflict and attempt to resolve it on that level. That is, he must modify his own concepts of reality.

Sullivan asserts that mental illness is a special strategy that the person invents to live in an unliveable situation. Laing[13] defines it in a similar way. Irresolvable contradictions, as in a double bind, are internalized and the individual feels himself in an untenable situation: 'in checkmate'. His case history of Ruby, age seventeen, describes such a checkmate. She was admitted to hospital in a catatonic stupor, and later diagnosed as paranoid.

> It was clear that the fabric of the girl's sense of reality was in shreds. . . . Ruby thought people were talking about her, and her family knew in fact they were, but when she told them about this, they tried to reassure her by telling her not to be silly, not to imagine things – of course, no one was talking about her. She guiltily suspected that they did not want her at home and accused them, in sudden outbursts, of wanting to get rid of her. They asked her how she could think of things like that. Yet they were extremely reluctant to have her at home. . . . They tried to make her feel mad, or bad, if she perceived they did not want her at home, when, in fact, they did not want her at home.
>
> The whole family was choked with a sense of shame and scandal (she had been pregnant). While emphasizing this to Ruby again and again, they told her she was only imagining things. . . . Their lives began to revolve around her. They fussed over her and, at the same time, accused her of being spoiled and pampered. When she tried to reject their pampering, they told her she was ungrateful and that she needed them.

> The girl was labelled paranoid, although her perceptions were accurate. When she was told that obvious facts were not true, she began to question all her other assumptions concerning reality and her identity: it followed that if the obvious was incorrect, so must be all her other assumptions. So she rejected the identity based on these assumptions, and became labelled as mentally ill. No matter what attempts she made to find external consistency, she was repeatedly faced with contradiction. So she internalized, and found at least the consistency that she had only herself to debate with.

Counteraction strategies

However, there are fortunately other strategies than internalization that the individual can adopt to meet the less extreme contradictions in his environment. This chapter will outline some of the counteractions that the individual employs in order to deal with his vulnerability in confronting reality.

Counteractions, as we define them here, are reactions to dependency: and we have already defined dependency as a reality phenomenon, imposed by authority figures on the 'autonomous' infant. Counteractions are thus related to, yet different from, the defence mechanisms such as projection, introjection, regression and reaction formation described by Freud: a defence mechanism is a self-protective reaction, whereas a counteraction has the additional component of an effort to regain lost autonomy.

Emotions are either a direct replica of those emotions experienced within the womb, such as rage, or they are modifications of those emotions, adapted to incorporate the reality of the new world – such as assertion. Modification takes place when transitional logic or logos is not consistent, as when there is maladaptive feedback from the environment, or when the expectations of others negate identity. Modified womb reactions are either logical or illogical, depending on feedback, and the degree of consistency that is perceived.

Counteractions incorporate distorted feedback from the environment into distorted modifications of womb responses. Among the distorted mechanisms developed to counteract loss of logos, or the disorder in reality, are guilt, narcissism, womb-return and magnified dependency.

When the child enters the world, he is subject to the needs and demands of the environment, and this is his first confrontation with vulnerability. No doubt all later counteraction strategies can be related back to his first response at this stage – narcissism, isolation and disrespect for others all reflect not only rejection of the world-self and the resurrection of the womb-self, but also passive dependency rather than an expression of autonomy. The implications of these choices are considerable.

The most extreme counteraction is full psychosis. More moderate strategies include creating order, developing theory, expressing sexuality, demanding freedom, blind ambition, goal setting, retreat into fantasy, aggression and other socially disapproved behaviour such as homosexuality, power hunger, fanatic money-making and martyrdom. Because these forms of resolution are anti-logos, they always defeat their own ends, since they are ineffective in dealing with disorder and only lead to more convoluted misdirections of energy. At their base they are all trying to contradict or deny the crisis umbilicus, and its associations of anxiety, helplessness, confusion and conflict.

Freud defined the principle behind the individual's attempt to organize the environment and adjust the self to reality, as the ego. But natal theory, as we have explained, maintains that there is an initial organization that begins in the womb and predates the emergence of ego, which we have called logos. Logos is differentiated from ego in that it does not have included in it the idea of reality. The extent to which this original drive towards organization is broken down at the stage of the umbilical crisis, is the degree to which the ego must become developed in order to aid logos in evolving a consistent order and compensate for that loss. And the ego develops its own strategies, one of which – as Freud again pointed out – is repression.

Repression

Repression is the process whereby maladaptive thoughts and experiences – those that deviate from logos – are rejected, and not retained in memory. We all know that material is best remembered when a logical connection can be made. In school, for instance, when memorizing vocabulary, retention increases if the word is associated with a digested idea or concrete visual image. It may be that memory and psychoanalytic sense depend upon the same requirement of logic – i.e. that repressed material is essentially inconsistent material.

It is the work of the ego to fill the gap in understanding created by repression, and make a new logical transition to connect the logos with correlant reality. The more distorted that reality is, and the more disconnected from the individual's internal organization, the more irrational and symbolic will be the 'symptom' devised by the ego to offset inconsistency. In the next few chapters, maladaptation of inconsistent and illogical feedback will be discussed further.

Sexuality is one of the forces most confusing to the child, as will be indicated in the chapter on seduction, and it is therefore much involved in the process of repression. Freud,[14] working with hysterics, in fact assumed that sexuality was at the root of all repressed trauma. In that sexuality is so frequently subject to illogic, natal theory would accept that it is in fact at the base of most repression in some form. But although sexuality *may* be a component of all material that is organizationally inconsistent and repressed, other processes, such as what I have called emotional prostitution, may be more overt manifestations of the mechanism of repression.

The moment that someone attempts to organize the world – that is, from the first second of birth – he has set a task for himself, a drive towards individual consistency which is the initiation of ego. In this sense, there is only one drive – logos, or the maintenance of order. The attempt to readjust the environment to accommodate and maintain order is *the primary* drive. The resolution of hunger, frustration, fear, and all the behaviour that leads to homeostasis, really represents attempts to rebalance when logos becomes disrupted. As things become clearer and more orderly after a crisis, we feel we are more 'there' and more ourselves. That is because in fact we become more the selves we were prior to the breakdown of order brought on by the crisis. Part of the function of natal therapy, and the feeling of being reborn when it succeeds, results from this elimination of disorder, and the reinstitution of the organization that existed originally – that is, before birth.

We might say that all behaviour is appropriate to some environment. Similarly, the individual's behaviour is always appropriate to him, in that it always fits the logical choice for that individual, given his past experience. If we see the behaviour as distorted, it is because we cannot see it in context of the whole scheme of that person's life. If the individual himself considers his behaviour inappropriate at any particular time, we must assume that it has developed out of past appropriate reactions, even though it is being repeated in circumstances which need a different response. That is, feedback has at some point been distorted and the behaviour is symptomatic of some form of behavioural regression, recurring when a confusion about environmental expectation has not been resolved. We must assume that the reason the behaviour persisted is that some misunderstanding took place in relation to expectations at the time – almost certainly in early life – when it was initiated, and that the individual's cognition was never able to locate the gap in his understanding or to learn how to create a transition into new behaviour more appropriate to his situation as an adult. There is a gap, in short, in the individual's transitional logic.

Development of Transitional Logic

The child who has not developed transitional logic to enable him to accept his vulnerability as a separate entity will experience conflict, and deal with it by inappropriate forms of coping. In some sense he has been jarred into world reality, where he must accept his mother as a separate person, too soon. If, however, he has been given ample opportunity to perceive the mother as an extension of himself in a symbiotic, fulfilling relationship, he can then make the transition slowly and give her up, when more logically consistent coping mechanisms for dealing with the separation have been developed. He must learn to accept the fact that his needs can be neglected, and yet he still remains a whole person. The only way he can assimilate this is by experiencing a total symbiotic relationship with a 'substitute cord', so that world-adjusted independence is not superimposed upon the trauma of the umbilical crisis, but is learned. He must learn to adapt and not be pushed into it.

If self-sufficiency comes too soon, and he has not had a chance to adjust to the birth experience, he will not be able to handle such differentiation. His mother will remain an object to him, and he will always see her as rejecting. Due to his own inadequacies, he will dwell persistently on the negative and unfulfilling aspects in life. He will always see others as inadequate objects, and will experience separation anxieties and problems in giving up anything. He will either compensate with deep feelings of inferiority, or feelings of narcissism that individualize him and lead him to believe that he is unique. He will isolate himself and reject communication with others, become dependent and passive and in general extremely unhappy. For once that first crisis hits him, unless it is late enough in life for experience to have afforded him appropriate coping mechanisms to offset the trauma, the initial loss can never be adjusted to or resolved.

Coping mechanisms evolve once the reality principle is established, in the later stages of the child's development. Once more cerebral development has taken place, and the corpus collosum has completed its physical connection between the two hemispheres, nonverbal emotional reactions to the environment can begin to evolve for the first time into verbal ones. And verbalization is the most beneficial and resolving form of coping mechanism we have. The younger the child, the more likely that this verbal mechanism is physiologically underdeveloped, and resolution of conflict is all the more difficult because feelings have attached themselves to the individual's identity.

Feelings can be resolved, expelled and made rational only if expressed. Until they are externalized in expression, they remain internalized, take over the child's identity and control his behaviour.

Pain

It is a curious phenomenon that there is some element of pain or punishment in all inappropriate adjustment. The point is that when he experiences pain the infant attempts to recreate, and get back to, the self-sufficiency of the womb. Pleasure and pressure were experienced there – pain was not, and nor was punishment.

The sensation of pain is to be avoided because it is anti-womb and counteracts the womb world. The infant strives to regain the old autonomy of the womb, or to seek new autonomy, which means additional adjustment and modification of behaviour to fit the new situation in the outer world.

Basically birth itself should not be painful to the infant, and may even, as we have seen, be extremely pleasurable. It is probable that only when there are complications in the birth that discomfort or trauma occur. Pain is thus probably more intensified, more unexpected and much more misunderstood – that is, traumatic – when it occurs shortly after birth, rather than later, after a transition period of adjustment. If this is so, it follows that the cutting of the umbilical cord immediately after birth has an extraordinary impact on the child, bringing blood and pain, and associations of violence.

Since we do not experience pain until after birth, its first impact must be illogical, inconsistent and undefined: totally confusing.

We should note here that since the first experience of vulnerability and the first experience of pain occur approximately at the same time, the two may become psychically associated: we define emotions that are unpleasant as 'painful'. And it is also possible that the initiation of the pain response affects the child's emotional predisposition to relationships, which is set up within the womb but symbolically transposed on to the real world in interaction with people. Pain can certainly effect changes in these relationships, and influence our modes of expression, as well as the energy we invest in others.

Langworthy[15] observed, as we have noted, that the birth experience serves as a stimulus to the deposit of myelin in the human infant's nervous system. The pressure during labour may initiate this new deposit of myelin thereby creating the new response of pain. He states, 'tracks on the nervous system become myelinated at the same time when they become functional'. These sensory tracks must function in some way before myelinization, but the sensory stimulation at birth may create the additional effects on the nerve fibre that stimulate the process. It is known that the optic and olfactory systems, like parts of the brain, receive myelinization only some weeks after birth, although organizational activity can occur inside the brain before myelinization.

If stimulation during birth is the process that creates myelinization of the nerves and the eventual degree of pain sensitivity, this also would effect consciousness. Pressure creates myelinization, which creates pain, which, in turn, creates greater awareness of the environment. Does this imply the greater the pain sensitivity, the greater the capacity for awareness? or the greater the pressure during contractions the greater the eventual development of emotional sensitivity?

Some confirmation of the conclusion that pain is a world phenomenon only is the fact that the lack of pain response noted in the newborn infant is even more evident in the premature infant: in one experiment a premature infant on the first day after birth was pricked until blood came without giving any response.*[16]

Recently, physiological research has discovered a substance in the pituitary gland that, when released, stops the pain response. This substance is called endorphin.[17] Can it be that nature did not intend for us to experience pain? Why else should it have created the potential for us to counteract it physiologically? Pain, in this sense, can be seen as unnatural and not a necessary part of the adjustment of life – that is, provided that the physiological apparatus is working appropriately.

Childbirth, for the mother, is frequently one of the most painful of experiences. It is sudden, rather than worked up to over a period of time to enable the body slowly to adjust to the pain, or to increase production of endorphin. The demand for the substance in this situation must substantially and suddenly increase and then decrease, thereby producing violent changes in the balance of

---

* This experiment is itself indicative of the total disregard in our society for the experience of the embryo, the foetus and the newborn; it also shows no understanding that lack of response does not necessarily mean no response, only no evident response.

chemical and emotional reactions. Researchers[18] have already found that excessive production of endorphin can produce depressive and even catatonic reactions, so post-natal depression becomes newly explicable. And if childbirth depression can be seen as the result of an excessive release of endorphin due to sudden pain, other forms of emotional distress too can perhaps bear new analysis.

One might hypothesize, for instance, as follows. Excessive emotional pain, as in trauma or in severe punishment, may, like physical pain, be expected to create a demand for abnormal amounts of endorphin, which in turn might result in a greater predisposition towards mental illness. In other words, the emotional situation does not create the illness but creates the change of chemical distribution of the endorphin which then creates the illness. People with lower pain thresholds due to more myelinization – that is, who are more sensitive – would need more of this substance to counteract pain and thereby have a greater predisposition to illness.

Another aspect of these research findings that can lead to further speculation is the fact that endorphin, when injected in large amounts in mice, produces an addictive reaction. Although self-addiction to a chemical within one's own body seems inherently improbable, the idea tempts one to take another look at the phenomenon of masochism, for example. If there is a history of excessive pain response throughout childhood, and if endorphin is in fact addictive, future pain might be sought out, in order to create the substance within the body.

Another interesting finding is that myelinization is incomplete in children with certain learning problems.[19] And here again there may be an implied connection with endorphin. With incomplete myelinization of the nerves, the production of endorphin may be greatly reduced because the pain response is reduced. This leads to the further speculation that creativity, originality and various processes of thinking may possibly be facilitated by endorphin, or similar substances in the brain structure. We find frequently that people who are extremely sensitive to their environment, who have been exposed to excessive narcissistic injury or other emotional trauma, can sublimate their reaction in creative and cognitive expression.

Punishment, as imposed pain, requires some comment at this point. Appropriate discipline and direction for the child is essential for its development, in that it identifies logical boundaries. It guides the child into adaptive attitudes and reflects love, concern and respect by the parent. Punishment, on the other hand, is by definition inappropriate and reflects the power needs of the parent. Suppose a child goes to the store, and instead of giving the change to the mother, stops to buy candy and toys for himself. To him, his behaviour is reasonable, since his mother has many times done the same. When he gets home, his mother can respond in a variety of ways. The punishing, authoritarian parent would be outraged and let him know that he is stupid, worthless, bad or selfish and then spank him to teach him not to do it again. Should this form of rejection occur regularly, one effect on the child might be the production of excessive amounts of endorphin in the system to offset his pain, thereby totally disrupting the chemical balance of his brain.

Direction, on the other hand, would involve the mother explaining the illogic of the child's act, and finding a correlant behaviour to offset it. With the second method, there is no personality disintegration or loss of self-esteem by the child, and he learns his lesson fully because the discipline is a realistic response to the behaviour. The process involves logic, and lacks any expression of maladaptive symptomology by the parent, such as power needs or sadism.

Autonomy
The drive towards autonomy in the world is one of the major motivating factors in emotional and cognitive development. It, along with the need to maintain a logical order for functioning, lies behind our orientation in human interaction, and helps define our tendencies toward adaptive or maladaptive processes.

When the umbilical cord is cut, the child loses the autonomy that he experienced in the womb. His drive will be towards establishing a new autonomy in the world, as consistent as possible with the one he has already known. If his sense of independence is facilitated by his environment and not threatened by it, he will develop an adult autonomy adjusted to reality. If, on the other hand, the environment negates him as an individual, prevents appropriate cognitive organization, and limits possibilities for adult forms of autonomy, he will attempt to regain the autonomy he once experienced within the womb. He will choose the alternative, more infantile, form of womb autonomy and settle for that.

How these primary (womb) or secondary (adult) forms of autonomy become manifest depends upon the kind of coping mechanisms the individual is able to develop. Individuals who use such mechanisms as regression, lying and emotional prostitution do not attain the adult autonomy that is devoid of dependency, and so tend to attempt primary autonomy; while those who develop healthy adjustments aim at secondary autonomy. Secure of their identity, they become assertive, functioning, relating adults with a sense of fulfilment and a well integrated personality structure.

Expressed in terms of umbilical theory, adult autonomy implies that the individual no longer needs a substitute cord and can relate to others as whole human beings.

Womb-return

Attaining adult autonomy takes much less energy than does regression to primary autonomy, for it involves dealing with reality as it is and interacting in a consistent way with it. To return to primary autonomy, detours must be made. Primary autonomy is outside the logical stream of behaviour, so distorted processes must evolve to connect the current reality with the infantile regression, and for this great expenditure of energy is demanded, which depletes the individual's capacity to function in the world. Such individuals are inevitably to some extent immobilized and passive.

The greater the passivity, the lesser becomes self-esteem and sense of identity or independence, which diminution further exacerbates the need for regression. Thus starts another vicious circle. So the person drifts further and further from his real goal, which is secondary or adult autonomy. Simultaneously, because of his lack of trust in his own perceptions, he becomes even more dependent on feedback from others. The more he depends on others for the definition of his behaviour, the more incomplete he feels and the more robbed of the experience of competence. So every time an individual is faced with an inconsistency in his environment that demands a response, he must create another detour, and so be pushed further and further away from secondary autonomy.

Womb-return, however, is by no means always negative. As Freud pointed out, sleep is one of the ways in which, even in healthy development, we return to the womb occasionally. It helps organize and resolve problems and so, with greater order and logic, to energize. Despite the regression in womb-return behaviour, there is also a healthy aspect that promotes autonomy and is even essential in stimulating mature integration of reality.

Fantasy is another example of womb-return behaviour, which can be either maladaptive and produce greater dysfunction, or adaptive and energizing. Fantasy regression and general withdrawal from the environment can be a rejection of the world that is also rejecting of the individual himself and his identity – it can be a form of isolation, and a way of regaining primary autonomy by avoiding reality. But another form of fantasy can be very productive, when it is used to rearrange the reality with which the individual is confronted and create a new order to suit his needs and make the logical transition he is looking for. Originality and creativity are thus alternate ways to deal with the environment when traditional modes of coping are not functioning. This use of fantasy is, in a sense, a thinking reaction formation: a reaching after the most unlikely combination of factors to find a new transition, because the cognitive means traditionally found useful for adaptation have failed.

Sexuality, like fantasy, reflects maladaptation, birth, and pre-natal organization, so it too can function in much the same manner to promote order and autonomy. We shall see in later chapters how sexuality reflects the birth episode, and is an attempt to master and resolve the conflicts surrounding it.

Dependency

Dependency must be specifically defined here. Rather than, as traditionally believed, inherent in the child till independence is achieved, dependency is here conceived of as a defence against confusion, and categorized along with other coping mechanisms.

Dependency is called into being by the demands of others, that is, of those in control. It never arises on its own. The child is born independent, which was his experience in the womb. There he was autonomous, and free. He had no restrictions imposed on him except the physical restrictions of the environment. Suddenly he was thrown into the world, where he was *expected* for the first time to be emotionally dependent. It is unnatural for him to feel dependent, not natural.

Simultaneously with becoming dependent, the child also becomes passive, because he must use an extra amount of energy to create the dependence within himself, to hold the self down and not express his real independence.

It is not the parent as an aid who requires dependency in the infant. It is the parent as an authority who does so. The more authoritarian the parent, the less directive or helpful, the more the child becomes dependent, for he is fulfilling the demand of the parent as the price he must pay for aid and acceptance.

Aid he does need, so dependency and the need for aid must be differentiated. One is the natural outcome of the birth process, and healthy. The baby needs the aids of food, shelter and love. The other is an imposed need from the environment, and a distortion. Children end up being dependent only in order to facilitate a logical interaction between themselves and the parents, if this is the condition they put on the provision of aid.

The more dependent we are made to feel in this world, the greater our difficulty in coping, so we have to find adaptation mechanisms. Finding these mechanisms is part of the parents' responsibility in aiding the child. They can point out to the child its autonomy, by offering direction, or its dependency, by offering authority. Yet those parents who create most necessity in the child for finding methods of coping, are the very ones most reluctant to direct the child towards the behaviours that would facilitate adjustment.

The child is totally unaware that he is dependent until he is shown so by the parents. And the parents have to work very hard to create a sense of incompetence within him. Yet in the end he will reflect back the emotional predilection of the parents, their power needs and other destructive feelings. The more dependent he is made to feel, the more competitive he becomes and the more difficult it will be for him to cope. Siblings or peers will threaten him because his need to return to the womb, where there were no others, will increase with each increase of awareness of dependency. He will become self-concentrated, and reject sharing with others in the environment.

If parents treat children as confident and capable of learning, as total beings who have their own perceptual viewpoint of reality and their own experiences which belong to them, the vulnerability and helplessness of childhood can be greatly modified.

So we find that part of the symptomology of the umbilical crisis is a rejection of others, with at the same time an overdependence on others. When there is both a need for and a withdrawal from others, a by-product is what we label loneliness. The inability to be by oneself, the need of another human being to supplement the indivdual in order to survive, relates to the umbilical crisis. The feeling that no one can ever be found who will supplement us sufficiently is the feeling that no one will be our life-support system.

Loneliness is wanting a cord and not having one. Lonely people many times do not like themselves, feel incomplete, incompetent, and vulnerable. This is because they cannot be their own cord and they cannot find an adequate substitute.

People who are successfully happy alone have transferred the need

for a cord on to themselves and have fully reached what we call
adult autonomy.

Autonomy, then, is the natural inclination of the child. And he
never, entirely, allows himself to give it up. When those around
him demand his submission, he attempts to fulfil the request. But
at the same time he devises behaviour patterns to maintain his
sense of self. For every required reaction that denies his identity,
he needs a counteraction to reinstate it. Some patterns permit the
accomplishment of both, simultaneously.

Drugs

Similarly, when the adult experiences dependence in the environment he attempts to counteract that behaviour with primary autonomy or a distorted form of adaptation. Drugs and alcohol are
potential means of directing behaviour in this way. One does not
become dependent on drinking, for example, but one drinks to
eliminate the dependency one experiences in the environment. As
his feeling of dependency increases, so the drinker will attempt to
offset this by increasing his consumption. The more self-sufficient
he becomes, the less he will feel the requirement for the drug.

None of these behaviours promotes dependency, but each is
motivated by the individual's drive to offset dependency while
adjusting to the demands of the environment. Although misdirected,
they are all attempts to attain the ultimate goal of self-sufficiency.

Homosexuality

Homosexuality too is a counteraction to offset feelings of vulnerability and confusion. Natal theory holds that the origin of a homosexual predisposition is in the crisis umbilicus, and thus involves
every maladaptive emotional response that evolves out of the crisis.

Homosexuality is of course defined here in a broader context
than the mere sexual preference for one's own gender. It is a whole
matrix of associations, an emotional syndrome. Latent homosexuality
when expressed heterosexually is just as much a coping mechanism
to offset maladaptation as is homosexual practice. And the he-man
or Don Juan who relates to women as objects, the husband who
desires his wife more when jealous, and the two female friends describing sexual exploits to each other are all expressing this same
counteraction.

Many authors have indicated that the penis, in the homosexual
experience, is a breast substitute. This is even clearer when we take

into account the concept that we have already examined in Chapter two: that the breast is a substitute umbilical connection, with the same feeding mechanism and emotional attachment associated. Only the penis, in fact, is a more appropriate substitute for the umbilicus.

We frequently find in homosexual syndrome symptomotology all the elements of hostility, regression, narcissism, intense feelings of vulnerability and inadequacy that we have already identified as emanating from the umbilical crisis. It is a unique form of maladaptation with its own dynamics, preceding many related formulations in its development, and when we discuss narcissism, which is one of the major components of homosexuality, we shall be able to throw further light on this topic.

There are three further areas with which we must deal as counteractions to dependency. However, they will be mentioned only briefly here, and expanded on in later chapters. They are aggression, control and use of power. None of these things exists in the womb, and all are counteractions to the environment. They arise to facilitate adjustment to inappropriate feedback.

Aggression
Most people assume that aggression is a biological need. However it might be more precise to say that we have fundamental *assertive* needs – which facilitate adaptation, understanding and fulfilment of individual needs. Aggression, however, although it is also in keeping with promoting recognition of the self, has destructive elements as well, so is maladaptive.

Hormones create predispositions towards aggression, but the aggression itself, in its maladaptive aspects, is related to environmental feedback rather than to internal physiology. The child goes through an aggressive-oral stage during nursing when he experiments with biting, destroys toys and tries to hit siblings or even parents. This stage has always been interpreted as aggressive, and it does have an element of apparent destructiveness. However, there is a distinction between aggressive behaviour that is destructive and malicious, and that which is experimental and geared to learning or mastering the environment for the eventual goal of expression of the self.

For example, the initial biting reaction of the child while nursing is facilitating – experimenting with the action of the jaw in response to the contact with the breast. He is learning about the reality of the object, and of the contact. There is no aggression here in terms of sadism or malice. If his action is dealt with realistically by those in authority, and treated as a simple expression, symptomatic of that stage of development, the aggression/assertion does not become destructive. However, when a child's actions are labelled as aggressive, and, in response, the child is aggressed upon by the parent, he learns for the first time what aggression is and it becomes part of his perception of himself. Thereafter he will have a greater tendency to perpetuate that part of behaviour. He imitates it. The next time that he breaks a toy or hits a parent it may indeed be with the malice and destructiveness that was initially interpreted. The aggression, as it evolves out of experimentation, becomes a reflection of what he receives, rather than something innate.

Aggression in this way is always learned, and maladaptive. It does not make for a cohesive, strong identity, nor does it facilitate communication. It does not in any way master the environment or protect the child, but extends misconception and further maladaptation.

Assertion is quite the reverse, and occurs with healthy transition and development. It facilitates communication, and mastery of the environment, and usually produces heightened self-esteem and reality adjustment.

Power and Control

One aspect of aggression is that it is not internally motivated by the needs of the individual to organize his environment and facilitate his own functioning, but is, even if indirectly, a demand produced from the environment and externally determined. In the same way, expressions of competition, power and control emanate not from the child, but from the individuals with whom he interacts. The need to aggress on a child is always a function of the adult's fear of losing control, and of his own potential inadequacy or ineffectualness. It is in a sense the adult's self-protective mechanism.

Competitiveness

One interpretation of parental aggression is that the adult is competing with the child for control. Competition is always based on fantasy. What drives one to compete is what one *imagines* the other person is doing, thinking or accomplishing as distinct from the healthy need for achievement which has only internal definitions and which develops out of the need for mastery of the environment. In competition there is the need to master reality of the world that another experiences and not one's own world.

Competitiveness never serves any purpose but to eliminate and destroy. It facilitates externalized goals that do not fulfil internal needs, and does not in any way produce contentment or self-realization. In that it was originally created by the individual for a purpose and a protection, it is a counteraction to facilitate adjustment. If the child feels at peace with himself, and sufficiently respected by his parents, he will not need to compete with others. Competition always implies a sense of inadequacy and a lack of trust in one's own needs – fearing that the definition of what is required to function in this world is better determined by others than by the self.

Dependency, because it involves externalization, is a requirement before competition can develop, and only in the resolution of dependency can competitiveness cease and the individual attempt to reach those goals that are satisfying to him specifically. Inherent in competition is the wish for another's defeat, another's dependency on you, and the need for power.

It is true that our society is set up so that certain professional achievements are impossible without competition because, with every success, that individual must prove himself better than another. However, there are also spheres where achievement is based on one's own individual expression, and success and goals are defined in terms of internalized values that do not necessitate competing, negating or destroying. Frequently these involve working in a situation where there is co-operation, creativity and some directed activity in the service of mastery of reality.

We may conclude this chapter by saying that man's perception of reality is always limited, in that he is confined to his own perspective. So he must attempt to eliminate that distortion that results from organizing only the fragments to which he is exposed. He has to meet the contradiction that he has inherent need of autonomy, yet has the requirement of dependency imposed upon him. To master his world, he must undertake the task of maintaining logos and adjust it to the environment so that he can survive peacefully.

7 EMOTIONAL PROSTITUTION

As we have seen, the child must learn new adaptation procedures to adjust him to reality after birth; and though his primary choice is to deal with consistencies, that reflect a natural transition and modification of the womb world, if the environment presents him with inconsistencies and illogic, he must adjust to these as well.

We have also already referred to Gregory Bateson's description of the 'double-bind'; that is, two simultaneous messages (usually from the parent) that are contradictory in nature and imply opposite forms of action. Here I propose to extend Bateson's theory, in the light of the research by Sperry on the role of the corpus callosum in monkeys, and the separate functioning of the two hemispheres of the brain. I have elsewhere called this extension the 'double mind' theory.[1]

When Sperry[2] found that monkeys with a severed corpus callosum could integrate material within each hemisphere separately, he established that they could actually do so with different material in each hemisphere *simultaneously*. Each hemisphere, he concluded, has its own mental sphere or cognitive system. 'It is as if each of the separate hemispheres is unaware of what is experienced in the other . . . it is as if the animal has two separate brains.'

Split-brain monkeys were able to learn opposite tasks in each hemisphere at the same time and also to display separate emotions simultaneously. Researchers suggest that one side could be taught to be passive and the other side aggressive, or vice versa, so that the animal could actually have two personalities.

Recently, split-brain surgery has been done on some human epileptic patients.[3] It seems that much the same occurs with humans as with animals: the two hemispheres can function independently. In one experiment, a board with two openings in it separated the patient from the experimenter. The subject would put his left hand through the appropriate opening in the board and be given a solid number shape (e.g. No. 3). He was then told to raise the same number of fingers on that hand as the number given. All subjects answered correctly. Then they were told to place the other hand through the board, locate the same number (3) among a selection of numbers on the experimenter's side and verbalize it. Virtually all picked the wrong number.

As in the animal studies, the right side of the brain did not know what the left was doing, even though each side had total cognition and recognition independently. The lack of co-ordination in recognition confirmed that the corpus callosum has the function of transferring perceptions and information from one side of the brain to the other. In human subjects, the verbal or speech-centred hemisphere on the left side was distinguished from the non-verbal hemisphere on the right side. Non-verbal hemispheric learning could not be verbalized after the operation.

The 'double-mind' hypothesis combines Bateson's conclusions with these on physiology. In the normal individual, information from the environment fed into one hemisphere is transferred through the corpus callosum into the other hemisphere, and integrated, so that there is consistency in attitudes and perceptions between the two hemispheres and they function jointly. If the new material or information is contradictory, as in a double bind, rejection by the alternate hemisphere may occur. For example, the verbal message from the mother is 'I love you', while the non-verbal message is 'Leave me alone'. Transfer of the non-verbal message is rejected by the verbal hemisphere since it contradicts what it is receiving directly. Repressed traumas and other such mental blocks may be examples of such rejections. If this is so, repeated double binds might actually lead to the development of a partially or totally autonomous personality within each hemisphere, a condition expressed in schizophrenia and possibly other psychoses. Each hemisphere would then have its own cognition, emotional response and reality interpretation. Mental health could then be defined as an integration between the hemispheres, and illness as distorted or obstructive transfer.

Included in this hypothesis is the belief that the non-verbal hemisphere has its own communication system and logic. The verbal side communicates in words and uses linear logic. The non-verbal hemisphere, on the other hand, communicates symbolically or metaphorically, for example through the patterns of posture and gestures. Its logic is that of dreams. And it follows that non-verbal communication, with its different language and different reality, may be distorted and misunderstood by the dominant verbal consciousness. Thus the behaviour of a schizophrenic is perceived as irrational – though it is understandable when deciphered, just as dreams show logic when interpreted.

Possibly something of the double-mind exists in us all: there is perhaps non-verbal dominance in impulse, compulsion, depression, withdrawal, indecision; and everyone has experienced conflicts of emotion. In extreme, the disjunction creates feeling quite detached from reality, as in Laing's schizoid robot[4] and Sullivan's 'not-me',[5] in whom the non-verbal hemisphere has perhaps taken over from, and lost its connection with, the verbal one.

Inappropriate feedback and illogic in the environment frequently has a double-minded component: that is, the individual receives messages that are logical on one level but not on the other. The only way he can handle contradictory expectations is by distorting behaviour, and his distortion creates further distortion.

One of the maladaptive forms which this process of surviving in the face of contradiction takes, we will label here 'emotional prostitution'. This occurs when the individual finds himself faced with a particular kind of contradiction: that between his need for his parents' approval, and his need for his own self-respect. His parents, in other words, offer him a view of the world that conflicts with his own 'logic'.

Primarily, in order to survive, the child must obey and win the favour of his parents. They are his extended umbilicus. If they reinforce their object role by demanding that he submit to behaviour that negates him as a person, he is being told in essence that he is a slave, inferior, and inadequate in this world. This automatically contradicts the child's experience – for in the womb he was unique, protected and autonomous. He must now reject his own needs and make a new, and of course distorted, consistency. The price for the love of his parents, in this illogical case, is indignity.

Let us look at two everyday incidents in the upbringing of a child. Suppose the child is told to make his bed. He feels that, since the bed will be slept in again shortly, the activity has no real purpose. But the parents insist, without giving a reason he can accept. He makes the bed, not because he feels it needs to be made, but to fulfil the wishes of his parents, and to avoid a reprimand. He prostitutes himself.

The parents could have taken the time to hear the child's point of view, and explain their own – such an approach would imply an integration of the belief that the child was a competent individual requiring their respect, and no emotional prostitution would be required.

In another case, the child paints the wall with his excreta. It is logical for him, since it is a form of creativity. The parents reprimand him and restrain him, instead of giving him his own activity space and expressing appreciation for his pictures. They feel negative, the child feels his creativity denied. He must give up the wall and succumb to the parents' demand for behaviour that they define as appropriate, but which makes nonsense to him.

Source of the First Lies

To survive, then, every child must win the favour of his parents. He is forced to prostitute himself if he is forced to relinquish what he believes to be consistent with his identity, his dignity, his self-confidence, in order to fulfil the demands of his parents. That is he lies to himself, for he knows the truth but denies it, to avoid the pain of rejection. The degree to which this is necessary will determine the extent of his eventual rebellion and identity crisis.

Every child must lie a little to himself, when he attempts to adapt to others' demands and convinces himself that he wants to do it. And each lie is a break from reality.

This inevitable inconsistency and confusion is compounded for the child if the parents' behaviour is itself contradictory. The dishonesty of a parent when role playing socially, or expressing advice he himself does not follow, multiplies the child's expectation that emotional prostitution is adaptive. Further magnification takes place when one parent negates or openly rejects the other parent. The child incorporates the values of those he respects, presuming that they have reality mastered. When this assumption is negated by another whom he similarly respects, the child is faced with a conflict that forces him to question his confidence in one or both parents. He may reject coping mechanisms associated with the criticized parent, even though they were effective. He may become confused as to what behaviour is acceptable. If he continues to mirror the behaviour of the criticized parent, he is in danger of assuming the criticized attributes himself; if he does the reverse, he strips himself of a valid adaptation. His decision-making process no longer functions on the basis of internal definitions but is externally determined.

Some adults actually feel free to dictate the child's sensory responses. They demand the child smile when he falls, insist bad-tasting food is delicious and in general discredit his ability to deter-

mine sensation or perception. The trained emotional prostitute not
only eats the distasteful food but says that it is good. Yet the only
one who can really know what the child hears, smells, tastes, sees
or feels is the child, and the task of the facilitating parent is not
only not to question the validity of the child's reaction but to reinforce his belief that only he is the authority on him. Saying one thing
and feeling another is illogical, and leads to a distorted image.

The requirements for emotional prostitution are built into our
society. Social lies, rituals that have lost their meaning, contradictory laws, value systems based on superficial appearance, all continually negate internal consistency. For example, people may choose
a gift according to its price, rather than its relevance to the interests
or needs of the other. Social lies make an environment more comfortable, and are almost universally accepted. Yet all lies threaten
logical transition to the world.

The more lies an individual tells, the greater will be the inconsistencies between that individual and reality, and the greater will
be the need for further dishonesty to recreate consistency. The lie
is an attempt to reinstate logic where there is none, but simultaneously it breaks down logic, so that it creates additional need for
more deception.

Truth on the other hand is easy because it does not need any
modification of what already exists: it just is, and therefore requires
very little energy. Since dishonesty involves work and effort, the
individual who must incessantly fabricate new transitions has a
greater tendency towards immobilization and passivity.

On the other hand, in therapy, with every lie that is uncovered,
additional energy is gained. Once the energy that was previously
used for hiding the truth is released, it can be directed towards other
more satisfying directions. For even if, as children, deception was a
necessary defence against our own vulnerability, when we grow
older we can modify and change this.

All societies have unwritten laws about loving and obeying one's
parents. As children do not love their parents or agree with them all
the time, at one point or another they must falsify their feelings
or face rejection. This leads to guilt, giving the parent that they lie
about a special power over them, which then turns to resentment,
rage or greater dependency. (Dependency is often the mirror of rage.)

Emotional prostitution, if expressed passively, in submission, is
always companioned by guilt; while if expressed actively, in defiance,
it tends to be narcissistic. And although both submission and defiance

distort, the former is the more complicated and destructive, since it includes self-deception.

Emotional prostitution is a modification of the truth in order to feel control of the environment. While overt lies attempt directly to counteract power displayed by another, and can actually reduce guilt feeling because narcissism is fed and the activity is rewarded, internalized lies actually revise the individual's self-concept. Because they are much harder to justify or modify, they enhance guilt and infect the liar like a disease, thus creating inactivity.

Dishonesty is always a cover for deep pain, ego injury and confusion. Thus the deepest internalized lie is often accompanied by a compulsion to tell the truth about everything else but when uncovered turns out to involve the individual's deepest core of security and identity. If the truth is complicated and terrifying enough, sanity itself may be at stake.

When dissected, this kind of lie frequently turns out to be about acknowledging lack of love from a parent. And once this is faced, the individual has further to confront his own lack of love for that parent – often the one he assumed he loved most. This parent that was not loved, but whom the child has pretended to love in order to gain acknowledgement, has usually been idealized in an attempt to depersonalize him or her so as to avoid the responsibility of dealing with the rejection that would ensue if the truth were to emerge. The individual formed by such a pattern in childhood then goes on to repeat it in adult relationships: he marries someone to whom he prostitutes his feelings, and in the process the mate becomes idealized – into a positive object, but an object none the less.

When the least loved is also the most demanding parent, the perception by the child of that parent is repressed and his internal reactions are negated and covered over by passivity and self-negation. An accepting parent, on the other hand, who is never demanding of love or blind obedience, does not provoke the conflict in the first place. For example, one patient hated her mother but believed consciously that she loved her mother more than her father. Since she was sure of her father's concern and affection and could risk it, she felt freedom to deny it. The maternal relationship was inadequate and controlling, but she could not face the truth of her mother's dislike for her. It was too painful. So she idealized the whole relationship. In effect, she gave fake love, and the inevitable fear of discovery was counteracted by excessive honesty in every other area. Honesty in this sense, is a form of compensation.

One way of getting approval is by emulation. Therefore, the child will often attempt to identify himself with the least loved and most rejected parent in an attempt to win his or her favour, and as a compensation for the internal, denied hostility. The really loved parent, who creates the least requirement for maladaptive response, can be virtually ignored, for there is nothing to be mastered. So too in romantic relationships. Too easy and successful a communi· cation leads to boredom and avoidance, while the difficult experience is passionately sought. The intensity remains only as long as the problem and the promise of resolution persist.

In a sense, the child does not love at all. He is not mature enough to be capable of real love. Only the adult, who is aware of himself and in a position of equality, can fully love. The child interprets his need for the parents as love, because it is identified as such by them. But he feels guilty and disoriented when he does not feel the appropriate emotions. When he feels unloving, he feels confused. In this way, a love-hate cycle begins. He resents being put into a position where he must fake love, and reacts with excessive loving or idealization because he feels guilt and fears rejection.

The greater the need to be dishonest in order to survive, the greater the discrepancy between healthy adjustment and the environment. Emotional prostitution is a defence. It is simply submitting, going along with whatever is demanded. But when we are passive, we have a debt to pay. Only when the debt has been paid, can we become active again. The passivity we feel passes when we have served our time and paid the debt, and can permit ourselves to be ourselves once more.

Dependency as Prostitution
Dependency is the same kind of reaction. It is a form of slavery, a selling of ourselves to a debtors' prison, and a form of prostitution. For we are all essentially independent and autonomous, no matter how young or how outwardly reliant on others for aid. The experience of helplessness is always a façade, and is perpetuated by dishonesty in dealing with those in our environment.

Despite the fact that the person lying feels he is controlling and fooling the other, inherent in the lie is the statement that he is dependent and involved. If he were not, he would not make the effort.

Repressing the Lie
Because power, emotional indignity, and seductive manipulation are all devoid of logical consistency with the life of the womb, they are all simultaneously protected by repression. Repression, as we have already seen, takes place when distorted feedback is found to lack transitional consistency with logos. The partial repression of the distortion involved, for example, in emotional prostitution, renders it impossible of resolution by the victim – patients often complain of difficulty in confronting opponents in argument, because they retain only a partial memory of the encounters. This dilutes the effect of their counter-attack, so they end by apologizing for having made an accusation, even though they know it was valid. Repeated impotent attempts at assertion reduce the victim to the depths of submission. Each episode has enough retention to ensure that the humiliation is remembered and enough repression to prohibit resolution.

The Emotional Pimp
The 'emotional pimp', on the other hand, feels he has conquered and defeated his opponent in intellectual mastery. The power contest inherent in the interaction magnifies the narcissistic-guilt dichotomy (which will be discussed later). When repeated frequently enough between parent and child, the interaction establishes patterns of insecurity and resentment that persist into adulthood. The quest for intellectual and verbal sophistication in the adult is frequently simply an attempt to equip the self with weapons for this contest.

The emotional pimp demands *performance* of his victim. He is quite indifferent to the feelings of the other, for his power needs have priority. He accomplishes his goal by obtaining proof of unconditional surrender when he wins. The more illogical and inappropriate the demand by him, the greater the verification of his success when it is fulfilled. In that this process deviates from logos it regresses, infantilizes, and promotes dependency. Having established his indispensability to the other, he finds ever new ways of stressing the incompetence of his victim, whose only retaliation is in the self-indulgence of guilt and fantasy. His technique is to obfuscate, so to break down the logic of the other to render thinking impossible. 'Obfuscators' pride themselves in presenting facts moulded to sound logical, when they are in fact rationalizations to justify what would otherwise be an untenable position. The verbalized statements, however, are often contradicted, thus further confusing the victim.

The emotional prostitute gravitates to such 'obfuscators' in the hope that eventually he will learn the key to the process and conquer. He is a gambler who plays to lose. When all order is lost because the game goes on, all that remains is anxiety.

One patient in therapy, whose marriage reflected this pattern, complained of severe anxiety to the point that he considered suicide. Although he claimed to love his wife and to want a successful relationship with her, he had avoided all sex for almost a year. The truth of the matter was that he felt trapped. He no longer desired any contact with her, but he was financially supported by her and was thus too dependent upon her to leave. His own exploitation was something he could not accept so he performed emotionally for her, and resented her all the more for accepting the lie. His anxiety arose when he began to confront the truth, for in so doing he would have to leave, or live with the contradiction to his self-esteem.

Once he became aware of the pattern of emotional prostitution to his mother in his childhood, which had been severe, he was able not only to see the same pattern in his marriage, but also to recognize that he had chosen his mate specifically because she would aid in re-enacting it. He had actually wanted the trap, and really did love and want her. The anxiety diminished, as the dishonesty, the performing, the resentment, and the power needs were reduced. He began to function sexually again, and his enraged frustrated wife reduced her hostility and dominance.

Begging and Pleading

Emotional prostitution taken to extreme is pitiful, where the individual is so defenceless and crippled that all dignity is lost. The coping mechanisms are either underdeveloped or ineffectual. This can have been caused only by a sadistic parent, who reinforced dependency and treated the child with emotional neglect by disregarding any affirmative assertion of his feelings, and giving positive feedback only when the child was humbled and self-depreciating.

There is always dishonesty in begging and pleading. Most beggars do not intend to carry out the promises they are making, and at bottom are dealing in power. In this sense, the lying inherent in the begging is active. And because we sense the dishonesty, we react with disgust both towards the person begging and towards the person being begged. When we beg or plead, we are letting the other know we are performing the most base form of adaptive reaction.

A begging individual is asking the other please not to hurt him, no matter what he has done. He attempts to seduce the other into distorted reaction.

Disgust

Disgust, in some way, is actually desired by the beggar, as the ultimate turn-off which at least defines boundaries and thus resolves the confusion. It is the opposite of idealization, yet those who idealize someone can also feel disgusted by them: for only with someone who does not come up to our idealized image, which is fantasy, does the emotion arise. Both idealization and disgust identify the interaction as being unrealistic and based on maladaptation, and permit neither self-realization nor healthy communication.

Disgust is based on pretence. You feel disgusted by those you fool emotionally or sexually. It is a reaction not to the person but to the dishonesty inherent in the emotional process.

At another level, however, disgust, like any other maladaptive response, is also an attempt to master and resolve some past interaction with authority figures in childhood. It is an indirect, ineffective way of doing so, but it is an attempt to gain adult autonomy. In that it contains a sense of mastery, control and power, it also is enjoyable. Dignity is the opposite of disgust. One is a reaction to the other. Therefore, both exist or neither do, in each individual. The cause is the same.

The type of individual who picks out a mate to re-enact this process will never deal with the negative feelings inherent in the relationship. His best hope is to find himself a mate who refuses to participate in the prostitution episodes, and who will admit negative feelings and attempt to deal with them rationally. Only by facing them can they be resolved and the relationship positively improved. Denying negative feelings is so complex, and so ingrained in the confusion and aggression of the emotional prostitute, that he cannot deal with them and must continue to deny them as he denied them as a child.

One patient, a bachelor in his forties who had prostituted himself emotionally to his mother in childhood, has continued to re-enact the prostitution of the self towards women in later life. He gets involved only with women with whom he cannot get fully involved. He acts the stud or the charmer, and prostitutes himself by professing love, self-negation and surrender well beyond what he feels they deserve. Internally he is rejecting them simultaneously as inferiors and as fools for being gullible. So he must detest and become disgusted by the very woman he initially idealized. Sexually, he suffers from impotence, because one cannot fully feel when in a state of conflict.

In fact, it is interesting that the more important has been the idealized person, the greater the reaction of disgust once idealization vanishes. The fantasy that that individual was once a complete and total substitute cord disintegrates, and the letdown creates all the more resentment because of the past dependency. The more the individual needs a substitute cord and feels vulnerable, the greater his drive to gain a substitute cord. Finding someone who he feels can maintain this fantasy creates the illusion of a full relationship – but since this is based on an interaction that never took place, it is liable to sudden dissipation. The very ingredients that created the magnetism and the importance of the relationship, are those that destroy it.

Paranoia

The relation between emotional prostitution and paranoia is obvious. Children who lie to their parents feel guilty, so they generalize and project their guilt on to others. The lie, and the cover-up, are what others do to them.

Also, the better one is at emotional prostitution, the greater one's contempt for others from whom one can hide the truth so successfully. A certain smugness comes from this form of pride, even a sense of omnipotence. When the child finds he can carry it off so successfully and fool grown-ups, who are supposed to be so smart, he considers himself as having capabilities above average. Once an adult this deviousness becomes even more sophisticated, and prohibitive to healthy interaction.

In this process, too, there is a particular element that we have called in a wide sense 'homosexual'. Homosexuality as we have defined it involves a rejection of the parent as a person and, too, a demand for performance. The submission of the self in the power struggle of the emotional prostitute is the same subjugation that takes place in most homosexual interactions. This is another example of how a homosexual symptom is latently expressed in maladaptive heterosexuality.

We often see emotional prostitution acted out in an overt manner on the stage. Originally, the actor puts on his performance for his parents, the child pretending to accept their values. In adulthood, the performer, by holding the audience, is indirectly winning back the parents' acceptance. And every time he receives applause, it is symbolically the applause of his parents whom he also attempted to fool.

In the ultimate sense, the requirement for prostitution begins when the substitute umbilical cord, which is of paramount interest to the survival of the child, makes demands that cannot honestly be fulfilled by the child, but which he feels he must fulfil to avoid rejection. Emotional prostitution is thus the eventual state of total surrender to helplessness and vulnerability, begging for help at any price. It is a counteraction of the most intense variety. Because of its intensity, it is one of the behavioural processes most self-perpetuating and hardest to resolve.

Emotional prostitution is a complex subject that has been dealt with only superficially here. However, in the next chapter, we will investigate one of the sub-components of this process, seduction. Susceptibility to the seduction episode arises out of a predisposition to emotional prostitution, and results in further maladaptation to the environment.

8 *HIDDEN SEDUCTION AND SADISM*

Violence and pain infliction are post-womb experiences; and because they negate womb logic, past coping mechanisms must be distorted, and counteractions evolved to offset the confusion they inevitably provoke.

In fact, no matter how often the individual is exposed to pain or violence, both will remain preposterous, and beyond ordinary communication. But some interactions are not only painful in themselves, but also involve subtle double messages which, as we have seen in Chapter seven, require time for mastery; while other painful responses include an underlying sexuality, and this too is a powerful source of confusion to the pre-puberty child. Adult sexuality is incomprehensible at this stage: in therapy we see this repeatedly confirmed when the adult recollects repressed material from, or regresses to that time, for he too has problems in comprehending sexual references.

These experiences of pain, because to the child they are unfathomable, tend to disrupt the sense of autonomy with which he is born and exposes him to new feelings of helplessness. This in turn creates dependence or passivity towards others, who are assumed to have mastered the skills that he feels lacking in himself. Yet the irony is that this proficiency at adjustment is particularly projected on to those very persons who have induced the confusion! Since they had the ability to create the incomprehensible, it is presumed that they also hold the key to its resolution.

This is the paradox that leads to the specific types of interactive tendencies which I shall label 'seductive susceptibilities'. These have their roots in patterns initiated in childhood, in response to parental demands; and when unresolved, they lead to maladaptive interaction in the adult. The vulnerability inherent in such a patterning is a by-product of the emotional prostitution discussed in the last chapter, and another manifestation of the umbilical crisis.

Forms of Sexuality
According to Freud,[1] sexuality, or 'libido', expresses itself in every

aspects of our lives. Much of this sexual energy however is not directly expressed but redirected by what he calls sublimation, into
creative, productive, and socially acceptable ways, such as in art,
thinking and work. However, I propose here to look at sexuality and
sublimation in a different way, and not to see art, thinking and work
as sublimations of sexuality, but sexuality as an attempt to master
problems in other aspects of our lives.

The process works something like this. An individual faced with
a problem, rather than deal with it cognitively, produces a sexual
fantasy that reproduces it symbolically. Then, by acting out the
fantasy, he gets a sense of release, and the peace associated with
the elimination of the problem, although the problem itself is not
resolved, only dissipated to the point where the anxiety and tension
connected with it are temporarily reduced. The anxiety-producing
confusion has been returned to a more primitive and basic language,
that expressed physiologically through the body in the form of action
and sensation. But to resolve the problem, the expressive mode must
be that of cognition.

Preverbal trauma, and illogic in its basic form, are particularly
related to bodily sensation, because that is the medium of expression
most accessible to the infant. It is also the most problematic. We
therefore find that it is preverbal problems that are most often the
subjects of attempts at sexually directed mastery, even in adulthood.

Based on my work with patients, I have become convinced that
most manifestations of sexuality in fact represent attempts to resolve
problems that are not sexual. 'Uncontaminated' sexuality – when
expressed simply as a physiological need, and a natural extension
of appropriate adjustment of reality to logos – is communicative and
loving only. Yet we find that the majority of people have other
motivations in their sexuality. We shall call these two forms of
sexuality 'confluence', meaning sexuality that is direct communication, and 'alligation', meaning sexuality used primarily as a means
for resolution of illogic.

Since it is virtually impossible for an individual to grow up within
our society without some contradiction and illogic confusing his
cognition, it follows that, if expressed sexuality can be used to master
problems, the majority of people will show some alternate forms of
sexuality delegated primarily to this process of attempting balance
or cohesiveness. The greater the maladaptation, the greater will be
this use of alligatory sexuality. This latter form of sexuality probably
comprises a good 80 per cent of what is considered libido, and this

is the part to which I would see Freud's concept of sublimation as referring. Mastery of a problem can take place in a variety of different ways – such as through creativity and work – so that part of sexuality can be sublimated; but only that part. Sublimation in this sense is therefore not evidence for a concept of sexuality as an energy that can be directed into various forms, but an expression of attempts at self-realization and adjustment.

The old double standard, which divides females into those for relationship and those for use as sexual objects, possibly reflects just these two different forms of sexuality. All forms of perversion, dysfunction and fantasy-oriented or masturbatory sexuality fall within the confines of the second category. In that the expression of alligatory behaviour reduces anxiety, tension, confusion, it is deeply rewarding and satisfying, so it need not be discouraged, at least until the problem creating the need has been reduced.

There has been much written on how the inhibition of sexual activity increases neurosis.[2] If in fact problems are dissipated by symbolic and metaphoric sexuality, then sexual activity may well decrease neurotic symptoms, and this phenomenon becomes explicable. Indeed, where there are severe problems that create excessive anxiety, the 'alligatory' form of sexuality is likely to be more satisfying than the 'confluential' type. On the other hand, the greater the adjustment of the individual and the less his need for problem dissipation, the more enjoyable will be 'confluential' forms. Generally we find that confluentiality is understated, and alligatory sexuality provocative and obvious.

Within all communication patterns there are indirect expressions of these two forms of sexuality. Confluence is expressed in affection, in love that is not self-serving or predicated upon the assumption that some gain must be received. It just exists because of the interaction itself. Because confluence does not reflect deprivation, it does not have the driven obsessiveness or the essential quality that alligatory sexuality has. On the other hand, it is only with confluence that the individual can attain what Freud has labelled genital primacy.

One of the indirect expressions of alligatory behaviour is seduction, with its overtones of sadism.*

* The appeal of many cults (with specific reference to the episode in Jonestown, Guyana, in November 1978) seems to involve some of the sexual components discussed here and in other chapters. The leader is frequently the major seducer, whom members follow blindly because of their seductive susceptibility needs.

Anal Origins of Sadism

Birth and the crisis umbilicus would almost by definition be among the most fundamental sources of metaphor and symbol in adult sexual behaviour. But the origin of seduction and sadism has most often been explained in terms of anality. This is a post-womb experience: anal excretion in the womb is toxic and therefore rarely occurs – if it does it may cause foetal death.[3]

Most pleasant feelings, as we have already pointed out, are reminiscent of the womb, while painful ones are totally world associated. Sucking, for example, has its sensual prototype in finger-sucking in the womb. The one pleasurable body sensation unfamiliar to the newborn is anal. But the first anal experience also coincides with the start of nerve myelinization – the first potential for pain – and with first feelings of hunger. It overlaps as well with the teething period in the first six months of life. So it is inseparable from a whole complex of physiological, sensual and emotional changes that must in some way affect consciousness. The affectual and sexual systems themselves require modification, depending upon what feedback the infant receives to his reactions to these new and unpleasant body experiences.

Interestingly, Freud[4] confirms that sadism originates during toilet training at about age two.

On the other hand, anal feeling is not entirely new, nor is it discontinuous with the womb. Anality in toilet training is clearly reminiscent of birth, the first separation, and consequently arouses any latent crisis in umbilical symptomology. Indeed, trauma during toilet training may be assumed to be traumatic mainly in the sense that it re-echoes umbilical trauma. Sadism can thus be traced back to birth.

Magnified anal symptoms, such as stinginess, obsessive orderliness, withholding and even narcissism, inevitably result in a sexuality that is alligatory. And if sexual expression is used as the primary means of dissipating problems, it must reflect the experience which created the problem. Let us examine how this may come about in practice.

Parent-Child Interaction

The mother may touch the child in various ways. Healthy touching expresses concentrated affection and relates to the needs of the child. Detached and indifferent touching, or hostile and aggressive touching,

are deeply destructive to the child; while seduction, though 'loving',
is sexual and self-serving, and it turns the child into an object. We
are here concerned with seductive manipulation[5] as a specific example of what is confusing or contradictory to the child, and thus
results in distorted interaction with others.

Seduction is sadistic in that it is manipulative, motivated by controlling and power needs. It usually comes from rejecting parents
who are incapable of making concrete their own demands, and who
are thus limited in healthy expressions of love. The types of parental
behaviour that can induce susceptibility in the child to seductive-
sadistic interaction include suffering exploitation (i.e. inducing guilt),
competitive or envious sarcasm, nagging, self-indulgent or narcissistic
exhibitionism, power games, violation of privacy of the child's body
or thoughts, critical judgmentalness, over-valuation of self, ridicule
of a mate's qualities compared with those of the child, reinforcing
dependency, requests for submission to prove love, and insistence
on blind acceptance by the child of the parents' irrational beliefs
or demands.

Physical contact by the sadistic mother or father is always seductive. Sadism and seduction have similar origins, symptoms and
expression, and there is always a sexual element in both.

The child learns to relate through any form of contact. If he is
beaten, he assumes that this is what contact is supposed to be like,
so this is what he sexualizes, and when he grows up he will respond
specifically to sadistic or painful forms of pleasure. If on the other
hand the child is treated with detachment, then this will become
his requirement in relating. Only if he is treated with love will he
learn to respond in that way, so that only lovingness will permit him
to experience himself sexually.

There are many differences between sexualized and desexualized
contact; not all necessarily on a conscious level, but certainly on a
subconscious one. A natural tone of voice can change to a sexual
and flirtatious tone; so, too, looks of the eye and touches of the hand
and body can change. The child can recognize these subtle differences, but he cannot separate the various responses into discrete units
of experience, at least not in a cognitive and defined way that he can
rationalize with his logic. Sexuality is an alien concept to him, until
he has attained puberty and can himself experience the emotions
surrounding sex, so he does not identify the expressions that he
receives from his parents as sexual. Instead he becomes confused
and anxious.

Seduction is contact most misunderstood, and leads to distorted interpretation of relationships. When a parent touches or talks seductively rather than affectionately, he has a sense of his own power and the child becomes the object, sexually and incestuously. It is manipulation, not love. Love or affection is desexualized contact and respectful of the other person, as a person. Once an adult, the seduced child distorts sexuality, and the child treated with love communicates. Freud has explained genital primacy as being the capacity to have a fully satisfying sexual experience in which there is both awareness of the other and awareness of the self. Only with non-self-concentrated communication, that is, not seductive, can the child learn from the parent to respond on a healthy sexual level and, thereby, reach genital primacy.

The type of seduction used by the parent will determine the types of response that follow the child as he matures. Parental seduction manipulates, humiliates, castrates or controls the child into behaving in a way that fulfils parental demands and rewards parental needs, while negating the child's. Seductive control is a way of obtaining co-operation from the child without a confrontation – which may threaten the parent's own, often maladaptive, personality foundation. If the child learns appropriate behaviour, it is not because he understands the reasoning behind it, but because he is passive to the requirement. Learning is thus inadequate, and creates a predilection for later maladaptive coping mechanisms.

The Seducer's Lie

Seduction to the child is undefined and without words. Some processes have words to describe them, such as love and hate; but some do not, and seduction is one of them. We never hear a child say 'Mummy seduced me or manipulated me last night', whereas we might hear him say 'Mummy loved me and needed me'. Seduction is not part of the child's verbal repertoire of understanding and, therefore, it needs reinterpretation and redefinition before resolution can take place.

The individual doing the seducing gives his object a promise, and that promise is the fulfilment of a fantasy wish that his object expresses verbally or nonverbally. Whenever someone is seductive, he is lying. He will not follow through on the promise, and indeed whatever he promises is exactly that which he will not give. He cannot follow through since this would complete the interaction and thus end the hold he has over the other. By keeping the promise just out of reach, he maintains power and control.

Symptomatic of seduction is its very deceptiveness. Yet just as when one makes love, one enters into the passion, into another level of consciousness, so, too, it seems that the seducee, and possibly the seducer too, enter another state of awareness during the seductive process; it is almost as if the seducee were hypnotized into blindness to the deception. Some relationships have as their major point of communication this ongoing process, where loving, sexuality, and verbal interaction all play secondary roles to the seductive episodes.

Individuals thus made vulnerable to seduction gravitate to all manner of equivalents in later life. For example, they may buy a product from a salesman only when seduced into the purchase: it is the seduction rather than the article that they are buying. Needing to be talked into anything in fact stems from seductive conditioning.

Seduction and Repetition Compulsion

Thus seduction fulfils all the elements of the repetition compulsion about which Freud[6] talks. One form of this repetition compulsion is represented by the person who once hurt someone else, feels guilty and permits a new seducer indirectly to get even. This happens particularly to the individual who had self-sacrificing, guilt-inducing parents. The seducer, on the other hand, may be getting even for a previous narcissistic injury, even attempting to re-enact the past episode for resolution.

In the seductive dyad, one partner is always an exaggerated umbilical substitute for the other, and is idealized or demonized – the seducer* feels in control and superior to his object, and uses the other as a tool. The seducee is vulnerable not because of lack of insight or stupidity, but because the sexuality within the seduction is so undefined. The seduction can be accomplished by words alone or through a series of behavioural responses. It can be just a twinkle in the eye, or a body movement; or it may proceed over days, weeks or even years. This process works by what behavioural psychologists would call partial reinforcement, which has indeed been found by experiment to be the most effective form of animal conditioning: if food is given only occasionally when the animal performs as trained,

---

* Most incest occurs between fathers and daughters, and does not include intercourse – it is mostly touching and oral sex. Interestingly it is those cases that do not involve intercourse that create the most emotional damage. Over 90 per cent of such abused children grow up to be adults who need deviant or dysfunctional sex.[7]

the animal always has the possibility of reward before him. The reward has to be given frequently enough to ensure maintained attention and motivation, but infrequently enough for the element of surprise to be sustained.

The corresponding emotional pattern in humans is in fact what we are calling seduction: acceptance occasionally given offsets the more prevalent pattern of rejection or detachment just enough to sustain the mate's interest, while simultaneously permitting the seducer to have control. He can be emotionally sadistic without risking rejection himself, and as time goes on he traps the other into submission. Seduction is thus a process and not a single act. It is not a means but an end.

Often, the seducee does not want to do what the seducer expects of him. He knows that he is being conned and controlled, yet feels helpless, or compelled to fulfil the wishes of the seducer. To justify his response, he may fool himself into believing he really wanted to respond in that way, thus diminishing his own identity in the process. Since there is then a breakdown in the internal integrity of his ego, he becomes more outer-oriented, his own self-worth becoming dependent upon the acceptance of the seducer; and this binds him further and makes him more vulnerable to future seductive episodes. The verbal rationalization that he needs to justify complying with the seducer's request becomes progressively more limited with every success of the seducer, till the seducee is totally dependent and defenceless, and feels the depersonalized object he has become.

The reason the child responds to the seduction in the first place is because it offers the affection he needs, and of which he would otherwise be deprived. Yet he is both responsive and withdrawing, for he is both being fed and confused. In other words, this is another example of Bateson's double-binding situation. However, by the time he reaches adulthood, he actually sets out to repeat the situation because it is something with which he is familiar. He looks for a replica of the seductive parent, or for someone with whom he can act the seductive parent, since this is love as he has experienced love in the past. Such perhaps was the relation between Elizabeth Barrett and her father – apparently an extreme symbiosis with a seductive element – which she replaced in the relationship with the young Browning.

Dependency and Passivity
Seduction always leads to dependency, as opposed to true affection,

which leads to independence. Seduction also inevitably includes some element of sadism, through the threat of force and punishment. Detachment, indifference or rejection are used by the seducer to encourage the seducee's dependency on him. The distance thus imposed prohibits the seducee from precipitating a verbal confrontation, which would be required to resolve the conflict, and the seducee opts for the sadism in preference for the detachment. He co-operates in setting himself up for further fulfilling the demands of the episode, and satisfying the seducer's power needs. Fear of abandonment by the seducer makes the seducee feel worthless, for part of the seduction involves convincing the seducee to delegate the criteria of his worth to the discretion of the seducer.

The seducer is an actor throughout the relationship, and this includes acting the underlying sexuality. Since he cannot follow through on his promises of sexual fulfilment, the seducing person does not usually experience the passion of sexuality. He is too wrapped up in the acting process, so he performs his own sexual response, and fakes. Frequently he is a person much aware of sexual technique, so he emphasizes this aspect of the contact. But because he performs a sexual response, whether in fictitious orgasms or in dramatic expressions of emotion which he does not feel, he must resent his mate. He must consider his mate a fool for believing his exhibition, and then responding in an honest way. He depreciates the value of his mate because his own performance is unreal. This in turn results in feelings of inadequacy for the seducer, who may become promiscuous to justify his own sexual coldness and to further negate his mate's response.

On the other hand the mate may recognize, on some nonverbal level, that the sexuality is a fraud, and become more dependent to try to negate the false emotionality by drawing the mate nearer. In this way, the sadism inherent in the seduction becomes even more exaggerated, and a typical sado-masochistic situation occurs.

Usually, people who see others as objects have trouble maintaining commitment, because commitment is a fraud based on fraudulent feelings. The seducer is incapable of feeling as long as he is busy playing his role, although his fakery may appear more real, more essential, more fulfilling, than true communication.

The seducer is only involved with forepleasure, which is all he can respond to. Within the forepleasure of a seductive act, is the end pleasure, since the seducer feels he is then in control. He cannot deal with real end-pleasure, since for him it signifies the relinquishing of the rewards of superiority and independence.

Seduction stunts growth, and renders a person impotent and passive. A person regresses with the seduction act by re-experiencing the same frozen helplessness, and counteracting it in the same way, as he did when originally overtaken by it as a child. The person was imprisoned by it when the episode originated in childhood. When re-enacted, he must again re-enact the immobilization and passivity with which it was first associated.

The passivity comes from having no concrete grasp of what is happening in the seductive episode. Since inactivity is a response to seduction, it also stimulates or seduces the seducer into repeating the interaction, thereby making the seducee also a seducer. Both the sadistic seduction and the passive dependent response, in short, are ways of manipulating. They can also both be viewed as self-protective mechanisms that originated to counteract problems in early childhood.

One male patient, who had the experience of a seductive mother, rendered himself passive to that mother by relinquishing his own sexuality. In that way he could avoid incest with her. As long as he remained infantile and male, or adult and feminized, he did not have to risk incest, which he felt would be imposed on him should he become a fully mature man. He gave up his sexuality, or his maturity, identifying with his mother and her needs, so as not to have to deny her should she want him as a functional man. In this way, the seductive parent can lead the child not only into emotional retardation, but also into psychosexual problems such as poor gender identification and homosexuality. One might even say that the very components of homosexuality include seduction, sadism and passivity.

The heterosexuality in adulthood of someone who was subject to this seduction as a child, is often impotent or nonfunctional because of latent fears of homosexuality, or incest; one male patient who had problems with sexual functioning was afraid to kiss his seventy-five-year-old mother for fear that he might get an erection. In discussion it became obvious that his real fear was that he would not get the erection. Inevitably there must be some form of rejection of the seductive parent by the child, for seduction creates so much confusion and contradictory emotional response in him, as well as making demands for imitation when the child is not yet equipped with the necessary mechanisms. Then, having rejected the parent, the child will either reject that portion of himself that identifies with him or her and become withdrawn, or incorporate the parental narcissism by emulation or reversion to feelings of inadequacy. This presents problems in superego development and the resolution of the Oedipal complex, so that seductive susceptibity becomes further magnified.

Seduction, as here described, requires adjustment by the individual to a reality that is disconnected, undefined and illogical. The only recourse for emotional survival is the development of counteractions that are equally maladaptive and irrational and which, in turn, lead to additional conflict. Only by recognition, labelling, and verbal dissection of seductive vulnerability can this distorted form of interaction cease. Yet we find all too frequently that this dissection meets with immense resistance. At the base is an even stronger coping mechanism that is stubborn to all attempts at resolution.

This is the bizarre mental malady that will be investigated next . . . the need to be God.

9 THE NEED TO BE GOD

In Chapter two we made reference to the 'fatigue' of the baby after birth, which we compared with a mourning reaction, and connected to the cutting of the umbilical cord and the first object lost. Later experiences of depression, abandonment and separation all, it seems, echo this first loss.

When a child realizes that the breast can be withdrawn at the will of his mother – not his own – he confronts again that original loss. And he reacts by striving to regain what he once experienced as his own omnipotence. In reality, his mother has the control he does not have, and if she meets his needs, she helps him adjust to his loss. But if she exaggerates her control because of her own power needs, he has no choice but to respond by mirroring the effect. That is, he not only begins to desire power but also all the distorted behaviour he sees associated with it, such as seductiveness, submission or manipulation. In becoming aware that he is not totally unique, that he is not in control, the child also becomes aware that if he were god he could regain his effectiveness.

The type of parental feedback he receives then becomes his definition of power. Power may be expressed in various ways: through money, sex, love or ability, depending on environmental teachings. He begins to seek out any rationale to enhance his power – and thereby becomes more and more dependent upon others for definition. For it is others, not himself, that define power. Whatever that rationale may be, it has destructive side effects, which will be discussed here.

The need to have control, or to be God, is a parallel development to that which I have called emotional prostitution. In both cases the power concept is learned after birth, the first time the infant has the experience of indignity; and the desired authority, power or omniscience is a defence against the subserviency that is imposed on him. Trauma during birth or after birth can thus initiate an over-evaluation of the self as a requirement for adjustment. But without a power-oriented environment, omniscient coping mechanisms would be rendered ineffective, and remain latent. If his caretakers are sensitive to his needs and recognize his individuality, the power drive and the need for omnipotence never develop. Power needs cannot be totally avoided, but they can be directed towards growth and mastery of the environment, that is the drive will be internalized. When the need for power is externalized, he becomes dependent upon his environment for encouragement, and when it is internalized, he becomes dependent upon himself for motivation. The latter makes for a functioning whole human being, with a strong identity, who can relate to his peers and his world with dignity and awareness of himself.

The physical presence of the parents and the kind of contact they offer can be loving or it can be aggressive, hostile and power-oriented. In no way can lovingness and power work simultaneously. Authority pushes away, demands submission and makes the other into an object, so any physical contact made at the same time must involve a subtle rejection. Seductive susceptibility is one maladaptive result of the attempt to unite love and authority. Real affection negates power.

People know what to expect from themselves. If they know they are capable of controlling their environment and defining the responses required of them, they can feel relatively secure in the face of possible rejection or criticism. But if they have been constantly rejected, or subjected to hurtful criticism, they may try to avoid it in future by imitating the manipulation to which they have been subjected. Since they have been taught to feel inferior for making an error, they opt for superiority or power. They need to be God, since gods do not make mistakes.

Denial
Yet only in the acknowledgement of one's faults can we overcome them, transcend them, and grow from them. One would suppose therefore that there would be more reward attached to the acknowledgement of a mistake than to the negation of it. With acknowledgement, mastery of reality increases; with denial, there is only a regression into fantasy. So denial of an error for fear of a drop in godliness is simultaneously denial of the transcending of that error, and the dynamic of over-self-evaluation goes on to deter other problems from resolution.

The need for power, or to be God, is thus clearly a negative, potentially incapacitating condition. Only those who feel insecure with their feelings and reactions are prone to it, for when you feel secure with yourself, it does not make any difference what another human being thinks. On the other hand, mutual insecurities create mutually reinforcing interactions. By being critical and judgemental one person can assert his own feelings of superiority, and put others on the defensive. He may even convince others, who wish to diminish anger or rejection because they too feel insecure, so that all become victims of a syndrome I have labelled 'Standing on the Roof'. Man A is standing on a roof and can see the whole city. Man B is standing on the street below, and he can see only a part of the street. Both think Man A sees more. In actuality they both have the same number of vision receptors in their eyes, and each has exactly the same angle of vision. The point is that Man A sees more area and Man B sees more detail. Their perceptions, though different, are equally valuable and can complement each other. Who is the greater fool? Man A who believes he sees more, or Man B who believes Man A sees more? It is a mutually dependent distortion, for without the ground fool the roof fool would not presume anything. In working with patients it has become obvious that such an analogy is mirrored in many emotional and interactive situations, where feelings of superiority and grandiose self-image are operating.

Competitition
The need to be God seems always to involve a competitive response and it can in fact only function when one human being is measuring himself against another. Yet competition is not necessary to achievement or growth. One can be encouraged to greater achievement through one's own need for mastery, through one's own need to eliminate confusion, through one's own need for expression.

Further, as we have already seen, competition is basically destructive and hostile. It is in no way loving nor does it encourage positive communication. Far from being an essential component in developing the self, it stops full development of identity or individuality. Real differences between people are without hierarchies.

Religiosity
Power needs can also be expressed in religiosity. Many patients who come to therapy for rebirths see the experience in terms of religious associations, and a need to be close to some spiritual authority figure. Invariably, there is a competitive hierarchy somewhere in their beliefs: those who are close to God are superior to those who are further away, and those who believe are superior to those who

do not. The question the therapist is tempted to ask is, If this person is God, who is the patient who just left?

Usually, the stronger the religiosity the stronger the fear of *not* loving God. The result is excessive devotion – God in short becomes a substitute umbilicus. The symptoms are certainly similar to those of the idealization of loved ones we discussed in the chapter on the Crisis Umbilicus, and also to some of the characteristics of emotional prostitution. Behind it all are power needs, competition and dependency.

Aggression and Assertion

The concept of aggression was discussed in the chapter on 'Adjustments to Reality', but it is also relevant here, for without comparison, and the need to defeat another, there would be no aggression. Assertion, on the other hand, which is the attempt to respond to reality to maintain self-esteem, is non-aggressive, and does not have as its underlying purpose the defeat of another, the submission of another or the control of another. The difference is clear in the behaviour of a mother lion when her young are attacked. She will kill to protect their survival, and if her territory is infringed upon she will preserve it. This is non-aggressive. But if the same lion were to attack a small animal and kill it for sheer enjoyment of conquest, this would be aggressive.

Assertion is self-determined, in that your own value system helps define what your reactions will be. Like the lioness, you act to maintain the balance of your own specific world. Aggression is other-determined, dependent on acknowledgement by the external world. And in that it is other-determined, and an externalization, it is not innate but learned. The individual can only express hostility in the way he has seen others exhibit it. Therefore, parents who are aggressive with children produce aggressive children, while parents who are nonaggressive have nonaggressive children. The irony is that the combative parent ends up punishing and negating the child for the offensive reactions the child has learned from him, thereby producing additional aggression.

Indeed, it seems as though the need to be God is one of the most universal of distortions. Even the most humble, in his very humility, may be acting out a role as superior – superior in humility. Yet it is not hard to see that it is much more serene and rewarding to be able to accept oneself as the equal of everyone, to be accepting of them and accepted by them. What do individuals feel that they are giving up by accepting this equality which is so universally rebelled against?

To some extent, all children are oppressed by their environment. The infant, prior to birth, is of course not faced with the question of whether he is powerful or powerless – it is only with birth contractions that the concept of comparison arises, upon entry into the real world. In that the contraction initiates the capacity to integrate behaviour in this way, all problems with control, power and narcissism stem from birth.

We have already seen that contractions are the beginning of comparative tools and that they teach the infant the boundaries of his environment, the boundaries of concept formation and the boundaries of feeling. In a distorted and deformed way, the experience of contractions teaches competitiveness too, for concepts of greater and lesser, inferior and superior, all begin here, as do delusions of grandeur and insecure feelings of depersonalization. In the last chapter, we will go further into such specific aspects of birth, and explain how a lack of self-control in the birth process can initiate power conflicts.

Fantasy Systems

Along with the need for superiority goes the demand for indulgence by others. This requirement of servility from others is of course a distortion of reality, and leads to disappointment when it in turn leads the 'god junkie' into confusion, spite, anger and vengeance. He meets any deviation from his fantasy with contempt. As a parent he usually demands total obedience, and as a mate, total devotion. He is a slave of his own needs, and value, justice, compromise are possible only provided they do not conflict with his fantasy. Each god junkie has his own criteria on which to validate his omniscience: his talent, wisdom, strength, will, charm, endurance, pride or frailty. Whatever the elements contained within his fantasy system, it rules more than he. As long as the system remains unchallenged, he can be kind, communicative and just; but the minute it is threatened, he becomes an illogical demanding child, self-concentrated and oblivious to the needs of others or the reality of the situation. Provided that the fantasy remains intact he can take all manner of disappointment or abuse, but penetrate this one proof of his importance and he falls apart.

The lengths to which such people will go to protect their system from disintegration is illustrated by a woman patient. She was thirty-eight years old, and a virgin. Her godliness was invested in her purity, and in her rejection of all suitors as inferior. She refused to modify her requirements for a mate because it was on her resistance and strength of will that her uniqueness depended. In all other areas she functioned well and communicated with sensitivity, but when it came to a sexual relationship she was a tyrant and devoid of reason. Yet it was her own judgement that her life was without real meaning.

Another god junkie patient appeared passive, charming and easygoing. His grandiose self-image first appeared when he discussed his tendency subtly to turn people against each other. It seems that he would report out of context the actions or words of one person to the other, a skill he had learned as a child when he had gained attention by setting his sibling against his mother.

A third example was a woman who was having three love affairs simultaneously. Each of the three mates was convinced that he had a monogamous relationship with her. When she became pregnant, herself not knowing who was the father, she convinced each one that he was. Even once married to one of the three lovers, she continued to feel power because of her secret, and thought her husband a fool for not knowing the truth. Her ridicule of him grew till their marriage was in a shambles. In therapy, once the truth was exposed, however, the combat was distanced enough to turn the marriage into a bonding of warmth and trust.

God and Secrecy
This last example demonstrates the need for truth in all relationships. Indeed in every communication, keeping a secret is an expression of the need to be God. We can act logically only when knowing all the facts. The 'obfuscator' distorts reality and the behaviour of others with whom he is in contact, either by outright dishonesty or by modification of the truth. He renders ineffective or inappropriate the response he receives, and thus devalues the authority of others so that he remains dominant, and unchallenged.

We have explained in Chapter six how perception of reality inevitably depends on fragments of the truth that we select out and incorporate into a system that makes logical our behaviour and beliefs. In our drive towards consistency, we attend especially to, and strive hardest to incorporate, those fragments that are inconsistent or out of the ordinary – so that a woman married ten times, a man sitting with a shoe on his head, and someone with a million dollars more attended to than other people because of their unusual quality. They have thus a greater influence over others' choice of what to attend to, and in that they are attended to, they have power.

On the other hand, those who render information misleading or incomplete, as does the obfuscator, also have the power to *alter* the perception of others, and thus control the world of their interaction. They have the information while those around them do not, so that they can make greater consistency in their world than can those with whom they relate.

Perhaps some examples will show more clearly how the need to be God manifests itself in maladaptive, destructive functions.

One patient, who had been a prostitute, was now working in an ordinary job. She always got involved with men whom she considered emotionally, racially, biologically, physically, chronologically, intellectually or in some other way inferior to her. Her grandiosity was reinforced by these men, who fed her ego to offset the lack of commitment she felt. Beyond this, she openly discussed a psychopathic pride in this deviation from social norms: she considered her social rebelliousness a verification of uniqueness, power and superiority. Despite the emotional hindrance of having to keep her romantic life secret, she could not give her practice up, though she frequently complained of guilt or isolation and said she wanted to change. The point was that she had not received enough emotional verification in her childhood to allow her to risk being 'unspecial'.

Another patient was thoroughly convinced that he was superior to and smarter and more capable than anyone else. However, his behaviour did not measure up to his self-image, so others did not respond to him as he felt he deserved, so he tended to become isolated and detached. When he did not gain the responses from others he expected, that would validate his fantasies of himself as superior, he did not question the reality of his self-concept, but instead claimed that others were deficient in failing to recognize his worth. So he was continually disappointed.

Rather similar was a young would-be scientist, who never took courses or went to school because he always felt he already knew more than the instructor, and would be lowering himself if in fact he did succumb to the requirements of the academic world. In this way, he remained totally incapable of asserting his fantasy, whether or not he had the intellectual capability. At the age of 40 he was still sitting at home dreaming up brilliant experiments – after coming home from waiting tables all day.

A third young man refused to get emotionally involved with anyone, because no woman was good enough – or willing to acknowledge his fantasy of his own grandiosity. He thus prevented himself from any meaningful contact, although devoured by an agony of loneliness.

Fear of Insignificance
All these people were standing on the roof, considering others around them inadequate fools: since they assumed that they really were as great as the fantasy they had about themselves, it was the inadequacy of the people around them or their lack of luck that created all the problems. Underneath, however, it was really their own inadequacy they feared. Their inability to accept limitation meant that recognition of any failing of their own would amount to a total breakdown of their fantasy about themselves. Underneath the grandiose dreams, then, was always an extremely negative self-image: these people felt it had to be either one or the other extreme; either they were as great as they wanted to be, or their utter insignificance would be verified, and they would be totally depersonalized.

Sometimes, like a young lady who could not maintain a job because to be told what to do by others destroyed her image of herself as in control, such people are fully aware cognitively of their deficiency. It is emotionally that they cannot accept it. Others acknowledge deficiencies, but insist that they should still receive the status, the money, the esteem that they wish. When asked why, they say 'Because I'm Melvin Schniedelhoffer!' Melvin Schniedelhoffer, in his own eyes, is worthy simply because he exists.

One young man, when asked what he intended to do with his life, said very specifically that he was waiting for someone to hand him a million dollars so that he could do whatever he wanted. In the meantime, he did nothing. One of his assumptions was that if he worked to get anything, he would be disproving his own infallibility and grandiosity. The concept that one has a destiny that will itself bring beautiful and exciting rewards simply because one is oneself, contains within it the seeds of procrastination, and thus self-imposed failure.

Any rejection of these people's grandiose fantasies is experienced by them as a total rejection. The god junkie always has the underlying fear that, on some level, he has some fundamental weakness that he does not understand and therefore cannot offset. Because he cannot maintain consistency cognitively, he delegates his potential to a fantasy world. The minute he becomes aware that he has some capability that is real, however, the grandiosity diminishes.

Most of us do not experience such obviously grandiose needs. But we are all familiar with subtle expressions of grandiosity in everyday life; in the charm of the flirt, the boasting of the vain person, the hyper-criticism of a boss or the rudeness of a waitress. We see it in the authority of the bureaucrat, for instance, or the doorman who ridicules a tenant's dress, or the construction worker who grades female passers-by, or the friend who lectures one about one's behaviour. Any time we insist that another come to us instead of extending ourselves, any time we choose to make a decision for another, where they rather than we must take the consequences, any time we assume the right to judge or evaluate another, we too are 'standing on the roof'.

That Can't Happen to Me

The insistence that 'That can't happen to me' is another symptom of grandiose thinking. Some women feel that rape can never happen to them. Other people find it hard to believe that they could be fired, robbed, hit by a car, get a disease or be left by a mate, and even judge negatively those that are. The feeling that somehow they are special, and immune to certain experiences, stems from the solipsistic concept of godliness. The devastation that results when this belief collapses exposes the most basic in god junkie tendencies.

Personally determined exemption of this kind can of course be both positive and negative. For some receiving love, gaining recognition or popularity, winning a contest, making a million or fulfilling a wish are beyond probability, and should any of these occur then reality organization too collapses. Immunities are a form of substitute umbilicus that are used to justify feelings of grandiosity. As long as imagined exemption from any life experience exists, reality is not confronted.

Major personality changes may be facilitated by a challenge to this immunity. A challenge can extend the client's awareness to encompass susceptibility both to failure and to tragedy, and susceptibility to success and happiness, for immunity not only protects the individual from life's misfortunes, it also sets up obstacles to satisfaction and reward. Immunity sustains unreachable dreams while making the reachable, unobtainable. It, like many defences, totally reverses reality.

Suppose there are two people sitting in a room, each quietly involved with his own project: one is reading a book, the other painting a picture. There is a certain calm, a certain serenity in the scene. The person with the picture shows his work and the other says, 'It's very good.' The person reading says, 'Listen to this,' and the other says, 'Hey, I never thought of that.' Each supplements the other, learns from the other; each is fuller for the experience with the other. Neither is better than the other for, if that were true, the other would not gain as much. One is not lesser than the other for, if that were true, the other could not gain as much. It is a peaceful, loving existence. Many people describe this as an ideal, but they do everything in their lives to create obstructions to just that harmony.

Basically we are all born with the predisposition to relate in this positive fashion, and we all desire such peaceful and constructive interaction just because it is what we are at the base. It is the expression of logos adjusted to reality in the easiest, least conflicting way. It is what people are about, when all the superimposed maladaptation is removed. Yet competition, which is destructive, constantly undermines this form of interaction.

Needing to feel important is part of dependency. You feel rejected by others because you depend on their assessment of you, and they have not taken you as seriously as your own feelings of importance dictate. The more important you feel, the greater the tendency to feel rejected by those around you who treat you casually. Expecting to be indulged by others inappropriately leads to much disappointment, depression and even confusion. Interestingly, successful individuals find the attention they receive as confusing as those who fail and are ignored, for even externally determined grandiosity is a distortion.

There is a sense in which, due to logos, each person is equally perfect. And dreams can be realized, provided they stem from ourselves and not from others. By adulthood we have all developed abilities that can be actualized and achieved. It is only the disruption of a healthy self-image by the outer environment, that results in some form of compensation, like the need for omnipotence, and the wish to attain the impossible. By concentrating on the unreachable we often overlook the possible. Fantasy and unreality substitute for activity and actuality. They prohibit accomplishment and create imagined limitation.

Most patients once they stop trying to get what they don't want, start to get what they do want. In the next chapter we will investigate this topic further.

10 *THE NARCISSISTIC-GUILT DICHOTOMY*

According to Freud,[1] guilt originates during the Oedipal stage of development, around five or six years old, when the child develops a superego and incorporates the values and attitudes of his parents. According to natal theory, however, guilt in the sense Freud describes it is anti-womb and 'illogical'. So if, in fact, guilt does originate at the Oedipal stage it must arise from a world experience – often a learning process whereby the child incorporates the methods by which his authority figures cope with illogic.

One might in addition suggest that, although guilt in its adult form originates around the age of five, it is really only an extension of various mechanisms that emerge at earlier points to facilitate maladaptive behaviour. These have to do with the original sensation that something does not make sense, the fear of abandonment or the experience of loss, all of which we have discussed as associated with the crisis umbilicus. When these experiences are repeatedly connected with maladaptive behaviour, we identify a particular emotional response and label it 'guilt'. Then the anxieties linked with vulnerability, dependency and the sense of loss continue to accompany guilt whenever the feeling is experienced. It is not the guilt itself, then, that is negatively experienced, but the old conflicts of the umbilical crisis which are aroused simultaneously.

The Oedipal Period
In terms of natal theory, Freud's interpretation of the Oedipal period clearly needs re-examination. First, it makes no sense for a child to feel guilty about having positive needs for the mother, because a taboo on sexual feelings is something he is simply not sophisticated enough at this point to understand. He may respond to power-oriented and competitive feelings in the parent, which are illogical; or he may be put in conflict by seductive responses to him. But real parental affection, such as was described as confluential in Chapter eight, cannot evoke an alligatory sexual response from the child – alligatory sexuality being the form that gives rise to Oedipal

problems, and guilt. Confluential affection toward the parent, which lacks any consciousness of taboo, tends to be guilt-free and leads to the capacity for fulfilling sexual relationship once adulthood is reached.

The parents, when exhibiting competition or seduction, also themselves exhibit guilt, because these are maladaptive behavioural forms. The child learns to reflect the guilt and to associate it with his own intense feelings at the time. The more competitively and seductively he is treated by his parental figures during the Oedipal interaction, the more traumatic the Oedipal period will be. So trauma is not inherent in the episode, but it can accompany it.

Guilt

Guilt itself has its origins not in sexuality but in dependency. Children don't need their parents (and certainly the adult does not really need them). We hang on to our need for our parents only out of a guilt – which they have created. So it is only in giving up their control over us that we can attain the individuality and the sense of freedom that we have a right to, that we were born with, and that we must have in order to function and feel content. Guilt implies a debt that must be paid back; a debt of future dependency and passivity to the demands of others – as we have already seen, we are passive when we have a debt to pay, and only when the debt has been paid, do we become active again. The debt can be imagined, or it can be imposed on us by those to whom we turn for direction. It is never natural, and just as it takes more energy to be dependent than to be independent, it also takes more energy to be passive than active. Passivity is a façade that is used to placate those who impose guilt.

In adulthood, this passivity can generalize throughout the personality structure. It is always associated with correlating feelings of hostility, judgementalness and disapproval, which, in turn, make the guilty person feel more guilty and then more passive. The whole process confirms dependence, because the individual's definition of his own behaviour is externalized, and dictated by the expectation of others rather than his own. Reactions to seductiveness in one parent, or competition in the other, do not occur for the first time when the child reaches five or six and the Oedipal stage begins; they were there all along. But they do emerge clearly at this time, when the child's ability to recognize these behavioural patterns as inappropriate evidently reaches a peak. It is possible that there is some corresponding development in brain physiology around this time, though there have been no neurological investigations to confirm this: certainly guilt as an adjustment to maladaptation represents higher cognitive levels than regression and some other mechanisms described here, in that it incorporates logic, and complex patterns of communication. Once established, it is not only maladaptive but often self-perpetuating, in that the individual tends to feel guilty about feeling guilty, the second form of guilt existing to protect the first.

Here, in the idea of guilt as a protector of maladaptive behaviour, is in fact a clue to its psychological function. Behaviour that fulfils our needs, that creates no conflict and is appropriate to increased functioning, maintains itself and is continually reinforced. But if behaviour that is inappropriate or unrewarding is to be sustained, there must be devices to protect the maladaptation from being extinguished. We are identifying two devices that have as their sole purpose the facilitation of distorted adjustment. These two are narcissism and guilt. But we see them not as distinct emotional entities, but, as we shall show through this chapter, as interdependent to the extent that they constitute a special psychological subdivision which will be labelled 'the narcissistic-guilt dichotomy'.*

So guilt, rather than an inhibitor of activity as it is traditionally held to be, in our experience turns out to be a facilitator: provided only that the behaviour is maladaptive. It is a mechanism which protects inappropriate behaviour, which at some point has been required for emotional survival. Guilt creates a logical order that justifies conduct that otherwise would appear irrational and unacceptable to the self. Guilt is thus distinct from regret, for with regret comes change, growth and healthy or adaptive behaviour.

Take, for example, an individual who is always late for appointments. As a child he had parents who were demanding and authoritarian, so he would be late as a gesture to assert his identity and protect some vestiges of autonomy. As an adult, this behaviour becomes inappropriate and illogical, but the guilt he feels forms a bridge to justify perpetuating his behaviour.

Another example is a man who was dating two women. He felt guilty but convinced himself that he suffered so deeply from guilt that he was justified in focusing his sympathy – and that of others – on himself rather than on the women. The situation thus remained

* Should early development be sequential rather than parallel, it is postulated that guilt, or its forerunner, precedes narcissism, rather than the reverse, which is traditionally assumed.

rewarding on all levels, and the guilt ensured its perpetuation.

This process can become even more complicated in situations where the guilt not only protects maladaptive behaviour and facilitates it, but also extends it. In his book *Compulsion to Confess*, Theodore Reik[2] identifies a process whereby criminals actually commit repeated crimes simply in order to be able to confess them.

The confession is symbolic of the resolution of a guilt that they felt years earlier towards their parents. The need to confess thus comes before the crime, and enables them to be punished not for the crime itself, but for an incident stemming from their childhood.

In the past, it has always been assumed that because guilt is associated with many defence reactions, such as compulsive cleaning or ritualized behaviour,[3] it actually causes these reactions. However, in terms of the above analysis, the truth is quite the reverse: the behaviour is protected from extinction and facilitated by the guilt. The guilt develops along with, or slightly after, the symptom.

In therapy, by severing the guilt-producing agent from current behaviour, resolution of the symptoms may take place. But the resolution of guilt does not get rid of the symptom. The resolution of symptoms, by showing that they are no longer necessary, gets rid of the guilt.

Guilt is not only a defence reaction; it is also used for the purpose of giving permission for the behaviour which the person otherwise would feel is forbidden. By imposing guilt on himself, the individual can do the act that he feels is inappropriate and still avoid responsibility for the action. He reasons that if he has been accused and must suffer the guilt (which he has imposed on himself) he may as well have the gain; he feels guilty about a fantasized accusation and then brings about the verification of the accusation. He may even set up a situation in which he manipulates a real accusation from someone else, in order to feel the unjustified guilt that then sanctions misconduct.

The Guiltist

When this kind of pattern becomes consistent, he is what could be labelled a 'guiltist'. A guiltist is not a masochist, for a masochist likes to suffer and a guiltist does not. His only suffering is the guilt which he imposes on himself, and which enables him to receive the reward of being able to do anything he wants. He can disregard the needs of others and not lose any self-esteem in the process. The masochist wants punishment to relieve guilt; the guiltist wants guilt to avoid punishment. The masochist says, 'I suffer.' The guiltist says, 'I feel guilt, therefore I am innocent no matter what terrible thing I do or how I behave.' He is self-indulgent and modifies the environment to fulfil his own narcissistic needs. He justifies himself by resenting the person whom he blames for producing the guilt within him.

One couple in therapy exemplified this. The man was a 'guiltist'. He felt submissive, yet continually acted out behaviour that created problems in the relationship. He had been brought up with strict religious beliefs, including rigid taboos on sex, and he had what traditionally would have been interpreted as a strong Oedipal fixation. He complained of tremendous guilt feelings, and said his superego was overdeveloped. However, all his values were externalized and he looked to his wife – and to his therapist – to define what was appropriate behaviour. Since he did not act accordingly, he then felt guilty for having deviated from the prescribed response. Outwardly, because of the definition of expectation he had received from others, he expressed excessive concern over loyalty, fidelity, and what was 'fair' or 'right', so that anyone not familiar with his history thought of him as concerned for others, with a stable, integrated and consistent superego. His behaviour, however, reflected the reverse. He did only that which came easily and did not conflict with instantaneous gratification. He always responded exactly as he wished despite his articulated values, and excused his behaviour by feelings of intense guilt.

His wife, on the other hand, was quite different. She came from a very liberal background with no guilt associated with sex and had a very strong, firm and defined sense of responsibility that was independent of external feedback. Her behaviour was always reflective of her values and she looked to herself rather than others for her definition of appropriate behaviour. Where he felt guilt, she felt regret. So she changed and he stayed the same. It is difficult to believe that the concept of superego as it is currently conceived can explain both these personalities, for two distinct processes seemed to be operative, with perhaps different origins, that up to now have been lumped together and called superego development.

One of the origins of guilt is disapproval from a parent of an act that according to the child's logic is appropriate. If the parent explains the reason for his reaction the child can internalize this, and blend it into his ego structure. But the 'guilter' parent rejects without explanation and leaves a gap in understanding, which shocks the child. To create order and explain the reaction of the parent, he fills the gap with guilt. Thereafter guilt is always associated with his own sense of inadequacy, as defined by the parents, and fears of being misjudged. The guilt is a form of seducer into the inappropriate behaviour, for it triggers off a variety of variously false expectations: of being criticized, of disproving the accusation, of re-establishing self-esteem, and resolving past mental confusion.

When the 'guilter' parent 'forgives' the child, the child feels a confused sense of relief that is rewarding. So the connected guilt becomes satisfying because of the reward of relief from anxiety that follows. The inappropriateness of the forgiveness is a contributing factor. The process is, in this way, self-perpetuating. Guilt is usually for behaviour that is unacceptable to others but which, based on logic for that individual, is appropriate. For this reason there is no regret. It is in the individual's justification of the act, rather than in the disapproval of others, that guilt arises: the individual himself does not recognize the inappropriateness of the behaviour, but he does recognize that another would judge it negatively. If he felt he could 'get away with it' and not risk punishment or rejection, there would be only satisfaction in the act. In this way the guilt represents permitting another to control and define behaviour, because of dependency or because appropriate social values were never internalized. It represents what Freud would define as a deficiency in superego development. Guilt is not only devoid of superego but devoid of responsibility.

Guilt also involves resentment, held in secret, for expression of it would be met with rejection, resulting in more guilt and more resentment. The passivity deepens further because emotions are held in check. These people gravitate to those who for them are 'guilters': that is, those who criticize and devalue just that behaviour that is appropriate to the guilty person's logos, and who are therefore guilt inducers specifically for them. If they chose to interact with someone whose values were compatible, they would eliminate guilt, resentment and passivity, but they would also never meet the challenge of mastering the incongruity of their early parental relationship.

The Guilter
A guilter is always someone admired, and symbolically similar to the authority figure who originally undermined competence. He is then endowed with the power of resurrection, or continued depletion, of the guiltist's self-esteem. The guilter ensures perpetuation of guilt

by an assertion of his own belief system, which he knows full well will be unacceptable, because he picked his partner for that reason.

The induction of guilt is, in itself, a complex process worth examining. Many parents discipline their child primarily through this method. Because the method is nonverbal, and confusing, it leads, as we have seen, to distorted response, including that of emotional prostitution. Such parents are usually the same ones who try simultaneously to perpetuate and negate feelings of dependency and worthlessness. They tell the child that they want him to be self-sufficient, responsible, a mature adult, while simultaneously indicating non-verbally that if he deviates one iota from their orders, he will be rejected. Dependency, in this sense, is a double-bind because the child feels guilty if he is dependent and he feels guilty if he is not dependent.

As long as the child must meet the demands of the parents in this way, and not initiate his own individualized pattern of responding, he remains reliant upon them for constant evaluation not only of his behaviour, but of himself as an individual. He is forced thus into a subservient role, and feels resentment because of it. He then feels guilty about his hostility, and reverts back to further dependency, passivity and immobilization. In this way, guilt is both a facilitator of dependency and a justification for its existence.

Shame

Our formulations are still in the stage of evaluation, and we have yet to reach a complete understanding of the origins of these adjustments to reality. But throughout this chapter, in discussing guilt, we recognise its connection with other feelings: just as narcissism, too, is assumed to represent a constellation of related feelings. Shame for instance, has been seen by some authors as distinct from guilt, and preceding it. It is thought of as entirely determined by external responses from important others, and its development has been traditionally associated with toilet training. However, shame in any case stems from loss of dignity associated with feelings of incompetence in the eyes of others, which are the components of emotional prostitution. As we have already seen, the crisis umbilicus often shows itself clearly just at the anal stage, when again an extension of the body must be given up, so shame, in that it means loss of self-esteem and dependence on externalized evaluation, could well be the natural outcome of this. This too can be traced back to a predisposition, in some form of negative self-concentration; but, unlike narcissism, it is reality orented, logical, cognitive, and other-directed. Emotional prostitution and seduction are other major maladaptations that become magnified at the Oedipal stage, and probably play their part in the development of guilt, though the mechanisms through which this happens are not yet clear. What we can suggest at this stage is that guilt is a rationalized magnification of shame, awareness of judgement by others, and projected fantasies of external evaluations; all interacting with a maladaptive self-absorption or mode of narcissism.

Value Systems
A child has different priorities from the adult; yet he must prostitute himself emotionally by overtly accepting their priorities even when they are in opposition to his own. He thus has two value systems: (1) what is appropriate to others; and (2) what is appropriate to him. If he develops healthily at the traditional Oedipal stage, what is appropriate to others becomes fused with what is appropriate to him, and he internalizes new priorities. But if he remains infantile due to guilt (which prevents maturation and introjection of values), he will retain two value systems, each in conflict with the other.

Guilt prevents maturation by covering up the inconsistency, and thus preventing mastery of it. It stops introjection of values by keeping them delegated to definition by others. The child learns the pattern of the adult's values, and if he deviates from this to accord with his infantile logos, he feels guilt. Any value that is discarded in this way and covered by guilt becomes fixated at that point, and will not mature. Only that which is inner-defined matures, for it has transitional cognition.

The guiltist is impulsive, infantile and intolerant of frustration or postponement of gratification – he is split in superego. When he does something appropriate to him and not others, he feels guilt; but when he does something appropriate for others and not him, he feels controlled and dependent – even if what he is doing is consistent with reality and healthy behaviour.

A question that this theory raises in terms of Oedipal development is that if, in fact, guilt is an unnecessary reaction and not essential to healthy maturation, how does one explain the superego which Freud saw as based on a reaction to guilt? Are there, in fact, two different forms of superego, that develop differently and have different dynamics in adjustment? Or is the superego a product only of a distorted environment? According to natal theory, a healthy logical conscience based on reality testing that is not other-determined, should require no Oedipal trauma to create it, only logic and life experience. Such a conscience, or healthy superego, contains awareness of others, appropriate adjustments to reality and healthy mechanisms of defence that are constructive as opposed to destructive. These are all consistent with ego functions. If the cognitive maturation of the child is the outcome of a positive inter-action with parents who give appropriate responses, the superego is devoid of guilt, hostility and competition. One could wonder if in fact is exists at all.

Guilt and Narcissism
The greater the discrepancy between the two sets of values – inner-directed and outer-directed – the greater the production of guilt. The infantile set is self-concentrated and narcissistic, in that it ex-cludes the socially adjusted adult set; but it remains the only set of values internalized. Guilt has thus retarded growth and prevented the emergence of mature values. Since only values that are not linked to guilt, but evolved for the purpose of self-defined mastery of life, are retained once guilt is removed, there is always an ego change in such people to narcissism and self-concentrated values when guilt is eliminated. From this we conclude that narcissism is a secondary formation to guilt with latent guilt at ts base.

We can now trace back the steps in development of the narcissistic-guilty personality. Self-stimulation in the womb encourages umbilical sensuality and the first sense of mastery. Then comes the umbilical crisis, followed by insecurity when, through others, the infant experiences loss in his sense of competence. This is the root of guilt. It is in demanding back what is lost that self-concentration occurs, because the deficiency must be exaggerated by the need. If the infant's demands are met with loving contact, his demands are rewarded: others are valued and can substitute for that loss, so he turns from self to other-concentration. But rebuke or control by others develops maladaptation. If contact is rewarding, yet promotes maladaptation, guilt results. If coping mechanisms cannot be used for compensation, or there is no reward in the interaction, then nar-cissism results. With very early onset or exaggeration of the umbilical crisis, for example because of abandonment, or overwhelming illogic that reduces the satisfaction of interaction, narcissism increases again. It must be recognized that even in the narcissism prior to developed guilt, which is a reaction to the crisis, there must be consciousness of others. This fluctuation between self- and other-concentration can be seen as reflecting an even earlier pattern: the concentration on the thumb and the breast.

We have already shown how thumb fixation comes before breast fixation, the thumb being 'self-cathected' and the breast 'other-cathected'. That is, the thumb concentrates energy on the self and the breast incorporates response toward others. So normal progression would have the infant substitute the breast for the thumb. This assumes that the breast is sufficiently satisfying, or the change would be rejected; but the breast is clearly more satisfying than the thumb, for it offers food as well as outlet for the sucking response. So a transfer from thumb and self to breast and other is natural and expected.

The thumb, however, has the advantage of accessibility. When the breast has negative attributes, or when it is withheld, this advantage acquires a new significance, and the infant reverts to thumb-sucking. A recathexis on to the thumb represents the beginning of narcissism. Only with the acceptance of the breast is the child capable of being other-oriented and developing the dependency that is a requirement for the evolvement of guilt.

Thus, both guilt and narcissism represent all the components of feeding, survival, competence, sexuality and orality that are associated with the self-stimulation of the cord in the womb. They are both emotionally masturbatory. They both arise from the experience of vulnerability and loss of self-esteem stemming from the umbilical crisis.

When the foetus has its umbilicus, its experience is total and complete. Only when deprived of it, only when functioning is subtracted, does he reach out to seek ways of compensating for that imbalance. He evaluates the attributes of others according to whether or not the component that he selects is effective in regaining his own feelings of competence. The greater the experienced loss, the greater his requirement to add attributes to restore and resurrect his identity. The greater the disparity between what he becomes with the loss and what he needs to supplement his deficiency, the more judgemental, critical and evaluative his decision-making process.

However, the degree to which he is aware of loss is dependent upon the reactions of others, who may convince him by criticism and rejection that he is now incomplete. This awareness is always other-determined rather than self-determined, and the resolution of the loss is predicated upon the perceived severity of the task. Success in making good the loss too is other-determined, for it is reflected in obtaining responses from others.

If the child is satisfied with his image because he has received acceptance, attention and support, he has no need to seek, compete or judge. He does not need to expand expectancies beyond that which exists, for he is content with what is. The dissatisfied child, who is convinced by others that he is inadequate, has however four choices. First, he can negate himself, by reflecting the received responses. Second, he can react in fantasy by seeking unrealizable goals (which lead to disappointment with each failure). Third he can integrate other-oriented definitions of competence, whether relevant to him or not, and attempt to adapt to them. And fourth, he can choose narcissism.

Narcissism

When rejection and injury to self-esteem reach unbearable extremes, in the terror of acknowledged abandonment, the child confronts his unresolved vulnerability. In a final sense, he has only himself. He rejects others as they reject him, and fills his fantasy of himself with all the unrealistic expectations he incorporated from contact with the world. He loves himself as he wishes to be loved. He is his own object, for there are not others who are willing to substitute without imposing an unacceptable price: that is, acknowledgement of his own inadequacy. The self-involvement of narcissism is thus always an evolved development, emanating from feelings of imposed inadequacy and from a dependency on definition by others. If the child receives sufficient acknowledgement and attention to offset the crisis umbilicus, narcissism, even on the most primary level, does not develop.

Many authorities[4] have included such concepts as self-esteem, aggression and self-protection as part of 'healthy' narcissism, assuming that some form of self-concentration is inherent, rather than reactive. But this idea depends on the concept of the foetus, infant and child as dependent, and learning to become self-sufficient only with maturation. This book attempts to reverse this perspective by perceiving both as counteractions to maladaptive environments.

Prior to birth, relationships with others are symbolized in the foetus's relationship with the umbilicus. Relationship is thus a womb-continuous experience and narcissism, which occurs after birth, means a loss of communication. It does not, as traditionally believed, precede object-relation formation, but is a regression in response to environmental vulnerability. A total rejection of that which is outside of the individual leads him to relate to himself as an isolated object, concentrating solely on his own identity. He would not do this unless previous contact proved unrewarding or painful.

Some confirmation of this thesis is to be found in the fact that the elimination of narcissism from an individual's personality in therapy results in an increase in feelings of inferiority and inadequacy; while diminished feelings of inferiority frequently increase narcissism rather than healthy ego functioning. This suggests that narcissism, like guilt, comes from superego, not ego, development.

Altruism

Several contemporary psychological and biological theories insist that all behaviour has to have a reinforcing base for it to exist at all; and that all generosity has thus, when dissected, narcissistic elements, so that complete altruism or selfless giving is impossible. It is perhaps important to try to explain altruism and 'absent' narcissism in terms of natal theory.

There are three different forms of altruism: 1) exploitative, 2) giving, and 3) responsive. In the first, the individual is altruistic for a purpose, such as reward, manipulative power (as in seductive episodes), or to maintain a certain self-image. In the second the individual does in fact act generously, and only as an unexpected byproduct may receive a reward. The third type is simply a logical reaction to the environment. And this is in general selected out, cognitively, for it lacks all psychic content or purpose.

If, as most psychological theory assumes, we remember only that which aids mastery and facilitates functioning – that which is traumatic is repressed and that which is valueless is simply overlooked – truly altruistic behaviour, of this third type, is simply disregarded as inconsequential and unnotable. Therefore, since we do not retain memory of these acts, we assume no such behaviour exists.

Freud's Primary and Secondary Narcissism

Narcissism must be distinguished from a component of ego which has the self as an investment. Here the need for communication, mastery, and maintaining rather than regaining lost self-sufficiency is healthy and strong. But narcissism, on the other hand, involves self-indulgence in negation of others. Freud[5] named narcissism from the myth of Narcissus, who fell so in love with his own image in a lake that he died of starvation. In his 1916 paper 'On Narcissism' he points out that in this fixation there is a lack of autonomy, yet isolation from others. The individual cathects himself, that is, he concentrates his energy on himself, which is 'primary narcissism'.

Traditional psychoanalytic theory has conceived of this primary narcissism as being inherent in the infant at birth. Later on, he can cathect this same energy on the mother's breast, which is called the first object-cathexis, the breast being the first love object. But according to cord theory, the first cathexis occurs in the womb when sucking produces sensation in the umbilical unit, so the mother's breast is seen as the second object-cathexis.

Freud calls 'secondary narcissism' the later rejection in the world when the infant turns away from others and puts his energies back on to himself. According to natal theory, this is really the first time the self becomes consciously cathected. It is a return to the same type of energy concentration that occurred within the womb, but with the addition of a reality component, so it is a regression as well as a new stage in development. Regression is thus differentiated from emotional or behavioural return: a full return is a going back to another psychological point in development, while regression is 'acting out' a previous developmental point, which this time includes elements of change that occurred thereafter.

For example, regression in an adult retains cognition, verbal skills, and awareness that belong to the adult's consciousness. A total return includes at least amnesiac elements and loss of perspective, and also excludes awareness that his state is one of return: he is not just acting five, he is five. In rebirth therapy, we find that when the experience is a true return, as distinct from a regression, the individual is frequently unaware of that part of the episode. He thinks nothing happened until it is identified by the therapist. In other words, this is repressed material, frequently extremely beneficial for diagnostic evaluation and gaining insights into uncharted psychic territory.

Narcissism is always regressive, that is, it never totally returns to the womb. It always has world characteristics, in that it includes elements of seductiveness, sadism and an intentional disregard for others. For without seductive episode vulnerability, narcissism cannot occur. Narcissism, like guilt, may remain latent initially and become manifest when an Oedipal situation is magnified. As we have already shown, excessive Oedipal trauma leaves the individual with these two psychological alternatives: to increase narcissism, so as to lack all conscience or superego and become psychopathic; or to develop excessive guilt and become what has diagnostically been described as an obsessive-compulsive. Which he chooses depends upon the rewards of interaction.

When the child needs to be loved or touched, to re-experience the closeness of the tight womb in the last few months prior to birth or the hug of the contraction during birth, he acts without seductiveness, without power and without any kind of maladaptive overtone. And if the response is positive, communication, which is constructive, takes place. But if there is no positive response, he withdraws and goes back to simulate the self-stimulation that he experienced in the womb. He reflects back the pushing away of his parents, for in not touching, the parent is not giving no response, he is always giving a rejection response.

Narcissism thus always has at its base the essential need to protect oneself and, in this way, it is a reaction and a counter-reaction. If it is a response to the environment, as is shown here, it cannot be innate but must be a developmental process arising from contact with the real world. According to Freud,[6] 'Increased narcissistic advancement is unhealthy in several ways . . . it falsifies all kinds of perception, reality adjustment, prevents relationships with others. It offends these others who are useful and a healthy basis for relations. As we have pointed out in general, specifically, there are narcissistic countercathexes to a multitude of objects of libidinous attachments.' We can be aware that there is a self only when we can differentiate between our own identity and that of another human being. As long as this distinction is predicated on dependency and on introjection of the values and attitudes of the outside world, there must be a lack of definition and identity. Such is the case with narcissism. In becoming aware of others, we become aware of ourselves, but only if we acknowledge that there are differences and that these differences are non-competitive. Narcissism *is* awareness of self by comparison with others, but just as with guilt, it begins with inadequate or distorted interaction.

The Ego-Ideal

The concept of the ego ideal as Freud[7] described it has been interpreted by some as the forerunner of the superego and the internalization of values and attitudes; and by others as a separate and distinct phenomenon. The ego-ideal as defined by Freud includes all our highest goals. He[7] says that when we are in love, the love object becomes part of our ego ideal; that is, love is a way of experiencing the ego ideal through another. So, we tend to overvalue the loved person, and express our own grandiosity through our interaction with their personality structure.

The author sees the ego-ideal as including all extremes of wished reality. When the ego-ideal goes beyond world possibility, it is fantasy. One manifestation, for instance, is an overestimation of one's own potential, so the individual is constantly dissatisfied with himself. When an ideal is disruptive to reality testing in this way, it seems to result from super-ego development, while when it facilitates accomplishment, it can be seen as an ego function.

Magnification of goals to the point of unreality is the result of parental interference, by denying the child's capability to reach real goals. The value of what is withheld, considered unobtainable or lost is always exaggerated. Freud[8] maintains that what one actually accomplishes is always minimal compared with one's highest ego-ideal. But the author concludes that within the concept of logos, it is possible to see the ego-ideal – the attainment of self-realization, self-control and effective functioning – as realistic, and not unobtainable. If the ego-ideal goes beyond these parameters, it must be a reaction to demands from the environment and the result of deprivation which tends to inflate the fantasy values in the ego-ideal. In the same way, if someone is sick and he gets attention deserving of his condition, he usually minimizes the symptoms. When his illness is ignored he will complain, and try to convince others that his suffering is worthy of response – and, in the process, increases his own awareness of discomfort.

In the literature,[9] narcissistic problems in adult life are often seen as arising from failures to maintain omnipotent control over the other, as in primary narcissism. That is, secondary forms of narcissism are to this extent agreed to involve a negative self-image, and to lead to a split in ego,* since the individual comes to perceive himself and others in extreme fantasies, as gods or devils. It is when the concept of the negative ego ideal† contains the assumption that primary narcissism is inherent, ego derived and preceding object relations that this book takes issue with other theories. Kernberg,[11] for instance, sees grandiosity as a maladaptive form of behaviour.

---

* The reader is reminded that a few pages back a similar split in superego was discussed. This substantiates the similarities between guilt and narcissism, and between both as superego manifestations.

† Theodore Reik discussed the same concept, labelling it 'the ego horror.[10]

However, he, like others[12] feels that there is a healthy narcissism.

Freud[13] states that 'narcissism is the libidinal component, the egotism of the infant's self-preservation, the measure of which may justifiably be attributed to every living creature.' Yet if narcissism is a defence against life, which is the world outside the womb, and necessary to counteract feelings of inferiority, it cannot be innate. Even if the definition of self-preservation is limited to the need for survival, narcissism remains a reaction, not only to others but to umbilical loss. The greater the maladaptation, the greater the separation anxiety.

In the beginning, the ego organization or concept of 'I'-ness in the libido was energized on to the self. The child perceived the mother's breast as part of him: because every time he cried, it was there. But the first time it is *not* there, he has to confront the idea of separateness, and with it the memory of the crisis umbilicus and the mourning connected with that loss. Only then, when he knows that he may *not* get the breast when he screams, is he aware that there is some logical component to control, that he must learn. It has not been sufficiently recognized by the theorists that this learning can take place only after the first experience of not having control.

By cathecting on to the self, the individual regains control and becomes his own umbilical cord. That this is the symbolic meaning of this urge to control has been confirmed by many patients in natal therapy, who describe feeling like a robot or a puppet hanging on a string: the very visual representation of the foetus hanging on the cord, and manipulated by the placenta or the puppeteer. Thus it is a return to the womb visualization that frequently accompanies the last stages of narcissistic, and then guilt, regression prior to psychosis.

Narcissism is the obverse of feelings of inferiority since, when the child is rejected, he recathects himself on to himself. Alternatively, he retains the inferiority feelings and the guilt part of the dichotomy comes into play. But he has first to experience a loss. Our hypothesis is that there is a distinct organization, or logos, at birth which is slowly chipped away by the environment.

The organization itself has a perfection with which the child identifies himself, but he is conscious of it only when something disrupts this concept of perfection, magnifies the crisis umbilicus, and becomes a threat. In all deprivation, including 'ego deprivation', there is an inflation value in that which is deficient. Greed is always a reaction to deprivation. Narcissism is ego greed.

Another concept that appears in the literature is the so-called narcissistic injury.[14] Narcissism is said to arise or increase as a reaction to the narcissistic injury – in other words, to a loss of self-esteem based on responses from the environment. Yet this theory confirms rather than refutes the idea that all narcissism refers ultimately to the crisis umbilicus, because some form of emotional dependency would have to exist prior to the narcissistic injury for the reactions of those in the environment to have the magnified value that they must have to create the injury.

Narcissism negates assvity in that it is active. Freud[15] claimed that we delight in the narcissism of others (others being children and women!), possibly because in narcissism, there is perceived freedom and pleasure. There is a smoothness to it, an energy that other maladaptive behaviours do not have. When denying the world, energy is put on to the self. Guilt, however, is passive, and energy is used primarily to control the self. Guilt means adjusting oneself to reality, even if in an ineffective way, and narcissism is an attempt to adjust reality to the self. But if this maladaptive evolution regresses past narcissism and guilt in a return to thumb fixation in the womb, we are in the boundaryless realms of insanity.

In narcissism, much of the environment must be selectively blocked out to ensure the continuation of the fantasy. In this sense, narcissism must always lead to distortion.

To summarize the concepts presented in this chapter, we have identified two possible directions of personality maladjustment in response to trauma, determined by the fixation point of the crisis umbilicus. A predisposition to one or other response pattern is first set up in the womb, imprinted during the birth process, and triggered when the umbilical crisis reaches a climax. Symptomology is then determined by the level of maturation at the time of the onset of the crisis, which can occur at birth or be held latent until a later stage.

These two directions are both expressed in the narcissistic-guilt dichotomy. Both guilt and narcissism protect inappropriate responses from being extinguished, both have inherent within them self-imposed rewards that reinforce them, both stunt psychological maturation and, depending upon the requirement of the environment, each can substitute for the other. One is always passive, while the other is active. Neither can exist without a precipitating maladjustment. Fluctuation in the predominance of one over the other is reflected in pathological dichotomies such as sado-masochism or manic-depression: the individual may actually reach some form of homeostasis by an equal balance of both. But only with the elimination of the dichotomy altogether can full autonomy and self-realization be achieved. It is through search, experience and insight that resolution becomes possible. Let us now turn to a discussion of therapy which can supplement that search.

11 THERAPIST AND PATIENT

Every therapy process has its own techniques. And natal therapy, although its own technique is in an early stage of development, has reached certain conclusions as to procedure and interaction between patients and therapists. To date most, although not all, of the patients who have gravitated to the therapy had similarities in development that led to an examination of the specific areas discussed in this book. Many were those I have described as 'borderline' and male homosexuals, though 'borderline' in this context simply means people who might be seen as obsessive compulsives without control or ritual to protect them.* Though experience with these people formed the basis of many of the theories discussed, we have found that these theories can be applied to personality problems generally, just as we have been able to identify the interactional patterns we have discovered in particular patients, in others.

Classical psychoanalysis[2] involves attempting to resolve unconscious problems by the verbal analysis and interpretation of defences. Supportive therapy[3] uses suggestions, and reflects back to the patient his verbal perceptions to increase ego strength. Some of the more *avante-garde* therapies[4] on the other hand concentrate on nonverbal interactions between patients, and stress emotional as distinct from cognitive confrontation, to develop insight and resolution of problems. Natal therapy attempts to do both: to communicate and deal with the emotional needs of the patient along with a cognitive interaction of insight. The value of verbal as well as of nonverbal patterns is identified, dissected and resolved.

Observers who attend group sessions, and are not familiar with natal therapy procedures during individual sessions, often get the impression that natal therapy is much the same as primal therapy – that is, that material is reached but not worked through. This is true of the group experience. But the working-through process does

* Borderline is a psychological label used by Kornberg.[1] It was found that these were the individuals most likely to gravitate towards natal therapy.

take place. It is delegated to individual sessions, where intense analysis through verbal encounter is used.

Our criticism of primal therapy is that it deals with the birth fantasy, but sidetracks the ego completely on the grounds that it is not needed. Primal treats the patient without the aid of cognition, will or strength. Thus whatever assistance can be received stays buried and is never incorporated into the conscious ego. Primal therapy seems to reach the feeling around birth, but not to connect it with the rest of the neuroses.

Principles of Natal Therapy

Although in natal therapy there is a concentration on past behaviour and the origin of emotional maladaptation, the 'here and now' is also stressed. In this sense, the individual sessions are extremely traditional in their psychoanalytic approach, using interpretation and dealing with dreams and other defences that have evolved. And we try to strike a balance between the two major orientations in current psychotherapy: one stressing the value of silence, postponing interpretations until the patient is hypothetically prepared to incorporate them;[5] the other involving confrontation, freely offered interpretations by the therapist and vigorous verbal interchange.[6] The individual sessions in natal therapy are extremely cognitive, in that behaviour and emotional patterns are dissected and interpreted and an intellectual mastery is attempted; but simultaneously, the feelings that a patient expresses are responded to and respected.

If a patient prefers one rather than another approach – intellectual or emotional rather than a combination of the two – this itself can be a source of insight. Some patients avoid dealing with problems by being hyper-intellectual and negating their feeling structure. Others, by being strictly emotional and wanting that part of their personality attended to, avoid any kind of cognitive integration of insight. In our experience, dealing with emotions tends to get to the problem but dealing with cognition seems to work it through. The elimination of one or the other approach renders the whole process inadequate.

So although silence, as a technique to promote response patterns in the patient, can be productive, it can also be a waste of time. Sitting silently seems to us an implicit judgement by the therapist that the patient is inadequate or unready to accept the interpretation – a withholding act, permitting the perpetuation of maladaptation. It represents his own fears of rejection by the patient, and it promotes the perception of him as an authority figure. It is his responsibility, if he perceives anything about the patient, to offer it for the patient to evaluate. A wrong interpretation by a therapist is in fact often useful, if the patient can then explain how that interpretation is inadequate, and the therapist then redirects his pattern of thinking. A verbal contract should be made between the two to ensure the continuation of the therapy despite such misleading directions, and if they stick with it, by a process of elimination, an appropriate interpretation will occur.

The process of therapy is often described as a puzzle. It is like the game you played as a child, when you were given a picture with animals hidden in it. Your task and joy was to seek them out. Some of them were little birds or fish; some of them were great wolves and lions and mean, growling dogs. Part of the therapy is to find the hidden patterns within the psychic structure. Awareness of these secret aspects of ourselves then becomes a tool for greater functioning. and consequent mental mastery is the reward that perpetuates the self search.

When the patient can face the horrors within himself objectively, and deal with them as simply hidden pictures of his mind, the ugly fantasies and behaviours that are too shameful to admit become nothing but silly symbolic re-enactments of past episodes in childhood that have never been totally understood. The pain has gone out of them.

When emotional pain is associated with an insight, it is often because that insight has not yet been mastered, and more work needs to be done. When an insight really is resolved it leads to change, and there is always relief and revitalization. The patient has the choice of rejecting the emotional pain connected with a partial resolution as horrendous and responding with resistance; or of seeing it as simply another game his unconscious mind is playing to keep the pictures hidden, and responding with more work.

The unconscious is inventive, filled with mischief and tricks to create detours and barriers to growth. Its great skill in counteracting insight is worthy of awe. The therapist can share this wonder, while simultaneously learning about each patient's unique way of fostering his own dysfunction. The therapy thus becomes an adventure into the realm of the unknown, and the excitement of discovering clues is a shared and satisfying experience for both.

The Therapist
Because a therapist in natal therapy is conceived of simply as having tools of investigation, as if he or she were a trained detective, in no

way is he or she considered healthier or better adjusted than the patient. In no way is he considered superior or more authoritative. And certainly in no way is his reality considered as being more valid than the patient's. Far from a doctor, an authority figure, a parent, he is more like a student of emotion and the patient a student of himself. The text of this course comprises the responses and experiences of the patient. It is a learning seminar for both rather than a cure for one.

The therapist is required to synthesize and create logical consistencies in the patient's presentation of his view of reality. When there is a loophole in the logic, some form of maladaptive formation is likely to be operative. However, each person has his own belief system consistent with his own life. What is credible, just and real to one person will be perceived quite differently by others.

The therapist has his own boundaries, excluding many possible sets of values based on realities to which he has not been exposed. So he cannot see everything. He must recognize that each and every patient with whom he deals knows things, perceives things and learns things that he does not know and may never even dream of. At the same time, there are many areas within his own reality that the patient cannot grasp. Therefore, the two must deal primarily with that which overlaps, and trust in the validity of that which does not.

What the therapist can do, which the patient probably cannot, is explain what specifically in the patient's perception does or does not correspond to his own current reality. For example, a patient tells the therapist that he sees little green men. The therapist does not have the experience, but he must assume that for that patient, the green men do exist.* He can, however, explain during the session

* The necessity for techniques to respond to patients' illogical needs – that the therapist himself cannot experience – is frequently overlooked. A colleague, Marlene Abrahams, developed a method for dealing with transference-based separation anxiety, by acknowledging that cognitive and emotional perceptions of time may be different and that time/space responses may vary among different people. When she went on vacation for ten days, she foresaw that one of her patients would experience anxiety and consequent loss of time perception during her absence. She gave him a pack of ten cigarettes, one to be smoked each day, as a transitional object. He thus had a concrete physical measure of time and could know, not only intellectually but also on a more primitive level (corresponding to the maturation level of the anxiety response), that when the pack of cigarettes was gone, her vacation would be over and the sessions would begin again. This offset any resistances that might otherwise follow the experience of abandonment by the therapist. Much anxiety concerns not the absence itself, but uncertainty about the ending of absence.

that he does not see them, and that there is a problem for him in accepting them as real. He can also point out how the patient may be hurting himself by retaining that particular belief – if, in fact, he is hurting himself.

The therapist thus never denies that a perception is valid, or thinks of it as ridiculous. He just shows that it doesn't work well for the patient's life at that particular point. Based upon the history as he learns it, he can trace the origin and development of percepts and try to dissolve any dysfunctional effect through re-interpretation. In this way he never threatens the dignity of the person who has entrusted his being to him and is hence exceptionally vulnerable to ridicule, manipulation and judgement.

Inner illogical beliefs, as we have seen, usually emerge for a purpose: that of mastering external illogic. They have value for the patient because they enable him to function amidst distortion. So when the distortions are dissolved, the primitive protections will be rendered obsolete and the belief will fade. However, there is always the chance that the belief is productive and that the therapist is not tuned in to that part of reality, since his unit of experience does not encompass it. He must admit to not knowing all truth.

Transference and Resistances

The concepts of transference and resistance dealt with in classical psychoanalysis are also major factors in natal therapy. In Freud's paper 'Analysis Terminable and Interminable'[7] he describes how resistances in therapy are related to castration anxiety and penis envy. Using the concept of the crisis umbilicus, however, we trace resistances and transferences to birth. We have already shown that all transferences are symbolic re-enactments of the initial tie with the umbilical cord, and that they are facilitated by the infant's vulnerability when it is removed. The therapist may become a temporary substitute cord until these problems can be worked through, but the dependency which is symptomatic of the umbilical crisis, although understood and responded to, does not have to be facilitated by him. He can suggest alternate forms of response that are more appropriate to maintaining autonomy: responses that are equally satisfying and, in the long run, ensure greater security.

Any dependency the patient exhibits should be seen as the externalization of a copying mechanism learned when relating to his parents in childhood, and should be treated as a symptom. In no way does the therapist have the right to manipulate or determine the behaviour of the patient, and should the patient request this, it must be denied, for it is presumed that he is the only one capable of directing his own behaviour. When the patient is encouraged to be dependent, or when his request for dependence is indulged, he becomes more infantile, passive and non-functioning.

Resistances are welcome, provided that the patient expresses the respect for the therapist that he, as a human being, deserves. They are interpreted within the context of the patient's history, and are usually symptomatic of a discovery that threatens the organization of maladaptive behaviour. They give a clue that the therapist is on the right track, and if the resistance is worked through, greater insight will be attained.

The therapist, in some sense, has the job of reflecting the society in which he lives, so that the patient may adjust misconceptions that have led to negative feedback in the past. The therapist, therefore, will respond as any other human being would to insults, manipulation and destructive demands. He is in no sense an emotional prostitute, existing solely for the service of the patient. Many therapists who play the part of the emotional prostitute end up resenting and mocking their own patients, who in the long run must suffer from the unexpressed ridicule.

Hearing the therapist assert himself may in fact teach the patient methods of doing the same. Emotional prostitution on the part of the patient should equally not be encouraged, but identified as a form of dishonesty presented during the session.

Other inappropriate responses in the therapist would be inattention, lack of enthusiasm, and the avoidance of sincere empathy when it is justified. A cold and distant or an indulging and pampering therapist would be as destructive, and as promoting of maladaptive behaviour, as the parents of the patient have been.

These techniques and attitudes encouraged in natal therapy differ in several ways from the principles of therapy as traditionally taught. For example, natal therapists see the practice of calling the therapist by his last name, particularly if the patient is called by his first name, as perpetuating the very maladaptation the therapy is supposed to correct. Similarly, a clinical sterile office, a ban even on the limited physical contact of a handshake, and indeed any insistence on formality such as is traditional in therapy, involve built-in distortions which encourage justifiable resistance from the patient. The contrived reactions of the therapist may actually reinforce the narcissistic-guilt cycle in the patient, for they represent control, and 'roof-standing' attitudes which re-enact the very attitudes that generated the pathology in the first place.

Submission, passivity and competition are all interpreted on the lines already described in the chapter on 'Adjustments to Reality'. As in traditional psychoanalysis, they are treated as mirror images of presenting problems. All patients lie during sessions in one manner or another and it is presumed that they will. If for instance a patient walks in and says he is confused about something, the therapist assumes that either he is lying about something in the present, or he has lied to himself about something in the past. Once the deception is identified, the confusion is dispelled and there is an increase in energy. When patients are compulsively honest, on the other hand, we usually find that they are denying a lack of love for a specific parent. One exercise that is often effective is to encourage such people to tell inconsequential lies in their environment, to reduce the compulsiveness and the false honesty, and thus get to the pertinent material at the base of the conflict.

Procedure on Entering Natal Therapy
If a patient has had a year or more of traditional therapy, then natal therapy can be offered in addition, if the ongoing therapist gives permission. However, if an individual requesting natal therapy has had very little other therapy, he is required to undergo treatment with a psychotherapist prior to and throughout the natal therapy experience. This can be with a therapist outside of the Institute, or with someone on staff. He is first given an outline from which he writes his own case history, and this, along with findings by the natal therapist, is sent in the form of a report to his ongoing therapist, if he has one, who is also invited to observe the birthing.

Usually, the material in the autobiography runs from ten to thirty typewritten pages. Below is a copy of the outline the patient receives.

Case History Outline

1. History of development.
   a. Birth – length of labour, complications, pregnancy history, type of birth (natural, breech, instrument etc.), mother/father's attitudes, birth order etc., post-natal reactions.
   b. Toilet training – age, method, attitudes of parents, present reactions (constipation, frequency, etc.).
   c. Nursing history.

d. Sexual history – parents' attitudes, masturbation attitudes and activity, any childhood sexual experiences, sexual fantasies, description of sexual initiation (where, with whom, emotional reactions etc.), how you learned the facts of life, adult sexual patterns/problems, length of relationships, degree of commitment, homosexual or incestuous experiences, fantasy of the perfect relationship etc.

2. Relationship with others.

   a. Parents – what do they look like, think like, their background, your perception of their problems, the way they treat you and perceive you and others that were important (i.e. siblings, relatives, etc.), how demonstrative with love, expressions of anger, fear, love, punishments.

   b. Siblings, friends, relatives (same as above).

3. Academic and work history.

4. Religious attitudes, death and related family beliefs. How do these influence you?

5. Medical history and therapy history.

6. Perception of self – Do you like yourself? Why? Describe yourself. Do you give, take, are you dependent/independent? What are your major problems/assets? What are your goals? What emotional changes do you want to make? What traumas have you experienced? What is your first memory? Any childhood dreams? How do you express: love, anger, fear, acceptance? Social ways of interacting.

7. Describe your daily routine – living habits (i.e. bedtime, etc.), eating habits, social habits, etc. Describe your environment; how is your home decorated? Degree of order, care, pride, comfort.

8. Dreams, fantasies, symptoms (i.e. rituals, panics, immobilization patterns, etc.).

Once the case history material is obtained the patient goes on to a waiting list, so that each group can start approximately at the same time. The patient's write-up is intensely studied, and will be incorporated in discussion in the individual sessions, of which there will be between three and ten.

The minimum qualification of the natal therapist who conducts these sessions is a master's degree in psychology, training at a training institute, and total familiarity with natal therapy itself. The sessions themselves run between one and four hours, depending on the severity of the problem and how much happens in the session. In fact, the best sessions often take place at two o'clock in the morning over the telephone! Our experience is that a session that lasts only an hour is too limited and superficial to reach the deeper material – it is as though the patient holds back initially, and responds to real interpretations only after time has elapsed. With longer sessions, formality between patient and therapist also has a chance to diminish, enabling greater freedom of expression. It is also important that the patient can relax fully, uninhibited by any feelings of deprivation, so cigarettes, candy, coffee, hot chocolate and a variety of other edibles are available. Warm slippers on a cold wet day and pillows to hold or lean on also contribute to comfort during the session.

The office should be friendly and warm. If the office reflects the personality of the therapist, it does not stop transference developing, as many traditional professionals feel, but, on the contrary, helps the patient perceive him as a person rather than an object.

Each patient keeps a journal summarizing each session, describing dreams, responses and experiences in between sessions, as well as reactions to the therapy and the therapist. These are mailed in, reviewed by the therapist prior to the next session, and discussed then.

The material to follow is a shortened example of one such journal kept by a patient. It is presented so that the reader can more deeply understand the procedure.

This patient came in depressed, quiet and passive. He had been rejected and sadistically abused as a boy by his parents and brothers. As an adult he felt hen-pecked by his wife and pushed around even by his six-year-old son. Though he had been working for twelve years for the same firm, he had been overtaken in salary and status by men who had been there only half as long. He had been through two years of regular therapy, and one year of supportive therapy, but found he had changed little. He complained of being trapped but did not know by what. On and off he thought about suicide but said he did not have the guts to go through with it.

The Therapy
Session 1 – 50 minutes long

I was nervous about what was going to happen. I felt reluctant to talk at first, but then I relaxed and found myself explaining my history in greater detail. I was amazed at how much I left out and that it was the information that was most important, in some cases. We covered a lot, to get an overview of how I think, feel and behave. Although I got a few ideas about myself that were new I must admit I felt shy about revealing everything. I know that this attitude can only hold things up. I feel impatient with Leslie because more didn't happen and a bit sceptical that anything will. What kind of therapy is this?

(Hostility expressed could be confronted and worked through. Proof that a transference was developing quickly and effectively came the following day with his telephone call. The next step was to get to the dependency feelings behind it.)

Telephone call Reaction
I'm so glad I called and we talked. My anger with my parents became clearer now. I really see how I set my wife up to create problems: my mother taught me to believe I was responsible for her marital problems. I realized this wasn't true.

Reaction at Work
I saw my boss differently today. Usually I feel resentful when he asks me to do anything and today it just seemed OK.

Fantasy
I am walking through a meadow. My wife is there but she is dressed like an Eurasian girl with flowing hair. We run towards each other and make love. I feel as though I'm melting.

Associations
Love-making is disappointing – it's never like I fantasize.

(He was beginning to open up and share his thoughts. The experience of anger apparently was a prerequisite to allow any closeness, which was a clue to a personality characteristic to be investigated. The sexual need of idealization of an object in fantasy, rather than wanting contact with a person, was symptomatic of the narcissistic-guilt dichotomy. It was furthered by wanting to melt – a longed for and unmet symbiotic need for his rejecting mother – and it suggested a love-hate conflict with those that were important. Finally it indicated an increase in transference and orgastic difficulty. I guessed that his first rebirth would end in depression and that he may have been held back with forceps at birth. This was all verified later.)

Session 3 – 2 hours 15 minutes
We talked about my birth, about Linda, my wife, and my childhood associations with sex. I feel better about Leslie now, and I realize that no way could she have fit my expectations, just as love-making never could. My feelings of failure and inadequacy toward my brother were discussed. I guess I was always angry at my mother for comparing me with him. The session was good but I am impatient for rebirth.

(This session was the beginning of a real rapport between the therapist and patient. He was no longer a dependent child wanting an authority to hand over change, but a man sharing the secrets of his mind.
In the next session we discussed his impatience, which correlated with sexual anxiety. A vague reference to cord trauma, which it also might symbolize, was made.)

Sunday Dinner at My Parents'!
I saw my mother clearly for the first time. How she always puts me down and prefers my brother. I suddenly hated her for this and afterwards I felt angry at Linda when she gave our son so much affection. But I caught it, and realized it was my anger at my mother. Later we made love. I didn't expect it to be much. I sort of did it because I felt guilty about feeling so much unjustified anger, and much to my surprise I felt very close and loving. She even noticed the difference, and for the first time admitted to me that she thought I had been having an affair because I had been so inattentive lately. Then we really talked. I found out I loved her more than I thought I did. I guess people stop being boring when you take time to share your thoughts with them.

(Here the parental emotional sadism and the child's seductive vulnerability came out clearly. Emotional prostitution, combined with performance in sexuality, emerged as the evolving pattern, and was to be the next topic. The therapist can always take the clue to discussion from material presented by the patient. The patient chooses what problem to work with next and thereby is more receptive. The following memory also indicated material on the crisis, and should be investigated further.)

Session 4 – 3 hours 10 minutes

I talked for the first time about Janice, the girl I'm having an affair with. I've decided to break it off but I still don't have the guts to tell Linda. We talked about my feelings of superiority and my guilt feelings. For the first time I even feel a bit of closeness to Leslie. I realize she is really trying to help and as I write this I can see she really *is* helping.

Memory

I remember being in the crib because I was in what seemed like a box with bars and my bottle dropped. I was crying and trying to get it. Nobody heard me and my fingers just didn't seem able to grasp it. I felt all shaky thinking of it.

Session 5 – 1 hour 55 minutes

We connected my memory to part of the history I had given Leslie about doing so poorly in school, and how I felt so helpless and scared when I got into fights in the 5th grade. She gave me a fake umbilical cord to wear, and when she did I felt silly but I put it on anyway. I have really begun to trust her, so I'll do it, but it sure seems silly.

Reaction

Wearing the cord felt awkward at first but I'm getting used to it. I'm also excited about going through the birthing next week. Linda's coming to help.

Homework

I found out more about my toilet training. I remember being afraid to flush because the noise might hurt me and swallow me up.

(His problems in sexual functioning and castration anxiety were metaphorically presented with his memory. The anality in sadism led to the following fantasy. It is quite usual that when repressed sadism is confronted and released, sexuality and loving feelings are also.)

Fantasy

I thought of my brother and how I wanted to hurt him. I imagined tying him up and slowly torturing him by cutting off one limb at a time so his suffering would be slow and painful. Instead of pushing my thoughts away I let myself think them, and suddenly I felt a rush of love and realized that although I may be angry with him, he was really important to me and I didn't want him hurt. I just want to get the same amount of attention. It was a very difficult thought to have.

Reaction to Birthing

I never realized how independent I felt and how much I hate control by others. Then I realized that the reason I hate being controlled by others is because I want to be in control. I really want everything to revolve around me and it never does. But in the birthing it did. I got lots of attention. I guess I need to work on not wanting it so much.

(Control and hostility, two of the components of seduction and sadism, were the major concentrations prior to his first birthing. It is quite common that whatever is the area of focus prior to birthing, is the very area acted out and partially mastered in the rebirth.)

First Post-birth Session – 2 hours 25 minutes

We went through my birthing step by step. Every tiny association and movement seemed to mean something. I hadn't realized it, but I had pushed Linda away when she tried to hug me afterwards. But I felt like she was taking away my moment and I hated her for it. I guess she wasn't. I wonder how often I push people away. I am feeling very depressed.

(The depression was the beginning of working through. Although he had resisted the cord prior to the birth he didn't want to let it be taken away. He acted more attached to it than to his wife, and felt its loss a threat. He had been quite passive in movement during the birthing and yet verbally gave orders and got angry when pressure was placed to aid his movement. He tried to double-bind the whole group. His birth took much longer than most and the release part was met with detachment by him. This behaviour was symptomatic of his original birth, yet also filled with reality adjustments which were made later. In combination it formed his present reaction.)

Dream
I am tied up to a tree and people are standing around it laughing and not noticing. I call out for help but I can't seem to make any sound.

(His intensely obvious attachment to the cord and simultaneous resentment is shown in the dream. Trees frequently represent the placenta in dreams. This could also be a memory going back to the womb of foetal distress in a tangled cord. Later in interaction with others he re-enacts the immobilization. Feels helpless and ridiculed for it.)

Love-making with Linda
I couldn't seem to get an erection and I felt disgusted by her.

(The sexual counterpart to emotional impotence is manifest. Frequently just before the resolution of a problem the symptoms become exaggerated.)

Second Post-Birth Session – 4 hours
Still felt very depressed. We talked about what happened with Linda. We also talked about my father criticizing me, and how I don't remember ever being hugged by him. I felt even more depressed.

(Homosexual anxiety and his relationship with his father had not been discussed previously. Cord as representing father was the next association, and another clue to problem roots. Although he felt his anxieties stemmed from his mother and obsessively connected everything with her, his father was a tougher connection to deal with. His mother, the tree in the dream, was giving him support. It was the cord-father that had him trapped and immobilized. It was in the follow-up phone call that he made that further investigation and finally relief occurred.)

Phone Call
I felt guilty about calling so late, but when Linda wanted to make love I just went into a panic. Leslie and I talked and it suddenly

made sense. Everything suddenly made sense. I can't stand being controlled and need the power myself because everyone is so fucking important. Only they're not. They're not any more important than I am: I felt so free. I tore off that fake cord I hadn't wanted to give up at the birthing and threw it out the window. I ran upstairs and made love to Linda for three hours because I wanted to, not because I felt guilty about not wanting to. I feel terrific. Tomorrow I'm going to ask my boss for that raise and this time I know I'll get it.

(He did indeed get that raise, which led to eventual assertion in his home and socially. This was just the beginning of the therapy. He had three more birthings and, including telephone calls that were one half hour or longer, eighteen more sessions. The total length of time was five months from beginning to end.

He now feels happier, untrapped and excited about self-discovery. His suicidal tendencies and sexual dysfunctions were eliminated. His life today is not perfect, but he respects himself and others, feels at peace, handles situations with competence, has gone successfully into business for himself, and enjoys his family and his life.)

The Birthing

As seen from this example, most sessions are verbal and psychoanalytic. However, the group rebirth is key to the therapy, and must be described in detail.

The patient comes in with his own pillow, blanket and slippers, and a package of his favourite food to share with the others. Usually, the larger the group where the non-verbal experience occurs, the more effective the therapy, and so visitors, friends and colleagues are invited to come as observers. Each patient as well brings along a companion to work with him during the therapy.

We sit in a circle, and each person introduces himself and explains his interest in natal therapy. Those who wish can summarize some of the effects they have felt in themselves as a result of previous sessions. The lights are dim and there is a heartbeat going in the background. Everyone is then required to lie down with a pillow and participate in a fantasy trip that helps relax the body and the mind.

Each patient in turn is mentally carried backwards through adulthood, childhood and then into infancy. After each memory, he is taught to contract his body, inhale, pull his body in, exhale, extend his body and relax. It is a movement that includes both freedom and tension very much like contractions during labour.

Just as anxiety follows trauma, to reverse the process and undo the neurosis, anxiety must precede the re-enactment of trauma. Patients going through natal therapy must thus be anxious before the rebirth episode or they will not experience proper relief from that anxiety. So they are prepared in advance to achieve high tension arousal. In addition, the tension of each group member will be communicated to the rest – this contagious quality facilitates each patient's readiness for his own birthing.

In watching another undergoing natal therapy, the patient identifies with or takes the role of the mother. His participation therefore begins before his own rebirthing, and those patients who do not experience this empathy have less successful natal experiences themselves. It is therefore advisable for an experienced patient to be the first birth in a new group.

In his first rebirth experience, the patient is primarily in control. He lies down on a mattress. His arms are folded and, while maintaining eye contact with the therapist, he takes three deep breaths. His hands are passed to another group member, as he closes his eyes. In this state he is quite aware of himself and his environment. Then he begins to push with his hands and feet. He begins to move as he does so, slowly, subtly, beginning to sink deeper within himself, until he reaches another state of consciousness: one similar to the point just prior to falling asleep. The world is both real and unreal. Voices are heard from others in the group, but only half attended to. The birth experience is superimposed upon reality but must be distinguished from it, like a double exposed photo, to dissolve into memory. And then he is born in triumph, or sadness or desperation.

The following three descriptions were written by patients about their experiences in natal therapy:

Debbie

I walked into the room. It was dark and the tension was calmed with the sound of a heart beating in the background. People were sitting in a circle and then we all lay down. What I liked was that even those that were friends and observers also participated in this initial phase, and I found out they also took active part as assistants to those undergoing the experience. Leslie's voice guided me to peacefulness and although we were supposed to think certain thoughts, all I kept thinking was of my expectations. Perhaps this was a way of resisting, for I caught myself falling into it occasionally and despite wanting it I was fighting it in a way. Tony was the first one. He screamed and yelled and I felt terrified that I might do the same. He kicked and pushed and seemed angry. Finally with his last push he melted exhausted into a pool of sweat. And then after he was hugged, his face had a glow and I relaxed. Then I went. My palms were sweaty, my whole body tensed. I felt like the time I was being examined by a gynaecologist in front of a group of residents, all tight and self-conscious. I closed my eyes and the deep breaths relaxed my tensions. I felt a bit dizzy and too weak to move. Sam pushed his hands against mine and somehow I found the courage to slowly push back. Then I was pushing quicker, harder, with more force. I felt an urgency. My body arched and I felt annoyed at Sam. He wasn't following my movement. He wasn't pushing hard enough. He was holding me back. I don't need anyone, I can do it myself. Why were they slowing me down.

I gave one big kick and my body suddenly felt free. Free and I seemed to almost float the rest of the way. Then I felt Jack's arms enfold me, hold me, and I felt as though I just fit perfectly into the shape of his body. I felt childlike. Yet somehow whole. I felt proud.

Dannie

I lay down on the mat and was aware of all the people around me. Leslie held my hand and told me to take deep breaths, but I didn't. I guess I shouldn't have undergone the whole thing because I didn't believe much would happen. I just took the breaths because I was told to. Leslie then told me more specifically to breathe and hold the breath, and although I did I still kept it shallow. Then Des began pushing me and I started to move. I opened my eyes and saw all those people staring at me. I stopped moving. Leslie came over and tried to reassure me and we started all over again. This was silly. Nothing was going to happen. The whole thing was a big farce and I was an ass to be there at all. But there I was and it would look even worse if I got up now. So I breathed and I pushed and I moved. I felt bored by the whole thing. OK, here I was doing what I was told and nothing was happening, just like I thought. Just like nothing ever happened any time. OK.

Peter

Excitedly I went over to the mat and lay down. All my life I had been waiting for this moment. The sessions taught me much, but I hadn't wanted them – all I wanted was to be born – to be born again. I had always felt so incomplete and I knew this was the answer to what I had been looking for. I had been ready for this for years and it was here.

I imagined going back over my life to younger and younger times. And then I imagined myself in the womb and felt my body curl and push. My thoughts were vague, fuzzy, as if someone at a distance was reversing my life and yet it was me thinking those thoughts. I felt myself growing smaller and smaller and more helpless. I sort of heard Leslie say 'push, push', but my body and its movements seem separate from my mind. I could feel what I was doing yet I was detached from it.

My head hurt suddenly, as though tons of pressure were pushing back, surrounding my temple, my eyes, my back and my ears. Oh that pressure. I pushed to get out of that entrapment but it wouldn't let go of me. I felt as though my brain would burst and it kept pushing back.

And then the air cleared and my head had a tingle and a looseness and I was hugged. Suddenly it was hard to breathe and I was coughing up something thick – saliva or mucus or something. It made me gag a little. Sandy tried to rock me but the contact was almost annoying. I wanted to be alone – to think. I broke loose from her and as I did I felt a strength and authority that I was truly me, full, complete and that I would be really me from then on.

After rebirth the patient is hugged into the world by his companion, his brow is wiped clean of sweat, his slippers are placed on his feet, he is wrapped in a blanket and then, when able, helped to the bathroom. Upon his return, he is given milk and baby food, and his reactions are discussed. We are currently experimenting with something new, where the individual is required to wear an artificial umbilical cord for a week prior to the therapy and it is cut off at the birthing.

The real value of the experience is not investigated in front of the group. Many feel they prefer privacy, and in any case need to absorb what has happened. When everyone who is to be birthed is finished, we all sit around in a group, talking casually and sharing food. One to three individual sessions follow, in which insights are integrated and hopefully resolutions of problems reached. Many times, in the first experience the individual is self-conscious and needs to repeat it. Every time the birthing is repeated, it becomes a different experience.

Those who expect the memory of birth to have the same character-istics as usual memory feel frustrated and disappointed. They forget that thinking in words, or awareness of the self, and even visual memory – the characteristics of our usual memory – were non-existent at birth. When the pre-fantasized expectation of birth memory does not occur, some individuals, even before the rebirth is terminated, get so involved with failure that they in fact prevent memory. This sense of failure is then treated symptomatically by the therapist. Some patients have clear awareness, while others retain only vague recollections. Some recall days later, although for others, whose trauma is too painful, the memory may never surface, even after many repetitions of natal therapy. But the value of the therapy is not contingent upon memory; only upon the coded messages the patient communicates. It is the movements that symbolize and piece together the problem.

In his first birth, the patient controls his own movements and speed of locomotion. The therapist observes his mode of behaviour and correlates it to his emotional life. In follow-up private sessions the observation of the therapist and reactions of the patient about the experience, as well as the happenings in his life in the days that follow, are discussed and integrated.

He then undergoes his second birthing. This time he is controlled in his speed and type of movement by the therapist. Hopefully this will modify patterns, and simultaneously change corresponding be-haviour outside of therapy. Again verbal sessions, to integrate the new awareness, follow.

A third birthing verifies and reinforces change, with the approp-riate concluding verbal sessions finishing the series. Each birth brings new insights and increased awareness; each birth is a new experience and quite different from the preceding one.

It is as if at birth we imprint the experience: each moment being a microcosm of emotional orientation. By concentrating on specific moments, we see a new section isolated and magnified. It is this magnification of each birth moment that creates the endless variety of experiences. The individual sessions have a value of their own, just as does the group session. Each deals with the material on a different level. Patients can have as many further individual sessions or group sessions as they choose, until they feel that they have got enough out of the technique.

Ideally, with the first birth, the therapist can reach an evaluation of what emotional responses in adulthood can be attributed to the patient's birth, and then, in later births, attempt to modify those responses, and thus facilitate greater adaptation in future behaviour patterns. Part of the function of natal therapy is to eliminate disorder, and reinstitute the organization that existed originally; and if this happens, this is what produces the marvellous feeling of being reborn.

Sex and Rebirth
One of the insights gained through the 'acting out', through physical representation of emotional predispositions, is into the individual's sexual orientation. Birth is considered the first sexual activity, although sexuality is initiated in the womb through the sensations surrounding the umbilical cord. With the completion of the birth episode, metaphorically correlating with orgasm, we can reach conclusions about the patient's predispositions for sexual response in adulthood. In that he acts out a replication of his own sexuality, the procedure is thus a valuable diagnostic tool. Because of this, interaction between couples participating together during rebirth provides material for determining problems in their sexual as well as their emotional interaction.

For example, one couple, who entered therapy primarily because of emotional problems, discovered that during rebirth the husband controlled and pressured his wife when he took the role of 'midwife'. She on the other hand, he complained, did not support his actions and expected him to do all the work. This was not only a physical replication of the emotional interaction between them, but it also metaphorically duplicated sexual misunderstandings that were at the base of their incompatibility. The episode greatly facilitated opening up for discussion in therapy sexual reactions and problems that had only slightly received attention previously.

Natal therapists are consistently struck by this consistent correlation between type of birth and sexual behaviour in adulthood. It is almost as though the trauma of birth is repeated every time we have sex, and the phenomenon recalls the repetition compulsion that Freud explained – in this case, an attempt to master and resolve the conflict of birth through repetition in intercourse. For example, lack of relaxation or relief in rebirth frequently means orgastic problems, and lack of feelings of competence; impotence and lack of movement in rebirth mean sexual passivity; and exceptional judgementalness of the therapy or therapist frequently reflects hostility shown to mates sexually. Since most emotional problems are reflected in sexual predilections, this aspect of the interpretation of the behaviour of patients should come as no surprise.

Even though the technique in the group experience can be modified slightly among individuals, basically the method is much the same. Yet we find not only that everyone has his own unique reaction, but that with each birthing, the same individual repeating rebirth will have different reactions. No matter what the reaction, the needs of the individual are respected. Sometimes, after the birthing, the individual feels like withdrawing and needs an extra amount of privacy. Other times, individuals become more gregarious and want to share their responses with others.

Within the weeks following the group experience, again reactions differ among individuals. With some, there is a response similar to a dope-induced high, and the individual feels elated, relieved and fulfilled. His sense of wholeness and serenity or elation is only transitory however, and usually inhibits the working through of the problems connected with the birth.

Other individuals go into a deep depression, where a mourning reaction occurs, followed shortly by insight. This reaction is an attempt by the individual to resolve the crisis umbilicus, or versions of it. The real purpose of the therapy is just this: to let go of maladaptive behaviour and work it through. My daughter at one point said to me, 'Mummy, how can people be reborn unless they die first?' And, in fact, this is why a mourning reaction does precede any non-transitory emotional change. In a sense, the more negative, the reaction, the greater the eventual prospect of change.

Other individuals have no reaction even after several rebirth sessions, and this reflects their lack of reaction to their environment in general. This leads to insight into the inadequacy of their response repertoire, and magnifies their dissatisfaction with it. Provided that the individual is willing to continue dealing with this particular manifestation, a greater involvement and stronger identity can evolve.

Reactions to natal group therapy thus seem to be magnifications of what already exists within the personality structure of the individual. By an analysis and a dissection of the minute fragments within each response, we can reach conclusions about each patient that are not possible within the realms of verbal interaction alone; each fragment being a symbolic re-enactment of an overall pattern that permeates the personality.

As many have remarked, repressed impulses are released in sleep[8] and problems enacted through the dream. So, toofi with natal therapy. It seems to energize, organize, and master unconscious material, while the individual is still awake enough to deal with it cognitively. During the natal therapy experience the individual is, in some sense, asleep and awake simultaneously, where both the unconscious and the conscious are functional and collaborating in the behaviour displayed.

And the most unusual thing about this condition is that it is contagious. Observers in the room, despite the fact that they are not participating in the experience, to some extent identify with the individual undergoing it and, through empathy, reach the same level of consciousness. The following is an excerpt from a Swedish article written by a woman reporter who came to observe: [9]

At the rebirth there were some other observers: a couple of psychologists and social workers – all sceptical. Those being re-born were an actor and his wife, a teacher, an academic and a psychohistorian.

We are all sitting on the floor in the basement room, mattresses around the walls, burning candles here and there on the floor. One at a time is made to lie down in the foetus position. In a soft suggestive voice Leslie Feher brings the person's thoughts backwards to the time of birth.

One helper is holding the feet with all his might. Another is pushing the head.

One cannot believe what one sees. As in a wild trance the child starts pushing forward, working round the room in a long passage on the mattresses.

The four I observed were born with quite different temperaments. All, with the exception of the actor who seemed dutifully to pretend, had orgasm-like outbreaks . . .

We observers were shaken, fascinated, embarrassed – but not sceptical. We got involved in that moment, we believed it to be a genuine experience. The babies were very different from one another. One was born with an enormous vitality and energy.

The teacher moved exactly as a jerking infant but did not want to be born, had to be pulled out. The academic screamed in a way I will never forget. Our hair literally stood on end, one left the room pale.

In this chapter, we have attempted some kind of cohesive explanation of the dynamics of natal therapy, distinguishing between the individual sessions that are verbally orientated, and the group experience which is non-verbal, since each reflects alternate aspects of the individual's psychological structure. Our belief is that a concentration specifically on one expression or another is a limited perspective on the dynamics of the emotional disposition of the patient; and that it is through integration and evaluation of a variety of different interrelated expressions that full interpretation becomes possible.

It will probably be years before a full grasp of the implications of natal therapy is possible. However, the beneficial effects have already been obvious and can only lead to more benefit in the future, when the process is further understood.

At present, how it works, why it works, and what it means, remain to some extent a mystery. What that other level of consciousness is, for instance, that becomes manifest during a group experience, is not completely comprehensible in any sense accessible to description. Only with repeated experience and continued experimentation can we eventually understand more. But we do know enough to have been able to evolve new theories on personality, and a new psychology of birth.

12   *THE PSYCHOLOGY OF BIRTH*

In chapters three and four, we took a partial look at birth. Now, in this final chapter, we shall attempt to bring together the concepts we have described throughout the book. What we aim to do is to make the theory relevant to the reader on a personal level, so that he can begin to understand the consequences of his own particular birth experience.

Studies of case histories, work with patients and broader surveys have all led us to the belief that certain personality structures relate to specific birth experiences. Much of the material, however, can be considered only hypothetical at this stage. It is based only on a handful of patient studies in each group, and there are so many variations on birth experience that only tests over a very large patient population, including proper controls, could give the conclusions any scientific validity. But we are not making dogmatic statements: we are describing the patterns we have observed, and attempting to initiate imaginative thinking about the subject, which can be correlated with future verification studies.

Many of our patients were in particular unable to obtain precise medical documentation about their own birth, and their mothers' recall is no adequate basis for accurate scientific conclusion. In this presentation the reader is expected to weigh the conclusions accordingly, and to recognize that there are limitations in this stage of study. The frequency, however, of correlation between the patients' sexual or emotional activity on the one hand, and birth experience on the other, has been so consistent that it is worth reporting despite the obvious lack of scientific method.

The Forceps, or Externally Controlled, Personality
Instrument babies tend to seek out dependency situations to correlate with the dependency imposed upon them originally. Brutal concentration on the head was their first contact with the world, and it remains metaphorically true that forceps babies, besides having a

higher degree of mental illness than others (possibly because of the ineptness of the physician attending the birth), have a greater tendency to intellectualize as a primary mode of adjustment. These two factors combine to make an individual prone to judgmentalness, grandiosity, guilt and idealization, such as we have described in earlier chapters.

Because external control was needed to complete the process of birth, external controls or attitudes become particularly important in later interaction. The transition from the womb to the world is broken, since neither the foetus nor the mother were in control, but the physician. This creates disruptions in early development, and most of the people in therapy who have been instrument babies have demonstrated what Freud would term an anal fixation.

Forceps are used with a range of complicated deliveries, including delayed births, when delivery is held up, usually for a matter of minutes, and prolonged births, which, if they involve prolonged heavy labour, are more traumatic.

Delayed birth (e.g. because the doctor is late to the delivery) prevents birth only in the last few moments. It predisposes individuals to be impatient and resent any restrictions ,and usually leads to severe dependency problems because such people also have a special need for closeness. They seem especially reactive to fears of abandonment because they feel that the very dependency they resent is a *requirement* for existence. The delayed birth experience is an externally controlled birth, and leads the child to expect subsequently to be held back by others, yet to feel guilt about independence, and about seeking responsibility and self-sufficiency.

In contrast, prolonged light labour, where the child is not held back but just takes longer to be born, results in a tendency to postpone tasks in later life. Order and ritual may be a strong requirement to functioning. Depending upon other birth and environmental variables, the individual may tend to avoid spontaneity. On the other hand, because of the longer preparation for birth change, the child may have a good capacity to adapt to change. Just as the Caesarean avoids process and wants only goals, prolonged-labour individuals may avoid goals and seek the process.

Multiple births involve even more complications. The infants must deal with extra confinement in the womb, and often with being held back in labour as well.

Late onset of labour, as with postmature infants, is yet another variation. These infants usually have overdevelopment of body parts, such as a large head, which complicates and brutalizes the birth in a tight canal.

For forceps births, re-enactment of needs for external control in personal relationships may lead to frustrated and distorted interaction. In therapy, if the therapist indulges these needs, he only facilitates greater maladaptive expectations. He has to point out the unrealized competence in the forceps-born patient. Since there are so many situations in life that need our own initiation for mastery, the instrument baby often has difficulties in coping.

Intervention by forceps, or any mechanical apparatus suddenly introduced at birth, must create negative associations to external sensation. The fact that forceps are made of cold hard metal and not of some material more familiar to the foetus, would reinforce this negative reaction. A little initiative and creativity could surely make the instruments required for safe delivery more sympathetic to the neonate.

The Breech Personality

In the breech birth personality, included in the expectation of being 'pulled through', there seems to be a need to set expectations of others very high. The consequences are continual disappointment, since these assumptions are often not verbalized but remain in fantasy, so that other people do not even know what they are. This uncommunicated requirement that others act out one's fantasies is an attribute, to a greater or lesser extent, of most people who have had external manipulation during birth, and when this is not achieved, dissatisfaction results, particularly sexual dissatisfaction. The kinds of expectation, and the ways of dealing with the disappointment, are functions of the other components of birth.

The breech who was turned and born in opposition to his own needs, although he needs to re-enact this turnabout by manipulating others, is always left with a lingering dissatisfaction when they comply. So he reacts with discontent either way. The breech who was not externally turned, and was in fact born buttocks or legs first, often feels on the other hand that he is 'kept dangling' by others. He also seems in general to undervalue cognition, since head pressure is reduced in these births. Many feel as though their bodies are divided in half, and feel disconnected emotionally. With all breech births, contractions are strong and violent, and this seems to manifest later in aggression, problems with control, ambiguity, and tendencies to overreact to environmental demands.

The Caesarean Personality

The Caesarean was pulled out also, but forceps were not used and the external contact was not as foreign nor as sustained as in other instrument births. He has dependency problems but they are quite different. His problems involve lack of contraction, arising from a lack of ability to define boundaries.

The Caesarean has bypassed much of the conflict of birth, so complications leading to goals are difficult for him to deal with in later life. The Caesarean adult will expect things to be handed to him. He is not irresponsible so much as confused if there are trials along the way, for he lacks the birth-learning others receive.

He needs the help of others to accomplish anything, and will blame any failures on others for not helping enough. Caesareans may not feel they should undergo any difficulties.

It is significant that in the Caesarean the umbilical cord is usually cut much more quickly than in other births, for fear of haemorrhaging in the mother. It is therefore easy to predict, based upon cord theory, an even stronger crisis of identity than with other births. For this child, transference to the second object cathexis, the mother, would also be more extreme and problematic.

The lack of the transitional phases during contraction would inhibit understanding of processes in general, making frustrations and responsibilities seem unbearable. Since a whole step in the birth is omitted, the individual will tend to omit other sequences necessary to achieving a goal. Thus therapeutically, Caesareans in general have problems in learning. The working through part of problem-solving is not assimilated easily, which in turn makes resolution the more difficult. Life requires organization, and attention to the means if the end is to be attained. This the Caesarean overlooks, which affects his functioning and creates dependency: he needs others to offset his blind spot.

Since Caesareans tend to have low tolerance of frustration, they tend to be enthusiastic yet insecure in interaction. They may also be violent and erratic, although this reaction may be repressed because of anxiety. While the instrument baby is often humourless and academic, the Caesarean can be dramatic, spontaneous and artistic.

The Pre- and Post-Mature Personality

A problem common to Caesarean and premature births is lack of stimulation in labour, for the premature, due to his size, was less confined in the womb than mature babies and had less pressure from contractions. Any limitation or restriction later in life is considered illogical, overlooked or denied. Denial is a mechanism employed, in general, when no past experience can logically connect something to that individual's reality. Regression and womb return are the premature baby's most common coping mechanisms, while his personality is often rather clinging: he feels pushed into things, resists change, tends to avoid responsibility and fears being grown up.

Particularly for the premature male child, the elimination of the cord took place too quickly. There is some loss of male identification, and an increase in identification as castrated female. Impotence or compulsive sexuality, here as with other extreme umbilical loss, is common. Many of the sexual and emotional patterns of the premature and the Caesarean are similar: their differences reflect the degree of contraction in one, and of physiological development in the other.*

If the parents tend to overprotect, and minimize any competence expressed, the child comes to feel guilt for his attempts at self-sufficiency, rather like the instrument baby does; but the premature baby does not have the extra cognitive capacity to cope with his guilt.

Overtime babies, in contrast, tend to feel independent and strong. They have clearly identified ego and body boundaries, and strong definition of reality. Others seem to look to them for direction and leadership. However, when feeling trapped or confined, they tend to overreact with intense emotion or to withdraw completely. They are usually large in size and therefore had good contraction contact. One personality orientation which they share with the premature, however, is avoidance of responsibility. With the premature, guilt and dependency motivated this, but with overtime babies it is the memory of being confined in the womb. The premature tends to be needy, and the post-mature tends to escape from confinement.

Some children just slip out. Others find this part of birth an ordeal, especially if instruments are used. The point of most traumatic climax in birth will predispose the person to a pattern, and mark the choice of symptom formation in any response.

---

* Medical complications, and hospital practice, often add contact deprivation after birth to the problems of Caesarean and premature babies, thus further hampering emotional development. The premature particularly may come to lack social skills.

One patient, when he felt emotionally trapped, as he often did when he visited his invalid father, would get a choking sensation in his throat. This symptom disappeared after his third rebirthing experience, when he discovered that the cord had been tied round his neck. In general the pressure and discomfort of being trapped, or of being held prisoner emotionally, can be traced back to a concrete origin of this kind.

Many patients have placed themselves in a situational trap and cannot find release from it. Often in these cases we find that they have been trapped in the womb with no exit, as in a delayed birth. Over-reaction to nagging is an example of this. The capacity to obtain relief and release is basic to learning, as is the acceptance that a process must take place before reaching a goal. Because such people make behavioural choices that are inappropriate to environmental demands, they become dependent upon others to define their behaviour, and subject to emotional prostitution and seduction. Forceps babies who show dependency towards the therapist feel this will clue the therapist into giving them approval. When this does not work, they will increase their dependency, unconsciously assuming that the degree has not been enough to produce results. Since there is no way for this to increase healthy functioning, it often leads to a lengthy and ineffective treatment process.

Claustrophobia and feeling trapped or confined, reflecting the tight quarters of the womb prior to birth, is remarkable in delayed birth personalities. Fears of riding or falling, particularly fear of elevators, often represent anxiety about going down the birth canal.[1]

Full-term infants who are the last in the birth order of many are like the premature, in that they have less experience with contraction, and similar reactions as adults.

Menopausal Birth Personality

Menopausal babies often underestimate their potential and feel inadequate. They also seem exceptionally hostile to people of the opposite gender, perceiving them as objects yet requiring excessive dependency once in a relationship. It is not clear at this stage whether these tendencies result from the particular chemical environment of the womb during the menopause; from environmental factors – having strong authority figures due to the age of the parent; or from birth complications. Frequently, such people seem to have what traditionally would be defined as a strong superego, tending to harsh judgements and to devaluing others.

Blue Babies and Oxygen Deprivation

Every baby faces a respiration trauma when transmission of oxygen changes from cord to lungs, and he has to breathe for the first time. Also the circulation of blood reverses direction simultaneously with the first intake of air, so his future attitudes to accepting or seeking alternative responses, rather than sticking with the familiar, will be in part determined by how terrifying this first physical reversal proved. But the blue baby has to cope with more – he comes near to death.

Oxygen deprivation is a risk at several points in the birth sequence. We know that in the womb it leads to foetal distress, whose symptoms are much like those of anxiety. Then during labour, the mother breathes differently, thus modifying oxygen supply through the placenta (the LaMaze technique for instance modifies the breathing pattern of the mother radically). We also know that anaesthetics produce sleepy despondent babies, while extra oxygen at birth has been shown to increase IQ and muscle co-ordination, and hasten development in general.[2]

A tied or restricted cord in the canal may be one cause of dangerously reduced oxygen supply. Then once the cord is cut, comes the moment when the inhale-exhale response, which echoes the pressure-release pattern of the contractions, must begin, and any delay can cause suffocation. The experience of feeling suffocated, and so close to death, can occur with all the births, even the easiest and most natural, though it is most extreme in blue babies. Laing[3] has concluded that asthma is a repetition of the suffocation resulting from a too quickly cut umbilical cord, and quotes his own birth experience as an example. Indeed, so closely connected is the first experience of anxiety with these problematic moments of birth that the author feels that all anxiety symptoms expressed in later life may be by-products of responses emanating from contractions and early respiration.

Problems with the cord can of course begin in the womb, and result in foetal distress there. But this distress, prior even to the anxiety response initiated in labour, is a pre-world experience so that it is qualitatively different from birth trauma in affecting emotional development.

The traumatic moment of suffocation, when source of oxygen changes from umbilicus to lungs, is later symbolically reflected in fears of smothering in life and dreams. One patient, for example, dreamt that she felt herself falling out of a window. She landed on the edge of a lake, with a tree branch hooked on to her clothing. Suddenly a waterfall appeared and began pulling her down. She could feel the water enveloping her. It was slimy, and she felt disgust and panic about breathing.

During the birth, a knotted cord, or a cord tied around the foot or neck, always carries with it emotional overtones of restricted movement and sensations of bondage. But it is most traumatic if it actually causes a break in consciousness. In this case, when a fragment in a series of events is eliminated, the effect on the psyche is similar to the loss of one piece of a puzzle which renders the whole picture unorganized. Later, this translates into faulty cognitive logic when dealing with reality: a predisposition perhaps to seeking confusion-producing people or situations (i.e. obfuscation). A similar effect may occur when the mother is given anaesthetic. Infants block out such noxious stimuli by going to sleep and losing consciousness, so should this occur during birth, whether at the start of labour or near to delivery, a pattern may be set up: that is, a predisposition to re-experience a form of repression or inattention in the face of threat in life.

Many authors, including Rank and Fodor, have pointed out that fear of tunnels, bridges or elevators can be traced back to birth. Dreams of creeping, going through narrow openings, sinking, drowning, being crushed, suffocated, pulled down or out, falling, being released, flying and being buried, violated, controlled or pressured are all birth associated too.[4] The author has concluded that in fact any sense of unreality, illogic, confusion, anything seeming irrational, can be traced back to birth in some way. Any loss of transition from womb to the external world is a loss in learning, and renders other later logical connections incomplete. So whether the break in logic is due to anaesthetic, faulty respiration, oxygen deprivation or awake-sleep modifications, it must lead to later cognitive distortions.

Emotional prostitution, for instance, can be facilitated by lack of transition during birth, for the individual already recognizes illogic as familiar, and will assimilate similar patterns more easily once in the world.

Anxiety and the Fear of Death
Death and birth are interchangeable symbols in the unconscious. Fear of death begins at birth. Freud's[5] concept of Thanatos is thus here thought of as inseparable from birth, for it deals with suffoca-

tion, loss of cord, and anxiety. Since no one fears death as itself, but only as a re-enactment of what has already been experienced at the end of womb-life, it is not a real fear but a disguised one. It is a defence, or 'return-to-the-womb', and is resorted to only when the narcissistic-guilt dichotomy loses effectiveness.

Suicide and homicide very often re-enact the major birth trauma exactly. Hanging, for example, represents being strangled by the cord; knife cuts (particularly to the limbs or navel) are reactions to loss of the cord. When all of life seems unresolvable and all defence useless, the individual turns more and more to past traumas, birth being the last world-connected experience.

Regression even further means return to the womb. This is why extremely depressed people rarely do kill themselves, and if they do commit suicide they do so only after an improvement. When a current situation is untenable and coping mechanisms ineffective the individual goes further and further back to seek out the primary cause creating his current reaction.

Fear of death, in short, does not exist. We can only be afraid of that which we have experienced. Just as castration anxiety in those who have not had a penis removed can be traced back to the cutting of the cord in its concrete form, so too all death anxiety is birth anxiety. The suffocation that occurred at the end of womb life, we all expect and fear at the end of world life. Hence many death rituals, like those the obsessive compulsive devises to protect himself from dying, can be traced back to the pattern of behaviour at birth following the diminishing of distress or suffocation.

Most unexplained fears – or phobias – have a concrete origin in anxiety experienced in the past. Anxiety associated with an experience sets up preconditioning patterns, so that whenever the experience is repeated, anxiety recurs. For example, if anxiety was associated with our 'new' experience at birth, we will continue to feel anxiety in the face of novelty. Impatience with novelty and fear in the anticipation of events are particular re-enactments of anxiety prior to birth; and any ways of approach to new experience similarly reflect the pattern of approach through the birth canal to the release into the world. Whether one meets novelty 'head on' or with caution is thus a literal metaphor.

Anxiety is very frequently correlated with anal activity: the illogic of pain, the confusion of pleasure and pain in anality, clearly recall anxiety during labour. Fears of cutting and blood phobias may be traced back to the cutting of the cord, as can fear of operations.

The symptoms of anxiety – dizziness, headaches, degrees of activity or passivity – all give clues to the specifics in the birth of which they are re-enactments. We have found, for example, that patients who respond to anxiety with headaches were usually forceps deliveries – that is, the sensation that accompanied anxiety was pressure on the head. A need for pressure in order to complete a task also very often reflects exceptional pressure in labour before birth. In the Caesarean, on the other hand, anxiety seems to manifest itself in detachment, and lack of contact with others.

Anxiety is an attempt to fill in the gaps of logical transition. During the birth when the body is jarred into new experience, there is inevitably anxiety. Birth is the most novel and unexpected of all our experiences. There has been no preparation for it in the infant's history, and even the concept of novelty itself is alien. Later, after the development of cognition, any sudden introduction of reality remains confusing, and produces the same reaction. The ways in which we cope with current surprises correlate closely with the degree of pleasantness or discomfort in the original one.

The Contraction: release, pressure, pain
The contraction combines two opposite processes – pressure and release – and is thus the forerunner of all later dichotomies. The alternate pressure and release of labour is the most active process to which the foetus has hitherto been exposed. It is then followed by the gigantic release of birth; and finally by sleep: the infant's first sleep is a sleep of exhaustion. This too must be novel in some way, and this first sleep may well condition future sleep responses. Anaesthetic during labour can cause an induced sleep in the infant, that would alter this later sleep response to release, and by association modify other responses to relaxation.

Many emotional problems reflect the pressure and release pattern of contractions: sado-masochism and manic-depression, for instance. But whether a problem can be traced back to birth and contractions, or is primarily the result of later environmental factors, will be ascertained, in part, by the degree of pain expressed. Since the pain response occurs only after birth, we can assume that any pathology that includes pain is a later development, so sado-masochistic behaviour is more complex and mature than manic-depression. Both have at their core the same symptoms, but their development would imply that in the first, physical pain is the source of trauma, while in the latter, the pressure part of the contraction process is significant. Both pathologies can be traced back to birth, but sado-masochism needs the refinement of post-birth maladaptation.

The interdependency of pressure and release symptoms also mirrors the relationship between reward and deprivation. The greater the reward, the more intense the deprivation; the greater the deprivation, the more satisfying the reward; the greater the loss, the more fulfilling the gain. Feelings of grandiosity, as we have seen, are a reaction-formation to hurt and loss, and since reaction-formation is a product of obsessive-compulsive behaviour it must also be a product of anal fixation. Narcissism, as we have also seen, is being deprived. The obsessive eater has the same deprivation fear so we can conclude that this kind of orality and narcissism have anal characteristics.

Narcissism and guilt
The effect, therefore, of the crisis umbilicus, when considered in connection with the release-pressure/pain process, explains what I have called the narcissistic-guilt dichotomy. And this argument also confirms the view that they must be mutually dependent, rather than different stages of development as traditional theory would have it. So does the fact that some Caesareans, particularly those who were also premature and had no contractions so that the release was without pressure, sometimes tend to be almost psychopathically narcissistic, lacking all superego or ego controls.

The narcissistic-guilt dichotomy, then, appears as first a reaction to womb or canal pressure (guilt), and birth release (narcissism). The contraction process is then repeated in the environment, with parental reaction and the degree of consequently *felt* abandonment and helplessness echoing the crisis umbilicus. The predisposition to select out and attend to that in the environment which would duplicate what happened initially is a major contributing factor, that may then condition those in the environment (i.e. parents) to respond back accordingly.

In this way, the father's response to the child is crucial. He alone can modify any predispositions that result from material chemical transmission through the placenta – the mother's responses during birth. He can expose the child to further magnification of that predisposition by responding in a way similar to the mother; or modify the predisposition by exposing the child to an alternative response.

The narcissistic-guilt dichotomy, which is one of the most universal of maladaptive expressions, present to some extent in all of us because we live in a society that perpetuates it, is thus dependent upon the birth episode to determine its degree and its direction. The nursing period, the type of interaction, the degree of abandonment or separation from the mother, are all variables that will affect what is subsequently attended to in the environment. But all must reflect back upon the conditioning of labour itself: activity and release are dormant in narcissism, and passivity or captivity in guilt.

The concept of orgasmic release is also first laid down at birth. It is next, in part, experienced when hunger is satisfied, and later with anal satisfaction. The pressure and release of pressure during contraction are essential to these developments. They begin a process of association with surrounding stimuli, which is later generalized in interaction with reality. Since world pressures include physical pain, pain is incorporated into the pressure part of the pattern. And this in turn affects the quality of orgasmic release. Most later maladaptive reactions can be traced back to the consequent extremes of feeling. For example, narcissism, elation, optimism, activity, generosity, sadism, manipulation, seduction, grandiosity and so on are developed from the release response; while guilt, depression, pessimism, passivity, withholding, masochism, submission, being seduced, feelings of inferiority, can be traced to the pressure and later pain part of the response.

For the Caesarean, and other births with limited contraction experience, the pressure-release process is underdeveloped, and requires alternative adaptation. The contraction birth personality is best adjusted to a society that has a structure, an order and expectations, while Caesarean personalities have difficulties in adjustment because they lack structure and order in their foundation.

In some births, such as the premature, the activation of the anal and intestinal functions is particularly traumatic, because of physical underdevelopment. The pain-release response is thus enhanced, rendering the infant more susceptible to later emotional seduction.

Myelinization of nerves is underdeveloped in the premature newborn, but in the postmature newborn may be overdeveloped, making the baby extra sensitive to the birth process and post-birth period. Again, inclinations to seductive-sadistic/masochistic orientations are enhanced.

The predisposition to passivity and dependency, which becomes manifest in the emotional prostitution process, is thus set up at birth. It is either a socially responsive expression, as in premature and Caesarean, or imposed by others as in the instrument birth.

Return to the Womb

Narcisism and guilt are world phenomena. But the need to return to the womb has a wholly different developmental source. The desire to avoid conflict and regress to a point of self-interaction, self-stimulation and self-definition is quite separate from the dichotomy, though very often it comes into operation when the rewards from the dichotomy (i.e. offsetting confusion or conflict) are no longer useful in protecting the ego. The individuals who found greatest satisfaction in the womb, such as the premature who bypassed the extremes of confinement, are most likely to choose this third alternative in coping. More incentive for this emotional mechanism also arises for those whose births were contraction free, and who thus cannot develop the dichotomy for coping as successfully as others. After all complicated births, the mother tends to be especially protective of the child, and less likely to acknowledge his competence, so this magnifies the crisis umbilicus. The additional burden that the mother feels in relation to such children also makes her more susceptible to other guilt-ridden behaviour, requiring further coping mechanisms in the child.

Orgasm, which so clearly echoes the birth release, has not only sexual or physical expressions, but emotional – as in the feeling of elation – and cognitive – as in a sudden intense insight. Mentally, confusion and resolution are counterparts of the pressure-release process, so an inability to have orgasm on one of these levels is very often reflected in a parallel orgastic inability on others. In therapy, when insight is required for change, any resistance to allowing insight is taken as possibly representing a negative birth, for the birth orgasm precipitated the change to a world environment. And it is also assumed to reflect sexual or emotional withholding as well. During toilet training, the refusal to let go has an obvious orgastic component.

We can generalize from this and say that there are two basic personality structures, one characterized by pressure-withholding and the other by release-letting go. The former can be further subdivided into pressure (womb, birth), and pain (anal) personalities. This concept changes much of traditional anal categorization. The obsessive-compulsive is generally described as anal-retentive, reflecting problems in the toilet training periods, and characterized by stubbornness, criticalness, judgementalness, needing order and ritual to protect him, tendencies towards paranoia, guilt and sadism.

But nothing has appeared in the literature about the reverse; an anal-releasive personality, who would be disorganized, giving, non-judgemental and creative. Yet such personalities do in fact exist and must be identified. The closest traditional description is of what has been called the oral personality, attributed to a fixation during nursing. But, based upon the perceptions of anal-oral and guilt-narcissistic development here, the whole concept of fixed stages of development and of personality structures as emanating from these stages clearly needs to be reviewed.

The intensity of the contraction is often defined by whether the birth is wet or dry. As Greenacre[6] has pointed out, there is a greater eroticization of the skin surface with a dry birth, creating much more friction and an intensification of pressure/relief reaction. Although breaking waters brings on labour quicker, the length of labour is extended, is more brutal, and results according to some observers in greater irritability in the neonate.

Loss of waters obviously creates sensation change; but at which point this occurs is also relevant. A dry birth restricts ease of movement for the baby, creating extra sensitivity to contact or pressure. It can change that which was pleasant into something rough and irritating, and magnify any jarring movement by the mother. Fear of being touched, which is a symptom in psychotics,[7] may be a replication of this experience.

Sexuality

The need for mastery, to regain a sense of competence, is a strong drive in all of us. And if the sense of being captive and passive in birth was especially traumatic, there will be a tendency in the individual to try to repeat it for resolution. The search for release and freedom, particularly when the individual has led a life of confinement, is thus a search for birth release. Orgasm, and the ability to accept or reject that experience, correlates with this first release.

Sexuality, as has been made clear earlier, is a process by which we can attempt to master the maladaptive or illogical aspects of birth and our later environment. Very often the sexual fantasy, and patterns of sexual functioning, can be traced back not only to childhood confusions, but even farther back to birth.

Sexuality is initiated at birth, but except for latent expressions it does not fully develop until after puberty. In its alligatory form, it can act out traumas, specifically any traumas of birth, and pre-verbal confusion.

Sexual fantasy is derived from birth and later trauma. It incorporates all novelty and illogic, and is an attempt to create consistency and mastery.

The first adult sexual experience is often marked with anxiety, arising from misconceptions that reinforce the primary anxiety that originated at birth. Such misconceptions prevalent in our culture that make for anxiety include beliefs that our sexuality is similar to that of animals, that intercourse brings immediate orgasm, that intercourse does not involve movement, that it must be violent or painful to be enjoyable, that it is a dreaded obligation, that it must be 'dirty' or 'forbidden' to be the real thing, that it brings with it power or narcissistic gratification, or that it must involve specific rituals.

If sexuality is used primarily for reality mastery and the resolution of conflict, it must result in a distortion of experience. In almost every case of sexual incompatibility or dysfunction that this author has heard about, sexual fantasy is used not only in masturbation but with a partner. And such pervasive fantasies must equally have roots in primary experience. One patient, for instance, had sexual fantasies of being tied by her feet. In her rebirth experience she relived umbilical cord restrictions in that precise area, and when we checked back with her mother we received verification that this had in fact occurred at her birth.

Excessive contraction, as in prolonged labour, may lead the individual later to reject opportunities for immediate gratification. Sexually, the requirement for excessive foreplay is much too frequent in such patients to be dismissed as coincidental. Although difficult to verify scientifically, other patterns of dysfunctional behaviour, such as orgasmic inhibition, are also too frequent for chance in people at whose birth anaesthetic has been used: if the infant is asleep at the final birth release, he has no sense of culmination to relate to. Severe handling by forceps or other extreme discomfort at birth can also contribute to rejection of release. And among blue babies the experience of suffocation upon entry into the world, with its associated fear of death, can clearly contribute to a terror of orgasm.

Premature ejaculation has been proved in many cases to be correlated to quick short labours. Caesareans and premature births are more distant lovers, while prolonged labour individuals seem to require relationships that are more intense.

Severe discomfort with contraction in the birth canal may set up a fear of entry, which may predispose a woman to tighten her vagina or a man to lose his erection just before intercourse. On the other hand, the infant who had the physical sensation of sliding easily out of the canal into freedom is predisposed to loving and satisfying orgasmic functioning.

Even anticipation, anger or violence as a requirement to sexual functioning reflects physiological symptoms of anxiety during the labour episode. Incestuous as it may seem, the child shared a monumental sexual experience with the mother, and whether her anxiety was transmitted chemically to the foetus through the placenta or simply through the excitement of her movement, her level of anticipation is relevant to his subsequent foundation, including his sexual foundation.

In the end of course, there is no dysfunction, there are just different types of functioning. We create too many criteria for what is 'good in bed', and values are irrelevant when discussing birth-correlated sexuality. Each of us is a product of our experience. The value judgement is a product of society and not of reality. If we could be generous enough with others, as well as with ourselves, we could dismiss external judgements of sexuality and realize that except for the guilt and anxiety it may cause us, which we and the environment inflict upon ourselves, there is no correct sexual function. If it expresses the self, it is correct – and it always does.

The greater the illogic and breaks in consistency during birth, the more the child will identify later illogic or novelty as reminiscent of birth, and respond with the anxiety patterns initiated then. His tendencies to react to novelty will in part be dependent upon his need to master the original new experience, and he will seek appropriate opportunities. The physiological experience of anxiety attributed to birth can thus be reinterpreted as a source of excitement in seeking out adventure and challenge. Racing-car driving, sexual escapades, mountain climbing and the like are examples of this form of re-enactment. Those who express themselves in cognition may study the occult, or follow radical political or social pursuits. Whether the point of entry into the world was perceived as negative or positive will determine the optimism or pessimism invested in these pursuits, and the degree of excitement or anxiety invested in them. For some, satisfaction is in the process of gaining the goal, for others the goal itself. A mountain climber enjoys the challenge of climbing but may actually feel depressed after reaching the peak, a gambler may play to lose, or a seducer feel disappointed after conquest: all these have in common a post-birth depression. Those who triumph in achievement also triumphed at birth.

It is too early as yet to study adults who have benefited from the many contemporary efforts to make the after-birth experience for infants a pleasure that is sensual and satisfying, such as described by Lewis Mehl in Chapter three of this book.[8] But we might guess that these children wil grow up to value the completion and not just the process of a task. Emotional development begins before birth. It is affected by birth and for individuals to develop fully cognisant of their own identity, they must transcend birth. To reach full maturity one must give up the womb state, and that means giving up those qualities within oneself that represent the womb – our omnipotence, omniscience, superiority. To accept the real world, we must be born, which means, we must function and experience and feel positive, even if not in charge of the whole universe. Sometimes by giving up being in charge of the universe, we regain charge of ourselves.

Birth and its trauma, although significant, even paramount, is not the only significant part of development. The birth experience is only the beginning. There is a whole range of physiological, neuro-logical, emotional and environmental experiences to follow, all of which help shape, modify and affect the eventual formation of the adult. But birth and womb experience have until recently been the great unknowns in human psychology, and we are only now begin-ning to understand them.

These pages have proved an adventure and challenge to the author. And this conclusion is a form of birth. It is hoped that for the reader the experience was equally stimulating, and that the material here presented will provide a stepping stone of insight to fuller awareness of the world and of ourselves.

CHAPTER NOTES

CHAPTER 1

1 FREUD, S., *A General Selection from the Works of Sigmund Freud*, Doubleday, New York, 1937; *New Introductory Lectures on Psychoanalysis*, Hogarth Press, London, 1933; *Problems of Anxiety*, Hogarth Press, London, 1936.
2 RANK, O., *The Trauma of Birth*, Routledge, London, 1929.
3 FERENCZI, S., and RANK, O. *The Development of Psychoanalysis*, Dover, New York, 1956.
4 FODOR, N., *In Search of the Beloved*, University Books, New York, 1949.
5 BETTELEHEIM, B., book review on *The Facts of Life*, by R. D. Laing, *New York Times*, May 1976.
6 MOTT, F. J., *The Universal Design of the Oedipus Complex*, Integration Publishing, New York, 1952.
7 DEMAUSE, L., 'The Independence of Psychohistory', *History of Childhood Quarterly*, 1975: 164–83.
8 MEHL, L. E., as discussed in Chapter three of this book.
9 LEBOYER, F., *Birth Without Violence*, Wildwood House, London, 1975.
10 GROF, S., *Realms of the Human Unconscious*, Souvenir Press, London, 1978; *The Human Encounter with Death*, Souvenir Press, London, 1977.
11 JANOV, A., *The Primal Scream*, Putnam, New York, 1970.
12 FEHER, LESLIE, 'Natal Therapy and Theory', *Journal of Psychohistory*, Winter, 1977; Special Birth Issue; Gross, Amy, 'Rebirthing', *Mademoiselle Magazine*, September, Conte Nest Publications, New York, 1976.
13 KEEN, S., 'Janov and Primal Therapy', *Psychology Today*, February, 1972; JANOV, A., op. cit.
14 JANOV, A., op. cit.
15 BREUER, J., and FREUD, S., *Studies in Hysteria*, Beacon, Boston, 1895.
16 SPERRY, R. W., 'Cerebral Organization and Behaviour',

Readings in Physiological Psychology, edited by Thomas K. Landauer, McGraw Hill, New York, 1967.

17 ORNSTEIN, R., and GALIN, D., Symposium, October 5–6, 1974, *The Psychology of Consciousness,* New York University.

18 WATSON, J., *Behaviorism,* Phoenix Book, Chicago, 1963.

19 RANK, O., op. cit.

CHAPTER 2

1 BEADLE, MURIEL, *A Child's Mind,* Doubleday, New York, 1970.

2 FLANAGAN, GERALDINE, *First Nine Months of Life,* Heinemann, London, 1963.

3 GREENACRE, PHYLLIS, *Trauma, Growth and Personality,* International University Press, New York, 1952.

4 THOMPSON, R. R., *Foundations of Physiological Psychology,* Harper & Row, New York, 1967.

5 COOLEY, D. G., *Family Medical Guide,* Meredith Press, New York, 1964.

6 BELLAK, L., *Schizophrenia,* Logos Press, New York, 1958.

7 COOLEY, D. G., op. cit.

8 CORLISS, C. E., Patten's Human Embriology, McGraw Hill, New York, 1976.

9 LANGWORTHY, O. R., 'Development of Behavior Paterns and Myelinisation of the Nervous System in The Human Fetus and Infant; *Contributions to Embriology,* XXIV, No. 139, Carnegie Institute, Washington, D.C., 1933.

10 WINDLE, W. F., *Physiology of the Fetus,* Saunders, Philadelphia, 1940.

11 WYNN, R. M., HELLMAN, L. M., and PRITCHARD, J., *Williams Obstetrics,* 14th edition, Appleton, Century Cross, New York, 1971.

12 CORLISS, C. E., op. cit.

13 GREENACRE, PHYLLIS, op. cit.

14 CORLISS, C. E., op. cit.

15 WHITE, R. W., *The Abnormal Personality,* Ronald Press, New York, 1964; ZAX, M., and STRICKER, G., *The Study of Abnormal Behavior,* MacMillan, New York, 1964.

16 KRECH, D., and CRUTCHFIELD, R. S., *Elements of Psychology,* Knopf, New York, 1962.

17 FLANAGAN, GERALDINE, op. cit.

18 WYNN, HELLMAN, PRITCHARD, op. cit.

19 Ibid.
20 ARIETI, S., *Interpretation of Schizophrenia*, Bruner, New York, 1955.
21 GREENACRE, PHYLLIS, op. cit.
22 FLANAGAN, GERALDINE, op. cit.
23 FREUD, S., *A General Selection*, op. cit.
24 LEBOYER, F., *Birth Without Violence*, op. cit.
25 GREENACRE, PHYLLIS, op. cit.
26 CORLISS, C. E., op. cit.
27 FREUD, S., *A General Selection*, op. cit.
28 FENICHEL, O., *The Psychoanalytical Theory of Neurosis*, Norton, New York, 1945.
29 PERLS, F. S., *Gestalt Therapy Verbatim*, Real People Press, California, 1969.

CHAPTER 3

1 LAING, R. D., *The Divided Self*, Tavistock Press, London; *The Self and Others*, Tavistock Press, London, 1970; *The Politics of Experience*, Allen Lane, London, 1970.
2 MITFORD, JESSICA, *The American Way of Death*, Simon and Schuster, 1978.
3 KÜBLER-ROSS, ELIZABETH, *Death: The Final Stage of Growth*. Prentice Hall, New York, 1975.
4 FRIERI, P., 'Cultural Action and Conscientization', *Harvard Educational Review*, 40 (3) pp. 452–77.
5 NORR, K. L., BLOCK, C. C., CHARLES, A., MEYERING, S., and MEYERS, E., 'Explaining Pain and Enjoyment in Childbirth', *Journal of Health and Social Behavior*, 18 (September): 260–75, 1977.
6 Twilight sleep is a drugged state in which the woman's inhibitions are removed, and the experience is like a dream/nightmare, with amnesia afterwards.
7 Forceps are spoon-like instruments which fit around the baby's head and are used to pull the baby out of the vagina.
8 An episiotomy is a cut made in the perineum (tissue between the rectum and the vagina) to speed up delivery.
9 Recent unpublished data from Great Britain show walking to be one of the best activities for labour.
10 BIENIARZ, J., MAQUEDA, E., HASHIMOTO, T., et al., 'Iotocaval Compression by the Uterus in Late Human Pregnancy', 2, in Arteriographic Study. *Am J. Obstet. Gynecol.* 100: 203–17,

1968; GOODLIN, R. J., 'Aortocaval Compression during Cesarean Section: A Cause of Newborn Depression', *Ob. Gyn.* 37: 702–5, 1979; HUMPHREY, M., HOUNSLOW, P., MORGAN, S., and WOOD, C. 'The Influence of Maternal Posture at Birth on the Fetus', *J. Ob. Gyn. Br. Commonw.* 80: 1075–80, 1973.

11 HAIRE, D., *The Cultural Warping of Childbirth*, ICEA Special Report, American Foundation for Maternal and Child Health, New York, N.Y., 1978.

12 Ibid.

13 BANDLER, R., and GRINDLER, J., *Patterns of the Hypnotic Techniques of Milton H. Erickson, M.D.*, Cupertino, California: Meta Publications, 1977.

14 ERICKSON, M. H., ROSSI, E. L., and ROSSI, S. I., *Hypnotic Realities*, New York: Irvington Publishers, Inc, 1976.

15 HAIRE, D., op. cit.

16 MEHL, L. E., 'Options in Maternity Care', *Women and Health*, 2(2): 29–42, 1977.

17 ARMS, S., *Immaculate Deception: A New Look at Childbirth in America*, San Francisco: San Francisco Books, 1975.

18 ETTNER, F. M., 'Hospital Technology Breeds Pathology', *Women and Health*, 2(2): 17–22, 1977.

19 DANZIGER, S. Socialization of Women during Childbirth, Ph.D. dissertation, Department of Sociology, Boston University, 1978.

20 ILLICH, I., *Medical Nemesis*, London, Calder & Boyars, 1977.

21 OXON, H., and FOOTE, W., *Human Labor and Birth*, New York: Appleton, Century, Crofts, 1975.

22 GREENHILL, J. P., FRIEDMAN, E. A., *Biological Principles and Modern Practice of Obstetrics*, Philadelphia: W. B. Saunders Co., 1974.

23 MYLES, M. S., *Textbook for Midwives*, London: Churchill & Livingstone, 1971.

24 Recent data from the Rhode Island Department of Public Health.

25 HELFER, R. E., 'The Relationship between Lack of Bonding and Child Abuse and Neglect' in KLAUS, M. H., LEJER, T. and TRAUSE, M., *Maternal Attachment and Mothering Disorders: A Roundtable*, sponsored by Johnson & Johnson Co., October 18–19, 1974, pp. 21–5.

26 MEHL, L. E., and PETERSON, G. H., Psychological Intervention During Labor. Report available from the Center for Research on Birth and Human Development, Berkeley, California, 1978.

27 FRIEDMAN, E. A., 'Patterns of Labor as Indicators of Risk', *Clin. Ob. Gyn.* Summer, 1974, pp. 172–83.

28 O'DRISCOLL, K. D., JACKSON, R. J. A. and GALLAGHER, J. T., 'Active Management of Labor and Cephalopelvic Disproportion', *J. Ob. Gyn. Brit. Commonw.* 77.

29 HAIRE, D., op at.; MEHL, L. E., 'Options in Maternity Care', op. cit.; ETTNER, op. cit.

30 HAVERKAMP, A. D., THOMPSON, H. E., McFEE, J. G., CETRULY, C., 'The evaluation of continuous fetal heart rate.'

31 KLAUS, M. H., and FANAROFF, A. A., *Care of the High Risk Neonate*, Philadelphia: W. B. Saunders, 1973.

32 KLOOSTERMAN, G. J., 'The Dutch System of Home Births' in KITZINGER, S., and DAVIS, J., *The Place of Birth*, Oxford: Oxford Univ. Press, 1978.

33 COLMAN, A., and COLMAN, L., *Pregnancy: The Psychological Experience*, Cambridge Mass., Howard Univ. Press, 1971; SHARASHEFSKY, S. and YARROW, I., *Psychological Aspects of a First Pregnancy*, New York: Ravenswood Press, 1973.

34 BARKER-BENFIELD, G. J., *The Horrors of the Half-Known Life*, New York: Harper & Row, 1975; EHRENREICH, D. and ENGLISH, D., *Witches, Midwives and Nurses*, Old Westbury, New York: Feminist Press, State Univ. of New York at Old Westbury, 1973; FOUCAULT, M., *The Birth of the Clinic*, New York: Vintage Books, 1975.

35 FOUCAULT, M., op. cit.

36 MEHL, L. E., 'The Relation of the Home Birth Movement to Medicine and Psychiatry', *World Journal of Psychosynthesis*, in press, 1978.

37 SCHNEIDER, J., quoted in *American Medical News*, p. 10, May 16, 1977, 'Cesarean Section Rate Increasing', paper presented at the annual meeting of the American College of Obstetricians and Gynecologists.

38 CHARLES, A., quoted in *American Medical News*, p. 10, May 16, 1977, 'Cesarean Section Rate Increasing', paper presented at the annual meeting of the American College of Obstetricians and Gynecologists.

39 HIBBARD, L. T., 'Changing Trends in Cesarean Section', *Am. J. Obstet. Gynecol.* 125: 798, 1976.

40 ENKIN, M. W., 'Having A Section is Having a Baby', *Birth and the Family Journal*, 4 (3); 99–105, 1977.

41 Ibid.
42 DE TOCQUEVILLE, A., *Democracy in America*, ed. Phillips Bradley, 2 vols., New York: Knopf, 1945, Vol. I, pp. 307, 308, 337.
43 BARKER-BENFIELD, G. J., op. cit.
44 COOPER, J. F., *Notions of the Americans*, 2 vols., London: Henry Colburn, 1828, Vol. I, pp. 36, 158; DE TOCQUEVILLE, op. cit.
45 BARKER-BENFIELD, G. J., op. cit.
46 Ibid.
47 Ibid.
48 TODD, J., *Women's Rights*, Boston: Lee and Shaphard, 1867; *Serpents in the Dove's Nest*, 1867.
49 WERTZ, D. and WERTZ, R., *Liying Dri: A History of Childbirth in America*, New York: Random House, 1975.
50 CALDEYRO-BARCIA, R., SCHWARTZ, R., BELIZAN, J. M., MARTELL, M., NEITO, F., SABATINO, H., and TENZER, S. M., 'Adverse Perinatal Effects of Early Amniotomy during Labor', in Gluck, L. (ed.), *Modern Perinatal Medicine*, Yearbook Medical Publishers, Inc., Chicago, Ill., pp. 431–49, 1974.
51 WERTZ, D. and WERTZ, R., op. cit.
52 BARKER-BENFIELD, G. J., op. cit.
53 CONNOR, L., 'Cesarean Birth', *Birth and the Family Journal*, 4 (3): 106–15, 1977.
54 PETERSON, G. H., and MEHL, L. E., 'The Effect of Some Birth Related Variables upon Infant Cognitive Development', paper presented at the 6th World Congress of Psychiatry, Honolulu, Hawaii, 1977. Available from the Center for Research on Birth and Human Development.
55 HELFER, R. E., op. cit.; LYNCH, N. A., 'Ill Health and Child Abuse', *The Lancet*, August 16, 1975.
56 HOBBINS, J., *Cesarean Births Are Healthier*, pres release, Yale University, Department of Obstetrics and Gynecology, New Haven, Connecticut, January 26, 1976 (Associated Press).
57 MOYER, L., 'What Obstetrical Journal Advertising Tells About Doctors and Women', *Birth and the Family Journal*, 2 (4): 111–15, 1975.
58 MEHL, L. E., CHRISTIENSEN, S., JOHNSON, L., PENSO, G., PETERSON, G., and SCADENG, B., 'Application of an Existential-Phenomenological Model to Childbirth: Needs Assessment', paper presented at the 3rd annual NAPSAC Conference, Atlanta Georgia, 1978. Available from the Center for Research on

Birth and Human Development. MEHL, L. E., CHRISTIENSEN, S., SOLZ, H., PETERSON, G. H., SCADENG, B., JOHNSON, L., 'Psychophysiological Risk Factor Screening to Further Delineate Risk in Low Risk Patients', paper presented at the annual meeting of the American Public Health Association, Los Angeles, California, 1978. Available from the Center for Research on Birth and Human Development.

59 KOESTENBAUM, P., 'Phenomenological Foundations for the Behavioral Sciences: The Nature of Facts', in *The Vitality of Death*, Westport, Connecticut: Greenwood Press, 1971.

60 NEWTON, N., FOSHEE, D., and NEWTON, M., 'Experimental Inhibition of Labor through Environmental Disturbances', *Ob. Gyn*, 27 (3); 371–7, March, 1966; NEWTON, N., PEELER, D., and NEWTON, M., 'Effect of Disturbance on Labor', *Am. J. Obstet. Gynecol.*, 101 (8): 1096–1102, August, 1968; KELLY, J. V., 'Effect of Fear on Uterine Motillity', *Am. J. Obstet. Gynecol.* 83 (5): 576–87, March, 1962.

61 ENKIN, N., et al., 'An Adequately Controlled Study of the Effectiveness of P.P.M. Training', 3rd International Congress of Psychosomatic Medicine in Ob-Gyn, London, April, 1971.

62 CHARLES, A. G., NORR, K. L., BLOCK, C. R., MEYERING, S., and MEYERS, E., 'Obstetric and Psychological Effects of Psychoprophylactic Preparation for Childbirth', *Am. J. Obstet. Gynecol.* 131: 44, 1978.

63 VELLAY, P., *Psychoprophylaxis in Obstetrics*, Paris: Seuill, 1956.

64 For more information, sec MEHL, L. E., *Foundations of Holistic Health*, Chap. 2, available from CRBDH.

65 NEWTON, N., PEELER, D., and NEWTON, M., 'Effect of Disturbance on Labor', *Am. J. Ob. Gyn.* 101: 1096–1102, 1968; NEWTON, FOSHEE and NEWTON, op. cit.

66 LEBOYER, F., *Birth Without Violence*, op. cit.; *Loving Hands*, New York: Alfred A. Knopf, 1977.

67 BRADLEY, R. M., and MISTRETTA, C. M., 'Fetal Sensory Receptors', *Physiological Reviews*, 55 (3): 352–82, 1975 (July); WALKER, B., GRIMWADE, J., and Wood, C., 'Intrauterine Noise: A Component of the Fetal Environment', *Amer J. Obstet. Gynecol.* 109 (1)L 91–5, 1971; READ, J. A., and MILLER, F. C., 'Fetal Heart Rate Acceleration in Response to Acoustic Stimulation as a Measure of Fetal Well-Being', *Am. J. Obstet. Gynecol.* 129 (5): 512–17, 1977.

68 HINDE, R. A., 'Mothers and Infants Roles: Distinguishing the

Questions to Be Asked' in HOFER, *CIBA Symposium on Attachment*, New York: Elsevier, 1976; HINDE, R. A., and SIMPSON, M. J. A., 'Qualities of Mother-Infant Relationships in Monkeys' in HOFER; NADLER, R. D., 'Periparturitional Behavior of a Primiparous Lowland Gorilla', *Primates*, 15 (1): 55–73, 1974; KLAUS, M. H., 'Is There A Sensitive Period for Bonding in Humans?', paper presented at the 4th Annual Maternal-Infant Life Conference, Great Plains Organization for Perinatal Care, Minneapolis, Minnesota, November 5, 1976.

69 CHEEK, D. B., LECRON, L. M., *Clinical Hypnotherapy*, New York: Grune & Stratton, 1968.

70 WAMBACH, H., *1000 Birth Experiences*, New York; Harper & Row, Inc., in press, 1978.

71 BUCHSBAUM, M., 'Self-Regulation of Stimulus Intensity: Augmenting/Reducing in the Average Evoked Response' in Schwartz, G, E. and Shapiro, D. (eds.), 'Consciousness and Self-Regulation', Vol. 1, *Advances in Research*, New York: Plenum, 1976.

72 EGBERT, L. D., BATTIT, G. E., WELCH, C. E., and BARTLETT, M. K., 'Reduction of Post-operative Pain by Encouragement and Instruction of Patients', *New England Journal of Medicine*, 270: 825–7, 1964

73 LUKAS, J., and SEIGEL, J., 'Cortical Mechanisms that Augment or Reduce Evoked Potentials in Cats', *Science*, 198 (4312), 1977.

74 PETRIE, ASEMATH, *Individuality in Pain and Suffering*, Chicago: University of Chicago Press, 2nd Edition, 1978.

75 GOLD, C., and GOLD, E. J., *Joyous Childbirth*, Berkeley: And/Or Press, 1977.

CHAPTER 4

1 ARIETI, S., op. cit.

2 MAHLER, MARGARET, *The Psychological Birth of the Human Infant*, Basic Books, New York, 1975.

3 NUNBERG, H., *Principles of Psychoanalysis*, International Universities Press, 1955.

4 FEDERN, P., *Ego Psychology and Psychosis*, Basic Books, New York, 1952.

5 BROWN, J. F., *Psychodynamics of Abnormal Behavior*, McGraw Hill, New York, 1940; COLEMAN, J. C., *Abnormal*

Psychology and Modern Life, Scott, Foresman & Co., Chicago, 1956.
6 RADO, S., 'Fear of Castration in Women', *Psychoanalytic Quarterly*, 1933.
7 GREENACRE, PHYLLIS, op. cit.
8 Ibid.
9 Ibid.
10 SPITZ, R. R., 'Hospitalism: An Inquiry into the Genesis of Psychotic Conditions in Early Childhood', *The Psychoanalytic Study of the Child*, Vol. I, International University Press, New York, 1962.
11 MEHL, L. E., 'Cesarian Births', paper delivered to Convention on Psychohistory, New York, June 1978.
12 COOLEY, D. G., *Family Medical Guide*, Meredith Press, New York, 1964.
13 FLANAGAN, GERALDINE, *First Nine Months of Life*, op. cit.
14 FREUD, S., *General Selection*, op. cit.
15 Ibid.
16 KLEIN, MELANIE, *The Psychoanalysis of Children*, Hogarth Press, London, 1949.
17 HALL, J. R., *The Psychology of Learning*, Lippincott, New York, 1966; WOODWORTH, R. S., SCHLOSBERG, H., *Experimental Psychology*, Holt, Rhinehart, and Winston, New York, 1938.

CHAPTER 5
1 LAING, R. D., *The Facts of Life*, Allen Lane, London, 1974.
2 ABRAHAM, K., *Selected Papers on Psychoanalysis*, Hogarth Press, London, 1927.
3 ABRAHAM, K., op. cit.; RADO, S., op. cit.
4 GOLDBERG, S., *The Inevitability of Patriarchy*, Morrow, New York, 1973.
5 DEUTSCH, HELENE, *The Psychology of Women*, Grune & Stratton, New York, 1944–5.
6 FREUD, S., *A General Selection*, op. cit.
7 GREENACRE, PHYLLIS, op. cit.
8 Ibid.
9 FREUD, S., *Character and Culture*, Collier Books, New York, 1963.
10 CORLISS, C. E., op. cit.
11 FREUD, S., *A General Introduction to Psychoanalysis*, Pocketbooks, New York, 1924.

12 FREUD, S., *Three Case Histories*, Collier Books, New York, 1963.
13 BEEBELL, A., personal communication.
14 TAUBER, GIESLER, 'Narcissism and the Borderline Personality', Lecture, October 1977, New York Center for Psychoanalytic Training.
15 FREUD, S., *Three Case Histories*, op. cit.
16 FREUD, S., *A General Selection*, op. cit.
17 Ibid.

CHAPTER 6

1 JAMES, W., *Principles of Psychology*, Holt, New York, 1890.
2 SHIBUTONI, T., *Society and Personality*, Prentice Hall, New York, 1961.
3 SULLIVAN, H. S., *The Interpersonal Theory of Psychiatry*, Norton, New York, 1963.
4 PIAGET, J., *Origin of Intelligence in the Child*, Routledge, London, 1953.
5 SHIBUTONI T., op. cit.
6 GOFFMAN, E., *Presentation of Self in Everyday Life*, Garden City, Doubleday, 1959.
7 SULLIVAN, H. S., op. cit.
8 BECKER, H., *The Other Side*, Free Press, Glencoe, New York, 1964.
9 ASH, S. E., *Readings in Social Psychology*, Holt, New York, 1952; SHERIF, M. and SHERIF, C. W., *An Outline of Social Psychology*, Harper & Row, New York, 1948.
10 MEAD, G. H., *Mind, Self and Society*, Chicago Press, 1970.
11 SULLIVAN, H. S., op. cit.
12 BATESON, G., 'Toward a Double Bind Theory of Schizophrenia', Smelser and Smelser, *Personality and Social Systems*, Wiley, 1963.
13 LAING, R. R., *Sanity, Madness and the Family*, Pelican, London, 1964.
14 BREUER, J., and FREUD, S., *Studies in Hysteria*, op. cit.
15 LANGWORTHY, O. R., op. cit.
16 CARMICHAEL, L., 'Origin and Prenatal Growth of Behavior', *Handbook of Child Psychology*, Clark University Press, Mass., 1933.
17 RESTAK, G., 'Brain Makes its own Narcotics', *Scientific Review*,

March 5, 1977, 4: 6–11; SCHMECK, H. M., 'Opiate-like Substances in Gland Shows Promise as Pain Reliever', *New York Times*, December 12, 1977, 22: 4; SNYDER, S. H., 'Opiate Receptors and Internal Opiates', *Scientific American*, March 1977, Vol. 236, 3, pp. 44–56; 'The Opiate Receptor', *Neurosciences Research Program Bulletin*, 1975, Vol. 13, Suppl. (1–27); 'The Opiate Receptor and Morphine-Like Peptides in the Brain', *American Journal of Psychiatry*, Vol. 135, 6, June 1978, p. 645. FLANAGAN, D. (editor), 'Internal Opiates', *Scientific American*, February 1977, Vol. 236, 2, pp. 50–6.
18 Ibid.
19 GOTTLIEB, B., 'Learning Disabilities Workshop', New York, University, Board of Education.

CHAPTER 7
1 FEHER, LESLIE, 'Double-Mind Theory', *American Journal of Psychoanalysis*, Vol. 33, No. 2, 1973.
2 SPERRY, R. W., op. cit.
3 CALDER, N., *Mind of Man*, BBC Publications, London, 1970.
4 LAING, R. D., *The Divided Self*, op. cit.
5 SULLIVAN, H. S., op. cit.

CHAPTER 8
1 FREUD, S., *Group Psychology and the Analysis of the Ego*, Bantam, 1960; New Introductory Lectures on Psychoanalysis, Norton, New York, 1965, p. 93; *Sexuality and the Psychology of Love*, Collier, New York, 1974.
2 THOMPSON, CLARA, and MULLAHY, P., *Psychoanalysis: Evolution and Development*, Grove Press, New York, 1950.
3 CORLISS, C. E., op. cit.
4 FREUD, S., *Character and Culture*, Collier Books, New York, 1963.
5 FEHER, LESLIE, 'Seductive Susceptibilities', presented at *6th World Poetry Therapy Conference*, April 1, 1978, New York City, Hunter-Bellevue School of Nursing.
6 FREUD, S., *Character and Culture*, op. cit.; REIK, T., *Compulsion to Confess*, Arno Press, New York, 1959; Wiley, 1966.
7 GIARRETO, H., Director, Child Sexual Abuse Treatment Center, *Donahue Show*, Channel 7-TV, March 22, 1978.

CHAPTER 10

1 FREUD, S., *Three Case Histories*, op. cit.
2 REIK, T., *Compulsion to Confess*, op. cit.
3 FREUD, S., *A General Introduction to Psychoanalysis*, op. cit.
4 FREUD, S., *Therapy and Technique*, Collier, New York, 1963; KERNBERG, O., *Borderline Conditions and Pathological Narcissism*, Aronson, Inc., New York, 1975; MAHLER, MARGARET, op. cit.
5 FREUD, S., *A General Selection*, op. cit.
6 Ibid.
7 FREUD, S., *Sexuality and the Psychology of Love*, op. cit.
8 FREUD, S., *Three Case Histories*, op. cit.
9 KERNBERG, O., op. cit.
10 REIK, T., *Masochism in Modern Man*, Giroux, New York, 1941.
11 KERNBERG, O., op. cit.
12 FEDERN, P., *Ego Psychology and Psychosis*, Basic Books, New York, 1952; KOHUT, H., *Analysis of the Self*, International University Press, New York, 1974.
13 FREUD, S., *A General Introduction to Psychoanalysis*, op. cit.
14 KERNBERG, O., op. cit.; KOHUT, H., op. cit.
15 FREUD, S., *A General Selection*, op cit.

CHAPTER 11

1 KERNBERG, O., op. cit.
2 THOMPSON, CLARA, and MULLAHY, P., op. cit.
3 GARFIELD, S. L., *Introductory Clinical Psychology*, MacMillan Co., New York, 1957.
4 ROSEY, S., *The Book of Highs*, New York Times Books, New York, 1973.
5 THOMPSON, CLARA, op. cit.
6 GREENSON, R. R., *The Techniques and Practice of Psychoanalysis*, International University Press, New York, 1967.
7 FREUD, S., *Therapy and Technique*, op. cit.
8 FREUD, S., *Interpretation of Dreams*, Discus, New York, 1965.
9 OHLIN, ANITA, 'Fodas om och bli av med livets grundlaggande angest?', *Svenska Dagladet*, May 23, 1977, translated by Yvonne Conaly.

CHAPTER 12

1 FODOR, N., *In Search of the Beloved*, University Books, New York, 1949.

2   FLANAGAN, GERALDINE, op. cit.; GUTTMACHER, A. F., *Pregnancy and Birth*, Signet, New York, 1956; RODALE, J. I., *Natural Health and Pregnancy*, Pyramid, New York, 1968.

3   LAING, R. D., personal communication with Elizabeth Fehr, November 1972.

4   FODOR, N., op. cit.; RANK, O., *The Trauma of Birth*, op. cit.

5   FREUD, S., *A General Introduction to Psychoanalysis*, op. cit.

6   GREENACRE, PHYLLIS, op. cit.

7   ARIETI, S., op. cit.

8   LEBOYER, E., *Birth Without Violence*, op. cit.; MEHL, L. E., 'Cesarian Births', Conference on Psychohistory, New York City, June, 1978.

NAME INDEX

Abraham, K., 82, *213*
Abrahams, M., 167n
Allich, I., *208*
Alport, F. H., *217*
Arieti, S., *206, 212, 217*
Arms, S., *208*
Ash, S. E., 94, *214*

Bandler, R., *208*
Barker-Benfield, 55, *209, 210*
Bartlett, M., *212*
Bateson, G., 95, 112, 113, 131, *214,*
    215
Beadle, M., *212*
Becker, H., 94, *213, 214*
Beebell, A., 87, *213*
Belizan, J. M., *210*
Bellak, L., *213*
Bergman, H., *216*
Bettelheim, B., 14, *205*
Bieniarz, J., *207*
Block, C., *207, 211*
Bradley, R., 62, *206, 211*
Breuer, J., *205*
Brown, J. F., *212*
Browning, Elizabeth, 131
Buchsbaum, M., 65, *212*

Calder, N., *215*
Caldeyro-Barcia, R., 57, *210*
Carmichael, L., *214*
Cetruly, C., *208*
Charles, A., *207, 209, 211*
Cheek, D., 64, *212*
Christiensen, S., *210*
Coleman, J. C., *212*
Colman, A., *209*
Colman, L., *209*
Conner, L., *210*
Connolly, Y., *216*
Cooley, D. G., *206, 213*
Cooper, J. R., 55, *209*
Corliss, C. E., *206, 215*
Crutchfield, R. S., *206*

Danziger, S., *208*
Davis, J., *209*
de Mause, L., 14, 80, *205*

De Lee, P., 58
De Tocqueville, A., 55, *209*
Deutsch, H., *213*
Dick-Read, G., 62

Egbert, L. D., *212*
Ehrenreich, D., *209*
English, D., *209*
Enkin, N., 61, *211*
Erickson, M. H., *208*
Ettner, F. M., *208*

Fanaroff, A. A., *209*
Federn, P., 72, *216*
Feher, L., 64, *205, 215*
Fehr, E., 16, 17
Fenichel, O., *207*
Ferenczi, S., 14, *205*
Flanagan, G., *206, 212, 216*
Fodor, N., 14, 194, *205, 216, 217*
Foshee, D., *211*
Foucault, M., *209*
Freud, S., 13, 17, 18, 27, 31, 36, 56,
    71, 76, 85, 88, 91, 92, 97, 98,
    105, 124, 126, 127, 129, 130,
    146, 151, 157, 158, 159, 160, 161,
    162, 168, 183, 194, *205, 207,*
    213, 214, 215, 216, 217
Friedman, E. A., 45, *208*
Frieri, P., 39, *207*

Galin, D., *206*
Gallagher, J. T., *208*
Gardner, A. K., 56
Giareto, H., *215*
Goffman, E., 93, *214*
Gold, C., 67, *212*
Gold, E. J., 67, *212*
Goldberg, S., *213*
Goolin, R. J., *207*
Gottlieb, B., *215*
Greenacre, P., 25, 72, 83, 84, 200,
    206, 207, 208, 212, 213, 217
Greenhill, J. P., *208*
Greenson, R. R., *216*
Grimwade, J., *211*
Grof, S., 15, *205*
Gross, A., *205*
Guttmacher, A. F., *216*

SUBJECT INDEX

Coping mechanisms, 100
  and aiding, 107
  denial, 121
  dependency, 106
  (see Guilt)
Cord, 69, 194, 195
  manipulation by foetus of, 27
  (see Umbilicus)
Counteraction, 97
Crisis umbilicus, *80–92*, 100, 168,
    197
  in dependency, 90, 107
  and guilt, 154
  in homosexuality, 109
  in infatuation, 90
  and sadism, 127
  and sexuality, 88
  in therapy, 184
  (see Umbilicus)

Death, 38, 86
Defences, 195
  (see Coping)
Delayed birth, 188
Denial, 136, 191
Dependency, 106
  in Caesarean birth, 190
  and competition, 111
  in delayed birth, 188
  and disgust, 122
  and emotional prostitution, 118
  in foetus, 35
  because of forceps, 187
  and grandiosity, 135
  and guilt, 153
  in habits, 87
  because of seduction, 131
  in therapy, 168
Depression, 198
  post-birth, 203
  post-natal, 103
Detachment, 196
Differentiation, 69
Dilute oxytocin, 45
Disgust, 121
Double-bind, 95, 112, 131, 176
  and seduction, 124
Dream, 86, 194
  logic of, 113
Drug addiction, 87
  and dependency, 108
Dry birth (see labour)

Ego, 31, 98, 160
  development, 71
  ego ideal, 159
  and guilt, 154
Emotional pimp, 119
Emotional prostitution, 33, *112–123*,
    135, 192, 198
  and shame, 153

in therapist, 169
Endorphin, 15, 102

Fantasy, 162
  birth, 16, 165
  in competitiveness, 110
  as defence, 105
  grandiosity, 139, 142
  infatuation as, 90
  projected, 90
  psychotic, 28
  of self, 156
  sexual, 200, 201
Father, 197
Fears, 192, 194, 195
Foetal distress, 45
Foetal monitoring, 47, 49, 51, 59
Foetal learning, 27–35
Foetus, 23–7, 63
Forceps, 40, 187, 188, 189, 196, 201
  delivery, 44
  and self image, 70
Freudian theory, 77, 82, 85, 92
  (see Freud in name index)

Gender identification, 82–5
Genital development, 85
God junkie, 139
Grandiosity, 197
  (see Narcissism)
Group therapy, 17
Guilt, 116, 146–53, 191, 197
  (see Narcissistic-guilt dichotomy)

Habit formation, 87
Homicide, 195
Homosexuality, 108–9, 122, 133, 164,
    177
Hunger, 198

Idealization, 121
Identification, 76
Incest, 130
Inferiority feelings, 198
  (see Self-image)
Instrument babies, 190, 198
  (see Forceps)
IQ, 193
Introjection, 76

Labour, 20, 39, 75, 196, 200
  in Caesarean birth, 190
  in dry birth, 200
  false, 76
  induced, 46
  premature, 190
  psychological factors in mice
    during, 61
  (see Contractions)
Libido, 161
  (see Sexuality)